MOTIVATING MINISTERS TO MORALITY

Motivating Ministers to Morality

JENNY FLEMING AND IAN HOLLAND
Key Centre for Ethics, Law, Justice and Governance
Griffith University

LONDON AND NEW YORK

First published 2001 by Dartmouth Publishing Company, Ashgate Publishing

Reissued 2018 by Routledge
2 Park Square, Milton Park, Abingdon, Oxon OX14 4RN
711 Third Avenue, New York, NY 10017, USA

Routledge is an imprint of the Taylor & Francis Group, an informa business

Copyright © Jenny Fleming and Ian Holland 2001

All rights reserved. No part of this book may be reprinted or reproduced or utilised in any form or by any electronic, mechanical, or other means, now known or hereafter invented, including photocopying and recording, or in any information storage or retrieval system, without permission in writing from the publishers.

Notice:
Product or corporate names may be trademarks or registered trademarks, and are used only for identification and explanation without intent to infringe.

Publisher's Note
The publisher has gone to great lengths to ensure the quality of this reprint but points out that some imperfections in the original copies may be apparent.

Disclaimer
The publisher has made every effort to trace copyright holders and welcomes correspondence from those they have been unable to contact.

A Library of Congress record exists under LC control number: 2001092647

ISBN 13: 978-1-138-70505-0 (hbk)
ISBN 13: 978-1-138-70496-1 (pbk)
ISBN 13: 978-1-315-20240-2 (ebk)

Contents

List of Contributors ix
Acknowledgements xiii
List of Abbreviations xv

PART I: MINISTERIAL ETHICS — THE PROBLEM AND THE THEORY

1 The Case for Ministerial Ethics 3
   Jenny Fleming and Ian Holland
2 Motivating Ministers to Morality 11
   The Right Hon. Lord Nolan
3 'Educating Devils': Theoretical Reflections on Ethics and Governance 21
   Haig Patapan

PART II: LESSONS FROM WESTMINSTER: CODES AND CONVENTIONS

4 The Role of Ministerial Responsibility in Motivating Ministers to Morality 37
   Diana Woodhouse
5 Ministerial Codes, Cabinet Rules and the Power of Prime Ministers 49
   Patrick Weller
6 Lessons from Westminster: The Scottish Executive and New Improved Codes of Conduct? 61
   Mark Shephard

PART III: WALKING THE TIGHTROPE: SERVING THE PARTY

7 Institutional Weaknesses, Ethical Misjudgement:
   German Christian Democrats and the Kohl Scandal   77
   Wolfgang Seibel
8 Problem or Solution? The Role of Ministerial Staff   91
   Anne Tiernan

PART IV: ETHICAL VIGILANCE: WATCHDOGS AND GUARD DOGS

9 Honesty and Corruption in the Canadian Federal Government:
   Regulating Ethics   107
   Robert J. Jackson
10 Integrity and Ministerial Office: The Queensland Integrity
   Commissioner   119
   Noel Preston
11 Conduct Unbecoming: Independent Commissions and
   Ministerial Adversaries   129
   Jenny Fleming
12 The Role of the Auditor-General in Scrutinizing Ministerial
   Ethics   145
   John Wanna and Alexander Gash
13 Ministerial Ethics and the Media   159
   Stephen Tanner

PART V: MOTIVATING MINISTERIAL BEHAVIOUR

14 Prior Advice is Better than Subsequent Investigation   173
   Charles Sampford
15 Moderating Ministerial Ethics: Putting Political Ethics
   in its Place   187
   John Uhr

16 Advancing Ministerial Ethics　　　　　　　　　　　　　201
   Ian Holland and Jenny Fleming

Bibliography　　　　　　　　　　　　　　　　　　　　　*215*
Index　　　　　　　　　　　　　　　　　　　　　　　　*229*

List of Contributors

Jenny Fleming is a Research Fellow in the Key Centre for Ethics, Law, Justice and Governance at Griffith University. She completed her doctorate at Griffith on public policy initiatives of new governments, and is a former lecturer in the University's Faculty of Commerce and Management. Her research interests include state politics and the politics of criminal justice and police unionism, on which she has published widely. She is co-editor of *Government Reformed: Values and New Political Institutions* (forthcoming).

Alexander Gash is a research assistant in the Centre for Australian Public Sector Management at Griffith University. During 2000 he assisted John Wanna, Chris Ryan and Chew Ng in writing a centenary history of the Australian National Audit Office.

Ian Holland is a Research Fellow in the Key Centre for Ethics, Law, Justice and Governance at Griffith University. He was formerly lecturer in environmental policy and politics at Griffith University's Faculty of Environmental Sciences. He has degrees from Sydney University, the University of New England and Griffith University and has published on environmental management regulatory strategies. He is co-editor of *Government Reformed: Values and New Political Institutions* (forthcoming).

Robert J. Jackson is Fletcher Jones Professor of Politics at the University of Redlands, California, and was formerly at Carleton University, Canada. He has been the Principal Private Secretary to the Leader of the Opposition in Canada. He has published extensively, including: (with Jackson and Baxter-Moore) *Politics in Canada: Culture, Institutions, Behaviour, and Public Policy* (1986); with Schendelen, co-editor of *The Politicisation of Business in Western Europe* (1987); and as editor, *Europe in Transition: The Management of Security After the Cold War* (1992).

The Right Hon. Lord Nolan is a distinguished British lawyer who reached the pinnacle of his profession, sitting on the United Kingdom's ultimate appellate court, the House of Lords. In 1994 he was appointed the first chairman of the Joint

Parliamentary Committee on Standards in Public Life. This committee was established following the 'cash for questions' scandal in which British MPs had been paid by lobbyists to ask questions in the house. The committee's landmark reports went beyond devising codes of ethics and suggested ways of building ethics into the operation of British institutions.

Haig Patapan is Research Fellow in the Key Centre for Ethics, Law, Justice and Governance, Griffith University. He holds degrees in economics and law from the University of Queensland and a masters and doctorate in political science from the University of Toronto. He has published articles and book chapters in political theory, jurisprudence, comparative constitutionalism and Australian politics. His book, *Judging Democracy* (2000), examines the way the High Court is shaping democracy in Australia.

Noel Preston is former president of the Australian Association of Professional and Applied Ethics and has held consultancies with the Queensland Electoral and Administrative Review Commission and the Western Australian government commission on codes of conduct. He is a regular commentator on ethics and political practice in the print and electronic media. His extensive publications include *Understanding Ethics* (1996) and as editor, *Ethics for the Public Sector: Education and Training* (1994). He is currently acting as consultant to the Key Centre for Ethics, Law, Justice and Governance, Griffith University.

Charles Sampford was the Foundation Professor of Law and is the Foundation Director of the National Institute for Law, Ethics and Public Affairs, Griffith University. He has written widely on constitutional law and theory, jurisprudence, applied ethics, human rights and legal education, including *The Disorder of Law* (1989) and *Legal Ethics and Legal Practice* (co-editor) (1995). He has undertaken consultancy work on codes of ethics and legal education in both Australia and internationally, including the Committee on Standards in Public Life in Britain in 1995, and is currently the legal adviser for the Queensland parliament's Scrutiny of Legislation Committee. He is a Director of the Key Centre for Ethics, Law, Justice and Governance, Griffith University.

Wolfgang Seibel is Professor of Politics at Konstanz University. He has been a visiting scholar at the Max-Planck Institute, Princeton, and University of California, Berkeley. He has published extensively on third-sector policy and administrative reform. His collaborative works include Seibel and Benz (eds), *Regierungssystem und Verwaltungspolitik. Beiträge zu Ehren von Thomas Ellwein* [*Political Systems & Administrative Politics: Essays in Honour of Thoman Ellwein*] (1995) and research in the area of ethics includes 'Corruption in the Federal Republic of Germany Before and in the Wake of Reunification' in Della Porta and Mény (eds) *Democracy and Corruption in Europe* (1997).

Mark Shephard completed his doctorate at Houston, and lectures in Scotland's premier politics department, at the University of Strathclyde. His recent publications include contributions to Norton (ed.), *Parliaments and Governments in Western Europe* (1998), Norton (ed.), *Parliaments and Pressure Groups in Western Europe* (1999), and *Parliaments and Citizens in Western Europe* (forthcoming).

Stephen Tanner lectures in journalism at the University of Queensland. He began his working career as a newspaper journalist in 1980. He was press secretary and researcher for Tasmanian Premier Robin Gray from 1984 to 1989. He has taught political science at the University of Tasmania, and conducts research on political and media ethics. His publications include 'The Media as an Anti-corruption Mechanism' in Deysine and Kesselman (eds) *Argent, Politique et Corruption* (1999) and 'Watchdog or Attack Dog? The Media, Politics and Ethics' in Preston *et al.* (eds), *Ethics and Political Practice: Perspectives on Legislative Ethics* (1998).

Anne Tiernan teaches at Griffith University, and has been a course convenor at Swinburne University of Technology. She has extensive experience in government, having held a variety of senior positions in the Australian and Queensland public sectors, including Director, Finance and General Services in the Department of Primary Industries. She returned to Queensland in 1994 as a senior officer in the Queensland Department of Housing, Local Government and Planning, where she managed the implementation of a package of significant legislative reform and industry improvement initiatives for the residential rental sector in Queensland.

John Uhr works with the Public Policy Program at the Australian National University. In 1995 he served as the Director of the Federalism Research Centre at the Australian National University. A part-time member of the Commonwealth Merit Protection and Review Agency since 1994, he has been involved with the Australian Senate in a number of capacities, including Director of Research. His consultancies have included the Department of Finance, national and state audit offices, and many parliamentary committees at Commonwealth and state level. In 1997 he was an adviser on public sector ethics for the OECD's public management committee (PUMA). He has published extensively on Australian government and public management, with a special focus on ethics in government, including *Ethical Practice in Government: Improving Organisational Management* (ed.) (1996) and *Deliberative Democracy in Australia* (1998).

John Wanna is Professor of Politics and principal researcher at the Centre for Australian Public Sector Management at Griffith University. He has written or edited several books on politics and public sector management including: *Budgetary Management and Control* (with J. Forster, 1990); *Public Policy in Australia* (with G. Davis, P. Weller and J. Warhurst, 1993); *Public Sector Management in Australia* (with P. Weller and C. O'Fairchealaigh, 1999); *Business Government Relations in Australia* (with S. Bell,

1992); and *Managing Public Expenditure in Australia* (with J. Kelly and J. Forster, 2000). He is currently engaged in a research project funded by the Australian Research Council on expenditure management in Australia and Canada and a history of the Australian National Audit Office (with Chris Ryan and Chew Ng) entitled, *From Accounting to Accountability* (2001).

Patrick Weller is Professor of Politics and Public Policy and a director of the Key Centre for Ethics, Law, Justice and Governance at Griffith University. He is a graduate of Oxford University, and gained a PhD in political science from the Australian National University in 1972. He was elected a fellow of the Academy of the Social Sciences in Australia in 1996. He is the author of a number of books and articles on Australia and comparative politics. He is, *inter alia*, author of *Can Ministers Cope* (1981); *Dodging Raindrops* (biography of John Button, 1999); *The Hollow Crown* (1997); *First Among Equals: Prime Ministers in Westminster Systems* (1985); *Malcolm Fraser, PM* (1989); co-author of *Treasury Control in Australia* (1976); *Politics and Policy in Australia* (1979); *Public Sector Management in Australia* (1999) and co-editor of *Menzies to Keating: The Development of the Australian Prime Ministership* (1992). His latest book, *Australia's Mandarins: The Frank and the Fearless*, was published in 2001.

Diana Woodhouse is Professor of Law at Oxford Brookes University, UK and Director of the Centre for Legal Research and Policy Studies. Her research interests centre on ministerial responsibility and judicial/executive relations, on which she has published widely. Her publications include *Ministers and Parliament* (1994), *In Pursuit of Good Administration* (1997); *Pinochet: A Constitutional and Legal Analysis* (ed., 2000) and *The Office of Lord Chancellor* 2001.

Acknowledgements

As an edited book, *Motivating Ministers to Morality* is a cooperative venture. The editors invited a number of authors both from Australia and overseas to contribute to a volume that would bring a broader understanding to issues relating to political morality, ethical reform and scandal at the highest levels of government.

The papers that emerged from this were aired at the Australian Political Studies Association Conference at the Australian National University in Canberra, Australia in October 2000. We appreciate the hospitality of John Warhurst and his colleagues at the Australian National University for providing the venue and for the extensive assistance offered to the contributors. Many people attended the sessions on ministerial ethics throughout the conference and gave us the benefit of their knowledge and experience, for which we thank them. Neal Blewett showed a great interest in the project and was particularly helpful throughout the conference. We enjoyed the company and conversation of Mr and Mrs Shephard throughout the week in Canberra. Mark Shephard wishes to thank the British Academy for its assistance in providing travel grants.

Early ideas about the issues discussed in this book were outlined in a session at the International Institute for Public Ethics Conference in Ottawa in September 2000. Our interactions with ethics professionals at that conference were tremendously constructive, and we were particularly assisted by the many ethics officers from the Canadian federal and provincial governments who talked to us during that conference. We very much appreciated Ottawa's hospitality, and the company of expatriate Australian Joanne Kelly.

The project was made possible through an Australian Research Grant to the Key Centre for Ethics, Law, Justice and Governance. Staff at the Key Centre contributed in a number of ways and particular thanks are extended to Susan, Barbara and Eileen. Pat Weller in his role as Director of the Centre was very supportive and encouraging. Thanks are due to our colleagues at the School of Politics and Public Policy at Griffith University for the endless reading of drafts, copious coffee sessions and general discussion of ideas. To Jennifer Coombs and Olwen Schubert for their painstaking editing and typesetting skills — thanks. It has been a pleasure to work with Valerie

Saunders, John Irwin, Ruth Peters and Suzanne Johnson from Ashgate Publishing, whose support has been invaluable.

As editors we would like to thank the contributors for their goodwill, cooperation and punctuality and above all for participating in this project.

List of Abbreviations

ABC	Australian Broadcasting Corporation
AFP	Australian Federal Police
AFR	Australian Financial Review
A-G	Auditor-General
ANAO	Australian National Audit Office
ASC	Australian Securities Commission
BMA	British Medical Association
CDU	Christian-Democratic Union (Germany)
CIE	Committee of Independent Experts
CJC	Criminal Justice Commission (Queensland)
CRTC	Canadian Radio-Television Corporation
CSU	Christian Socialist Union (Germany)
DAS	Department of Administrative Services (Australia)
DM	deutschmark
DoFA	Department of Finance and Administration (Australia)
DTM	Daily Telegraph Mirror
EA	Ethics Advisor (Canada)
EARC	Electoral and Administrative Review Commission (Queensland)
EC	Ethics Counsellor (Canada)
EPA	Environmental Protection Authority (NSW)
FDP	Free Democratic Party (Liberal Party) (Germany)
FOI	freedom of information
HC	House of Commons
HCPC	House of Commons Parliamentary Committee (UK)
HOG	Head of government
ICAC	Independent Commission Against Corruption (New South Wales)
MAPS	Ministerial and parliamentary services (division of DAS)
MC	Ministerial Code (Westminster)
MEPPC	Members' Ethics and Parliamentary Privileges Committee (Queensland)
MoPS	members of parliament staff (Australia)

MOU	memorandum of understanding
MP	Member of Parliament
MRI	Magnetic Resonance Imaging
NHS	National Health Service (UK)
NSW	New South Wales
OGE	Office of Government Ethics (United States)
ORC	Operations Review Committee (New South Wales)
PC	Parliamentary commissioner (Queensland)
PCJC	Parliamentary Criminal Justice Committee (Queensland)
PJC	Parliamentary Joint Committee (New South Wales)
PM&C	Department of Prime Minister and Cabinet (Australia)
PMO	Prime Minister's Office (Australia)
PPS	private parliamentary secretaries
PSC	Public Service Committee
QPM	Questions of Procedure for Ministers (UK)
QPU	Queensland Police Union
SMC	Scottish Ministerial Code
SMH	Sydney Morning Herald
SPD	Social-Democratic Party (Germany)
TCSC	Treasury and Civil Service Committee (UK)

PART I:
MINISTERIAL ETHICS —
THE PROBLEM AND THE THEORY

Chapter 1

The Case for Ministerial Ethics

Jenny Fleming and Ian Holland

Public regard for politicians' behaviour in most Western industrialised countries has fallen significantly in the past decade. The political scandal of Germany's public financing rorts in the 1990s unleashed public demands for greater transparency in politics and the business community. In the USA the Whitewater land deals of the 1980s followed by President Clinton's sexual indiscretions have reduced the public's confidence in politicians in that country. In Britain there have been ministerial resignations caused by indiscreet business practice or inappropriate personal behaviour. In New Zealand the perceived ministerial negligence associated with the Cave Creek tragedy heightened the debate about whether or not ministers have moral obligations beyond mere legal liability. In Australia allegations ranging from sexual abuse to the mismanagement of travel and accommodation expenses have dominated the media in recent years. Every country has its scandals.

Particular scandals such as those mentioned above spark great public and media reaction. These are, however, embedded in a broader picture of declining public confidence in political institutions and élites (Mancuso, 1995; McAllister, 2000; Rosenthal, 1998; Walsh and Richardson, 1995). Surveys show that public regard for politicians in most Western industrial countries has fallen significantly in recent decades. Australians, for example, view the honesty and ethics of parliamentarians as 'only slightly better than those of car salesmen', and only 7 per cent believe that members of both state and federal parliaments have high or very high standards of honesty and ethics (Morgan, 1998). Other research foreshadowed such dismal indications. McAllister's analysis of the 1996 Australian Election Study survey demonstrated that while Australian voters were not as cynical as their British counterparts, one in three Australians believed that 'politicians made a lot of money from using their public offices improperly'. Other damning observations included that citizens believed most federal parliamentarians will 'tell lies if they feel the truth will hurt them politically' and that they care more about 'special interests than about the general public' (McAllister, 2000, pp. 23–4).

Mancuso's work in Canada yielded comparable results. Her nationwide survey on public opinions about politicians showed that the public was 'unconvinced and resentful' about its government representatives with 74 per cent stating that corruption was a major issue. A further 71 per cent of respondents argued that political corruption would always be a feature of Canadian politics regardless of efforts to correct it. Over 60 per cent believed that politicians were only 'out for themselves' (Mancuso, 2000). Mancuso's (1995) work on British parliamentarians generated similar findings.

Political scandal and public disaffection make ethics in politics a pressing concern. Electoral volatility in all Western democratic countries suggests citizens' confidence in their governments is declining, even if they appear to have delivered sound economic outcomes. Voters are turning to minor parties and independents rather than support the major parties. Empirical research suggests that this disaffection with politicians and political parties has much to do with the way in which politicians behave.

This book is a response to these trends. It looks at ethics in public life, and in particular at the conduct of the political executive. As Uhr has pointed out, the study of political ethics concerns 'the standards of conduct which are appropriate to political life' (1998a, p. 11). The study of ministerial ethics then is concerned with the appropriate conduct of ministers. Within this context, two distinct, though related, questions arise. The first question is 'what constitutes the right thing to do?' The second question is 'how do we ensure that ministers do the right thing?'

Until recently much of the literature in the field of legislative ethics has been preoccupied with aspects of the first question. The issue is made more complicated by the fact that those in public life are unclear themselves what signifies the ethical path in politics, a point made by the Nolan Committee established in 1994 in response to allegations relating to inappropriate parliamentary behaviour in the UK (Nolan, 1995). Over the past decade much scholarly effort has been put into establishing what constitutes the 'right thing to do'. Goodin (1992) argues that everyone inherently holds moral principles as to what is fundamentally right or wrong behaviour. Davis argues that these will be broadly consistent among political actors: there is 'a reasonable consensus about what [ethics] entails ... [and] ... a good measure of compliance' (Davis, 1995, pp. 437–8). However, there are difficulties associated with reconciling voter expectations with the ethical perspectives of parliamentarians (see, for example, Mancuso, 1995; Rosenthal, 1998; Smith, 1998, 1999; Jackson and Smith, 1995). Their research has highlighted the diversity of ethical views among politicians. Others have also argued that historical factors and significant variation in political culture act as barriers to acknowledging and dealing with questions of government ethics, challenging the presumption that there is either clarity of or commitment to ethics in political life (della Porta and Mény, 1997; Mény, 1996; Seibel, 1997).

While there may not be universal agreement on what might be the right thing to do, political scandals tend to produce at least temporary consensus about the kinds of actions we should expect from our politicians (see, for example Smith, 1999). This does not, however, help address the problem of how to elicit such actions. This book takes as its starting point Goodin's observation that there is a distinction between having a 'keen appreciation ... of the right moral principles' and 'persuading [people] to act upon those principles' (1992, p. 3). We should not presume that an awareness of ethical matters is sufficient guarantee of ethical conduct. It may be necessary, but it is not a sufficient condition for securing what a community might regard as satisfactory conduct. Having made this distinction, the key question is then one of *motivation*. This brings us to the second question: how do we ensure that ministers do the right thing?

Many countries now have institutions and procedures committed to maintaining standards of conduct deemed appropriate to political life. They seek to restore public confidence in the political process by providing assurances that those in public life meet a high standard of ethical conduct. These institutions and procedures have aroused public interest but little effort has been made to evaluate the comparative success of the diverse methods employed to bring about ethical conduct. Indeed there is increasing scepticism about these methods, the way they are administered and their general effectiveness in motivating ministers to morality. It is the need to evaluate these institutions and methods that provides this book with its central focus — to what extent do they motivate ministers to do the right thing?

Before we continue we should clear some ground about terminology. It is not our intention to set a standard and measure ministers against it. Nor do we intend to debate at length the philosophical dimensions of what constitutes morality (see Goodin, 1992). In this book morality simply refers to a mode of behaviour that is acceptable to the public and at some level amends the public perception that all politicians are untrustworthy and self-serving. The public is not easily convinced. In politics, perception is vital and politicians, particularly senior politicians, need to be seen to be 'doing the right thing'. This has more chance of taking place if the public are aware of checks and balances within the political system that effectively monitor politicians' behaviour and seek to enforce conformity and encourage accountability. The 'ballot box' solution is not necessarily the only answer. A US study has suggested that enforcing appropriate behaviour through the electoral system is a 'blunt, and usually ineffective, instrument' (McAllister, 2000, p. 25).

The Special Circumstances of the Executive

Initiatives designed to set standards of conduct appropriate to political life have concentrated on establishing guidelines and institutions for the legislature or for the public service, yet ministers face different motivations and carry different responsibilities to parliamentarians in general. Although the public perceives a decline in government accountability, and with it the capacity to hold ministers to ethical standards, little work has been done specifically on ethics and the executive.

Why ministers? Why do they warrant attention as a distinct class of political actor? What distinguishes the executive from backbenchers? If we are to evaluate effectively the effects of various guidelines, codes of conduct and other institutions that seek to regulate political behaviour, it is imperative that we evaluate the extent to which they take into account the different motivations and different responsibilities that ministers face.

In most countries, ministers are not accountable to parliament in the ways they were once expected to be. This declining parliamentary oversight of the executive has eroded Westminster doctrines of ministerial responsibility. There are numerous examples of how conventions of collective and individual ministerial responsibility in Westminster systems have been ignored and where ministers have not had to answer for breaches of these conventions (Page, 1990; Sutherland, 1991; Woodhouse, 1993; Jaensch, 1997; Thompson and Tillotsen, 1999).

Most political commentators also agree that the development of discipline in the cabinet room has meant that responsibility for individual ministerial behaviour has swung 'almost exclusively to the cabinet itself, the prime minister and the executive' (Jaensch, 1997, p. 150). Despite the existence of established accountability mechanisms such as parliamentary committees and parliamentary procedures, it is with great difficulty that parliaments police the executive. This is a problem for Westminster parliamentary systems. Ministerial responsibility, particularly individual ministerial responsibility, is 'a key link in a "chain", the functioning of which is crucial to a parliamentary system' (Jaensch, 1997, p. 151). The chain linking the public service to ministers, ministers to cabinet, cabinet to parliament and parliament to the people is weakened considerably by the attenuation of individual ministerial responsibility. In these circumstances, strengthening this link requires special attention.

What else makes ministers a special case for ethical consideration? First and foremost is the level of power that ministers enjoy. Uhr points out that 'different public offices ... bring with them different sets of political power as well as ethical responsibilities' (Uhr, 1998a, pp. 11–12). It is the different degrees of power that distinguish ministers significantly from their parliamentary colleagues. Much of that power is derived from the political party of which they are a member. As senior figures in their parties they wield influence both inside and outside of the parliament, exercising autonomy and discretion in their dealings with colleagues and the public in general. The central place of cabinet and the ministry in the political system itself puts the power of ministers on another plane from parliamentarians as a whole.

Ministers, unlike their parliamentary colleagues, draw on the protective power of cabinet convention. Their decisions, mistakes and errors of judgement may be protected by cabinet secrecy, in circumstances where documentary evidence might otherwise be available. Away from media, parliamentary and public scrutiny, confidential cabinet discussions are an essential feature of effective government, but equally they present ministers with ethical challenges no other parliamentarian faces. Collective responsibility ensures that ministers will as a group support cabinet decisions and defend colleagues from external critics. Those seeking information under freedom of information (FOI) legislation find that requests for information relating to cabinet decisions are denied because the relevant documents are lying on the cabinet table and cannot be released until cabinet has no further use of them. It is not difficult to envisage how this situation can be manipulated in an unethical manner.

There are other things that set ministers apart from their backbench colleagues. Ministers, as the heads of departments, will have a number of temptations not accessible to backbenchers and Opposition members. Their status gives them wide access to public sector confidential files and other privileged information. A minister also has the right to expert advice on matters pertaining to his/her portfolio and ready access to lobby groups with whom policy is discussed. Overall, the minister is in a very powerful, information-rich position. The potential abuses of this often-confidential information make ministers vulnerable to temptation.

A minister's untrammelled access to opinion leaders and interest groups provides a fertile ground for potential conflicts of interest and unethical behaviour. Ironically, this may not be because ministers solicit favours, but rather because they, far more than their backbench counterparts, are likely to confront offers of bribery and influence peddling in their daily working life. Accepting them can, in some political cultures, simply appear to be 'the done thing' (della Porta and Vannucci, 1999). There is little question, however, that ministers, through their management and decision-making responsibilities and as heads of their departments, are more likely to be exposed than others in the political system to this kind of risk. Power brings temptation. Additionally, ministers are subject to a variety of pressures — answerable not only to their constituents but, unlike their backbench counterparts, also to the cabinet, the prime minister, the party, special interest groups and parliament. These often conflicting pressures in a party political system can be particularly onerous to reconcile and arguably expose ministers to potentially unethical situations.

Leaving aside their special vulnerability to corrupt exchanges, there is also the issue of how ministers manage the effects of their discretionary powers. It has been noted by the Independent Commission Against Corruption (ICAC) that a 'high level of delegated authority, significant autonomy and routine exercise of wide discretion' (ICAC, 1998–99, p. 1) puts public officials at a greater risk of exposure to corruption. Of all the public's paid servants, ministers have the most discretion of all, through their 'legislative and political authority to oversee the actions of the officials' (Weller, 1999, p. 63). There is no question that their powers ensure that government is possible, but it presents them with unique opportunities to influence policy implementation. That influence can seem so powerful that officials may make inappropriate discretionary judgements in favour of politicians without even being asked, placing an extra burden of ethical responsibility on ministers. In 1981 an Australian government minister entered the country carrying a television set on which duty needed to be paid. It was alleged that during the minister's interchange with customs officials, a senior customs officer may have given the minister preferential treatment (Page, 1990; Weller, 1989). The subsequent failure of the minister responsible for customs properly to deal with his fellow minister later forced both ministers' resignations (Page, 1990). Thus the distinctive authority of ministers for operational matters places special burdens upon them to be aware of ethical dilemmas, including those not of their own making, and to appreciate the proper response.

Ministers also have a unique role in being the *de facto* selectors of people for public offices, particularly on boards and statutory authorities. This exposes them to the moral hazards of both trying to appoint friends to positions and trying improperly to interfere in the operations of such independent entities (Menadue, 2000). Again the issue of discretion is pertinent.

Finally, ministers are distinguished by the support of a distinctive staff cohort whose functions and employment relations set them apart from the public service. Ministerial staffers play an important role in government activity, but are only to varying degrees governed by the rules and procedures under which the rest of the machinery of government operates. Ministers' reliance on their staff places them in both a privileged and parlous position that, as Tiernan demonstrates in the Australian case, requires special attention.

These are the many and important ways in which ministers occupy a distinctive, especially powerful, place in political life, exposing them to unique and frequent ethical dangers. There are, of course, some arguments to suggest a minister's power is limited by a number of institutional developments, such as FOI and administrative law, and that these initiatives have by and large ensured the continuance of ministerial responsibility and accountability (Blick, 1999). Indeed some suggest matters have gone too far, and that the range of control and check mechanisms limits ministers' ability to respond properly to their constituents and 'do their job' (Hayden, 1998, p. 64). The prevailing view, however, remains that traditional mechanisms of ministerial accountability have been eroded, and have not been adequately complemented by these new measures to ensure ministerial conduct is ethical and transparent. The very distinctive situation of ministers means that parliamentary or public-sector-wide measures are unlikely to capture fully the nature of the challenges ministers face. The question then is what responses might rectify these problems?

Institutional Strategies for the Executive

There are many ways to address ethics in politics. As Patapan points out in Chapter 3, they can range from education-based strategies to quasi-judicial regulation and constitutional rules. Various of these approaches have been adopted in different countries at different times. Most have been intended to support parliamentarians as a whole or to deal with specific classes of unethical conduct whether occurring within or beyond the parliamentary walls (such as the New South Wales ICAC). A few are targeted specifically at ministers. These include doctrines of ministerial responsibility, and codes of conducts directed specifically at the executive, such as that introduced in Australia in 1996.

All of these structures may have the potential to mitigate or even prevent the moral lapses of executive government. On the other hand, if badly designed or implemented, they might have the capacity to exacerbate the problem. We need analysis of these options, to give insights into what might be fruitful avenues for reform.

In exploring these options, this book is divided into five parts. The book opens with some reflections of Lord Nolan, inaugural Chair of the UK Committee on

Standards in Public Life. Speaking 'from the foothills of experience', Lord Nolan recounts his attempts to improve standards of conduct among ministers and others in public life generally and reflects on the measures adopted as a response to what he calls the 'crisis of confidence' in public figures. His committee had no constitutional standing, no legal powers or privileges and yet the principal elements for a government ethics regime recommended by his committee have been officially accepted by governments and serve to remind public figures that there are indeed standards to which politicians must aspire.

Following Nolan, Patapan demonstrates that a preoccupation with honest government is not a modern phenomenon but is in fact of ancient lineage. His chapter considers the question of institutionalizing ethics, distinguishes between classical and contemporary understandings of how to bring about 'good government' and provides a historical and theoretical basis for considering the issue of how we can motivate ministers to morality.

Part II examines the traditional parliamentary conventions and the codes of conduct established in more recent times in Westminster systems. Woodhouse and Weller illustrate how the conventions developed. Woodhouse looks at the doctrine of ministerial responsibility across two nations, emphasizing its contingent nature and the reliance on the prime minister to make judgements. Weller traces the emergence of cabinet rules and asks what impact these rules have on ministerial behaviour. He argues that prime ministers, and only prime ministers, can be judge, jury and executioner.

When it comes to establishing the rules for political conduct, very occasionally an opportunity arises to start with, if not a clean slate, at least a chance to create a palimpsest. What can be the result in the area of ministerial codes? Shephard discusses one such opportunity, created by the granting of partial self-government to Scotland by Tony Blair's incoming Labour government. Shephard demonstrates that one of the opportunities (and threats) that written rules present is not only that they are more explicit and fixed in the short term, but also that they are more amenable to change. Only an explicit set of rules can then be explicitly rewritten through a conscious, planned process. This has happened in Scotland, with some interesting twists. Shephard, Woodhouse and Weller all throw doubt on the adequacy of relying completely on conventional regulation.

The issue of internal regulation is highlighted in Part III where Tiernan and Seibel consider the significance and centrality of political parties. Adversarial in nature, political parties are necessarily partisan and this partisanship has important effects on ministers' ethical choices. Tiernan investigates the role of political staffers in Australia's travel rorts scandal, while Seibel examines Germany's Christian Democratic Union party and the scandal of illegal party financing. Both demonstrate the difficulties of the dual allegiances of party functionaries to the party and the state. Tiernan shows that the trend of the last two decades has been toward the increasing use of, and reliance upon, partisan ministerial staff. Valued for their commitment, finely tuned political antennae and problem-solving orientation, staffers are not without their vulnerabilities. Tiernan documents the adverse consequences of this for ministers. Seibel's evaluation of Chancellor Helmut Kohl's behaviour makes the point that the 'strength of the democratic political culture determines whether a society will or will not tolerate the unethical political behaviour' of senior politicians. Both authors illustrate the daily pressures faced by ministers and identify the difficulties of separating loyalty for the party and the public commitment to serving the public.

Existing and new institutions are the subject of Part IV. Jackson, Preston and Fleming assess organizations established in the last decade primarily to oversee the ethical behaviour of those in public office. Jackson and Preston consider the roles of advisory offices established in Canada and Queensland respectively in response to public concerns about unethical behaviour in public life. Fleming considers the relatively new independent institutions of the Criminal Justice Commission (CJC) in Queensland and the ICAC in New South Wales. The responsibilities of both organizations include the investigation of misconduct by public officials and elected members of parliament. Fleming demonstrates that while both the CJC and ICAC have had considerable success in identifying unethical practice among ministers, the organizations are to varying degrees restrained by their reliance on governments for funding and resources. Wanna and Gash look at the role of the Australian Auditor-General and assess its relevance in contemporary debates about conflict of interest and accountability. Tanner considers the oldest institution of all in the context of various scandals. How significant are the media and positive media coverage to senior politicians? How wary are they of critical media coverage? How does the media's investigative presence act as a deterrent to those ministers considering 'crossing the line'?

In Part V Sampford and Uhr's chapters take a more general approach. Sampford evaluates a number of existing institutions committed to providing advice, and identifies some of the potential problems of political accountability and responsibility that arise from them. He concludes that the availability of prior advice to ministers supported by legal sanction where necessary will motivate ministers to consider the issue of ethical behaviour more closely. In the context of the classic debate between Friedrich and Finer over administrative responsibility in democratic governance, Uhr cautions against an 'unrealistic reliance on chief ministers to regulate ministerial conduct' and 'idealistic over-reactions against [an] executive-centred model' and urges a return to parliamentary responsibility and the institutional capacity of accountability agencies.

In the conclusion we argue that there are no simple institutional solutions. There is in fact a suite of solutions — all of them with something to contribute but none of them sufficient on their own. In combination they may have the potential to be very powerful. That, we suggest, is the principal lesson. There are options that may work, but they have to be adopted with care.

Chapter 2

Motivating Ministers to Morality

The Right Hon. Lord Nolan

I propose to look at 'motivation' and 'morality' from the foothills of practical experience — the experience of Britain during the last six years and its attempts to improve standards of conduct in public life generally and in particular among ministers. I choose the last six years because it was in October 1994 that Britain faced up to a growing crisis of public confidence in the probity of the then government, of politicians generally and even of our historic democratic institutions. This was the background against which the prime minister set up the Committee on Standards in Public Life, of which I was the chairman until 1997.

The gravity of the crisis of confidence that the committee faced at its inception was vividly illustrated by opinion polls which had recently been taken and were put before us. With the proposition 'Most Members of Parliament make a lot of money by using public office improperly' 64 per cent of those polled agreed, and only 22 per cent disagreed. Eighty-seven per cent thought that most MPs will tell lies if they feel the truth will hurt them politically. Only 8 per cent disagreed. Of the categories of people generally trusted by those polled to tell the truth doctors and teachers came top with an 84 per cent vote. The category of 'politicians generally' scored 14 per cent. In the case of government ministers, the proportion of those trusting them generally to speak the truth was an appalling 11 per cent. The message from the polls, in short, was that most Britons regarded their elected representatives as venal and mendacious.

Most of those best placed to know — by which I mean the police, the auditors, the academics and the political journalists — thought that the public perception of MPs was unfair, and did not reflect the reality. All agreed, however, that the extent of public disaffection was itself a very grave problem and one that needed to be tackled without delay. I have always felt that as long as the people of our country have confidence in parliament, and in particular in the elected House of Commons, nothing much can go wrong. Without that confidence, nothing much can go right, and this was the danger we faced.

Why were our politicians more unpopular than they deserved to be? It would have been comforting to be able to discount public anxiety as the result of excessive media concentration on the failings of public figures. There was clearly some truth in this, but no one could sensibly argue that it was a complete explanation. Our politicians were, and still are, primarily responsible for their own public image. I believe that what I might call their excessive unpopularity was, and is, due to a number of causes which fall into two separate groups, one founded in reality, the other in perception. The 'reality' group consists of real, specific flaws and abuses in the system of government. These can readily be identified and, if not cured, at least contained by reform or by codes of conduct or by legal sanctions as appropriate. The 'perception' group is more elusive and intractable. It includes causes for some of which the politicians are themselves to blame, and which vary in importance from politician to politician and from administration to administration. But it also includes causes which simply go with the job and which are, I suspect, common to all modern democracies.

The first and most obvious cause for the perception of politicians as dishonest and untruthful is that is how they so often describe each other, especially at election times. It is hardly surprising if the public tend to take the same view, thinking that, after all, the politicians themselves ought to know.

Second, quite apart from the name calling, it is demonstrable that even the best politicians are, at times, economical with the truth. There may be perfectly valid excuses for this — the need for secrecy over national security, or diplomatic negotiations, or positively to deny an actual intention to devalue the national currency — but it hardly encourages a reputation for frankness. Third, and again demonstrably, politicians tend to make promises which in the event they are unable, or unwilling, to keep.

These political faults are generic and, I suspect, ineradicable. They are magnified in the public mind by four additional factors. One, the media need to sell their product. Bad news sells better than good news. Therefore the public tends to be given an unduly pessimistic picture of events. Two, journalism is, by definition, an ephemeral art. It serves up today's news for tonight's broadcasts or tomorrow's headlines. The news is generally obtained in conditions such as a live interview, which does not lend itself to a full and balanced account of events. Inevitably, the journalistic product tends to lack perspective and to produce a distorted picture. Three, politicians nowadays lead lives like goldfish in a bowl, constantly visible from all angles. How many of us can be confident that our lives would stand up creditably to that level of scrutiny? This brings me to my fourth and final factor, which is the share of the blame which we, the public, must bear. We, the armchair cynics, who rather like reading bad things about other people, and would soon become bored with the virtuous truth. We get the media we choose to support and encourage. It was interesting to find that individual politicians were more highly regarded in their own constituencies, particularly by those who knew them personally. This supports the proposition that the poor public perception of politicians is at least partly due to the ignorance and laziness of the perceivers. My own experience of urging those who think that politicians are corrupt to go and talk to their MP is that the invitation is virtually never taken up. The plain truth is that the armchair will always be the most comfortable seat of judgement. We waste our breath and our energy if we try to ensure that our elected leaders are fairly assessed in the public mind on their real merits. We do better to take comfort in the reflection that a degree of scepticism is healthier than blind adulation. The general unpopularity of politicians is something which we and they have to live with, and which must be kept in perspective.

So the committee turned its attention to the specific factors which were raising the distrust of politicians to dangerous levels. There were three that stood out. The first was the extent to which MPs were in receipt of payments from outside bodies for parliamentary services rendered or to be rendered. The catalyst was a well-publicized case in which journalists from the *Sunday Times*, posing as businessmen persuaded two MPs (both of whom later repented) to accept £1 000 each for putting down parliamentary questions for the benefit of non-existent companies which the journalists claimed to represent. The case came to be known as the 'cash for questions' case. Upon inquiry the committee found that 26 members had consultancy agreements with public relations or lobbying firms, a further 142 had consultancies with other types of company or with trade associations, and 184 had sponsorship arrangements with trade unions. One way and another nearly 70 per cent of eligible MPs — that is to say MPs other than the Speaker and government ministers, who are precluded from having outside commercial interests during their period of office — had financial relationships with outside bodies which directly related to their membership of the House.

The rule preventing ministers from having outside commercial interests had held firm throughout, with rare exceptions. It did not, however, stop ministers taking employment after their retirement with companies with which they had had dealings while in office. The matter was left to the conscience of the individual minister. For civil servants and the armed forces, on the other hand, there were long-standing arrangements under which any employment taken up within two years after leaving the government service had to be approved by an independent advisory committee. The disparity between civil servants and ministers, coupled with the suspicion that ministers had been using their powers in office to feather their retirement nests, was the second of the specific causes of disquiet most often raised by the committee's witnesses. The third consisted of repeated allegations that appointments by ministers to well-paid posts on the boards of high-spending quangos were too often being made, not on merit, but to friends of the government, and that there was no adequate means of supervising them.

These, then, were the principal faults that the committee had to address. Whatever the faults of the politicians, the central civil service, by which the system of government is mainly administered, remained free from corruption, and had maintained its tradition of political impartiality. The judges, too, were free from corruption and wholly independent of government. Standards of conduct in the accountancy and legal professions were high. The same was generally true of the police, particularly at senior levels. The media, though often lacking in discretion and objectivity, were healthily vigilant. Theirs was, as always, a vital role in keeping public figures up to the mark.

Finally, our voluntary sector, a crucial element in the public life of Britain, was as vigorous and influential as ever. Thus, despite the suspicions that well-paid jobs on quangos were going to government cronies, the committee found that some two thirds of the 27 000 board posts on the major quangoes are unpaid. The board members of our universities, further education colleges, grant-maintained schools, training and enterprise councils and housing associations, some 66 000 of them in total, are unpaid. Add to that the 30 000-odd unpaid Justices of the Peace, who hear more than 90 per cent of the criminal cases tried in England and Wales, and you have well over 100 000 important posts in Britain filled by volunteers. These people not only set a good example, they rightly demand very high standards from those who are paid for their public service. They were prominent among our witnesses and were not so much cynical as angry at the level of disrepute to which our politicians had fallen.

These were the circumstances in which I was able to write to the prime minister, when sending in the committee's first report, that 'the public anxiety which led you to set up the committee was widely shared and deeply felt. But we found that it was matched on all sides by a resolute determination to see that things are put right'.

I do not mention these facts out of any sense of complacency. Complacency had been one of our most conspicuous weaknesses. Even since the major reforms of the system which have followed the committee's reports, it is apparent that the need for vigilance is as great as ever. The process is a bit like squeezing a balloon. Compression and containment of misconduct at one point leads to its expansion at another. Informed opinion suggests that there has been an overall improvement in standards as a consequence of the committee's work but I am by no means sure that public confidence in politicians has significantly increased. The most I would say is that the rapid decline of 1994 seems to have been arrested. The lack of a positive increase is mainly due to the emergence of new factors which lie outside the ambit of the committee as an ethical workshop, such as the increase in violent crime, the shortcomings of the National Health Service (NHS) and the failure of the government, as seen by many, to produce their promised improvements in these areas. But even within the scope of the committee's work, problems both old and new continue to surface.

At all events, complacency was never justified, and is not now. My reason for referring to the strong foundations underpinning standards of conduct in British public life is to explain why we did not need to embark upon fundamental structural reforms, and also, in a broader context, to illustrate the proposition that although the problems being experienced by the advanced democracies are similar, and we have much to learn from each other, the solutions will vary from country to country, depending on their national character, traditions and institutions, and on the severity and the precise nature of the problems.

The starting point, though, in all countries must be the criminal law, the basic rules for the protection of the weak against oppression by the strong, the foundation of all law and order. Unless the criminal law and its administration are in a state in which people in the street are prepared to move along when asked to do so by the police you can forget all your luxuries like habeas corpus and judicial review. In its study of the criminal law in Britain the committee found serious weaknesses in the field of public sector corruption. These weaknesses did not threaten the maintenance of law and order, nor did they directly reflect the three specific faults that were at the top of the committee's agenda. The nearest to the mark was the total absence of any law directed against the bribery of members of parliament. No one knew if it was an offence, because the corruption laws were framed in terms of bribing officials or office holders, and the generally accepted view is that an MP does not hold an office. No one knew where or how the offence, if that is what it was, should be tried, because Article Nine of the Bill of Rights 1689 prevents the courts from questioning things said or done in parliament. In 1976 a Royal Commission on Standards in Public Life had recommended that the law should be clarified, and had pointed in particular to the difficulty of the House of Commons trying to act as a criminal court for its own members, but the recommendation had been ignored.

If it had been put into effect we might well have avoided the cash for questions affair, and the more general allegations of sleaze which did so much to damage the reputation of parliament and bring down the last administration. Instead, the House of Commons had confused the issue further by setting up a register of members' interests in 1992 with rules which provided under the heading 'Clients' for the registration of (and thus implicitly sanctioned), *inter alia*, the provision for payment of 'services which depend essentially upon, or arise out of, membership of the House; for example ... making representations to government departments ...'. Thus, while the historic rule against advocacy in the House for reward remained untouched, approaches to government departments, including ministers, for the benefit of 'clients', a most effective source of indirect advocacy, was expressly contemplated as falling within the rules. That being so, it would have been difficult to treat cash for questions as a criminal offence.

Since the committee's first report, the rules governing the registration of interests have been clarified and strengthened. Their observation is ensured by a senior officer of the House, the Parliamentary Commissioner for Standards, and is supported by a code of conduct, and the number of consultancy or similar agreements has sharply declined. The need for legislation on the bribery of members is therefore no longer so acute, but has at last been fully addressed by a joint committee of both Houses under the chair of another Law Lord, Lord Nicholls, and a draft Bill is awaited.

The two other relevant areas of weakness in the criminal law both affected the position of ministers. As office holders, ministers fell within the terms of our Prevention of Corruption Acts, but the Law Commission, having studied this legislation at the committee's suggestion, described them in their January 1998 report as 'obscure, complex, inconsistent, and insufficiently comprehensive'. The commission produced a draft Bill consolidating the law and bringing it up to date, and the government has promised legislation. Again, however, this weakness in the law did not directly reflect the specific allegations against ministers.

The third area of weakness, as the committee saw it, was the absence of a comprehensive remedy against the misuse of public office in cases where the office holder received no personal benefit as a result, and thus there was no bribery involved. An example of this would be the expenditure by the office holder of public funds for party political or other unauthorised purposes. Again, though, this fell some way away from the specific faults with which the committee was concerned. I suppose it might cover flagrant nepotism in the making of appointments — Caligula making his horse a consul, for example — but the need for reform emerged most clearly in the area of local government. There the committee found that local councillors or council officials could be ordered by the District Auditor to make good out of their own pockets any expenditure authorized by them either without legal justification or through wilful misconduct. In one recent case a lady councillor and a colleague were surcharged the sum of more than £27 million. The further surprise was that she reputedly had the means to pay it, though liability is still contested. Here too legislation is proposed to bring such cases under the umbrella of misuse of public office, a new statutory version of the old common law misdemeanour of that name, with the court determining liability and imposing an appropriate penalty.

For the House of Commons, the remedies (as I have already mentioned) were new rules for the registration of interests, fortified by the appointment of the Parliamentary Commissioner for Standards and the adoption of a code of conduct. For ministers taking up employment after leaving office the committee recommended that the same rules should apply as for civil servants and the armed forces, and this recommendation, though contrary to the view expressed by the government in its evidence, was accepted by the House and seems to have worked well.

For appointments to major quangos and NHS trusts the committee recommended that the ultimate responsibility should remain in the hands of ministers, but that a Commissioner for Public Appointments should be appointed to regulate, monitor and report upon the public appointments process. Again the recommendation was accepted, and the first two commissioners have performed their role with tact and firmness. The strictures of Dame Rennie Fritchie, the present commissioner, upon the preponderance of Labour supporters among appointees to NHS trusts has already led to significant changes in the appointments process, and more are under consideration.

What about those aspects of political and executive behaviour which call for the observance of high standards but which cannot suitably be dealt with by the heavy hand of the law or by improvements in the system? How do we stand on ethics? What *are* ethics? This much used and much abused word has a number of definitions in the dictionary, but the one I would choose is 'the rules of conduct recognized in certain limited departments of human life'. I like that definition because it puts ethics in the setting where, for practical purposes, it belongs, and that is to say in a department of life which has its own distinctive ethos, such as a particular administration, or the civil service, or the Bar, or for that matter the inhabitants of a prison.

So far as public life is concerned, the committee took the view that the ethos of any particular department must be based on the acceptance of certain fundamental principles.

With some diffidence we proposed that these should consist of, or at least include, selflessness, integrity, objectivity, accountability, openness, honesty and leadership. Taken together, they represented our idea of morality in the relevant sense. There was no magic in having seven of them. It might be felt that the last three, openness, honesty and leadership, cover the whole ground. At the risk of labouring the obvious, we added a few words of explanation to each of them. Thus 'selflessness' we explained by saying:

> Holders of public office should take decisions solely in terms of the public interest. They should not do so in order to gain financial or other material benefits for themselves, their family, or their friends.

The committee's fears that its proposals would be dismissed as merely trite were dispelled when the House of Commons included them verbatim, explanatory words and all, in its code of conduct. Many other organizations have done the same. To many people of my age, and of even greater age, who grew up in a time of simpler and more certain values, the very notion of codes of conduct was novel, and even faintly ridiculous. In its recent study of the House of Lords, that most ancient of our democratic institutions — it was, after all, the barons who compelled King John to sign the Magna Carta — the committee has encountered those who think that codes of conduct are all very well for boy scouts but hardly right for mature legislators. They have a point. There are still many who need no code to guide them. But in advocating these codes the committee was following the lead given by the professions, the civil service and many business organizations, and I am convinced that it was right to do so. Experience has shown that codes of conduct can fill an ethical vacuum, and in doing so can point to the solution of everyday practical problems.

What is essential is that each organization should have its own code, embodying the fundamental principles and applying them to the particular requirements of that organisation. The code should be the written expression of the ethos of the organization.

This cannot be emphasised too strongly. The key to maintaining ethical standards in any organisation is to build those standards into the day to day running of the organisation, and the day to day attitudes of staff. There must be total commitment to it, and the lead must come from the top.

This brings me directly to the subject of ministers, and the code of conduct that governs them. As the committee said in its first report (Nolan, 1995, Chapter 3, para. 4):

> The public is entitled to expect very high standards of behaviour from Ministers, as they have profound influence over the daily lives of us all. As [Professor] Bogdanor told us, 'it is from Ministers that standards in public life must flow'.

At the time of that report such guidance as there was for ministers was contained in a document called *Questions of Procedure for Ministers* (*QPM*). The original of this document dated from 1945, but it had been gradually and substantially augmented over the years as new problems arose. Initially confidential, it was made public in 1992 by the then prime minister, John Major. The committee recommended that it should form the basis of a new document, drawing out from the *QPM* the ethical principles and rules to form a free-standing code of conduct. This recommendation was accepted and a new ministerial code was produced in 1997. It runs to 131 pages, and the foreword begins with the proclamation that:

> Ministers of the Crown are expected to behave according to the highest standards of constitutional and personal conduct in the performance of their duties.

In its description of the more detailed principles which must be observed, the foreword continues:

> It is of paramount importance that Ministers give accurate and truthful information to Parliament, correcting any inadvertent error at the first opportunity. Ministers who knowingly mislead Parliament will be expected to offer their resignation to the Prime Minister.

The foreword concludes with the words:

> It will be for individual Ministers to judge how best to act in order to uphold the highest standards. They are responsible for justifying their conduct to Parliament. And they can only remain in office for so long as they retain the Prime Minister's confidence.

The sentiments expressed throughout the code are unexceptionable. The means by which it should be enforced are more problematical. The committee's recommendations for enforcement in other areas have been based on the twin principles of openness and independent scrutiny, and this mixture has worked well in such cases as the Parliamentary Commissioner for Standards, the Business Appointments' Committee for ex-ministers accepting employment, and the Commissioner for Public Appointments for Ministerial Appointments. But vital as the work of these independent scrutineers is, it does not and cannot cover the full range of ministerial conduct, much of which, unless exposed, inevitably remains out of sight.

The problem was fully aired before the Committee on Standards in Public Life when it was preparing its sixth report, *Reinforcing Standards*, which was published in January 2000 (Neill, 2000). The case for an ethics commissioner was strongly argued. The Committee concluded, however, that this would not be a satisfactory solution. It did so principally on three grounds. One was that calls for allegations to be referred to the commissioner would become a party political game. The second was the undesirability of leaving a minister 'dangling in the air' while the commissioner investigated, unless the complications of the case were such that a lengthy independent inquiry was unavoidable. The third was that the prime minister is the 'can-carrier in chief', and it must therefore be his/her right to decide in every case how the allegation should be handled. The appointment of an ethics commissioner would fetter the prime minister's discretion in these respects. Investigation of the facts could be carried out, as appropriate, and ordinarily in private, by the Cabinet Secretary, the Attorney General, the Chief Whip or, in criminal cases, by the police, but the ultimate judgement must be that of the prime minister alone — a conclusion which the committee felt should be more clearly spelt out in the code.

So far, at least, this view seems to have prevailed, and there has been no more talk of an ethics commissioner. It is true to say also that, so far at least, the matter has not been seriously put to the test. On the few occasions during the current administration, or for the last administration after the 1994 crisis, when the conduct of ministers had been widely criticized because of the revelation of questionable financial arrangements or of sexual affairs too eccentric to be consistent with ministerial office, the minister has resigned with little apparent pressure from the prime minister.

What does this atmosphere of relative calm tell us about the motivation of ministers? Or, to put it more generally, what improvements in motivation, if any, can be detected as having occurred since the committee's first report in the early summer of 1995? I would prefer to approach the questions on this broader basis, because that is the way in which they have been approached by most commentators, and it is difficult, as I have said earlier, to consider the position of ministers without reference to the parliamentary, administrative, legal, public opinion and electoral factors which influence their behaviour.

The importance of this last factor is obvious. Self-preservation is one of the strongest of human motives, for ministers as for the rest of us. I doubt whether morality ever won an election, but its conspicuous absence can play a major part in bringing a government down and putting ministers out of their jobs, as the last British election showed. On the parliamentary front, the effects of the first report have been more apparent, and in the long term much more important. This is because of the acceptance by the House of Commons of the committee's main recommendations — leadership is vital and the House gave it — and the introduction of new rules for openness and independent scrutiny administered with great skill by Sir Gordon Downey, the first Parliamentary Commissioner for Standards, and his successor, Elizabeth Filkin. These rules do not bear directly upon the conduct of ministers, but they certainly influence the parliamentary climate within which ministers operate.

The work of the Commissioner for Public Appointments *does* bear directly on ministerial conduct in a crucial, albeit limited, sphere. Its effect upon ministerial morality has been motivational, if only in the sense of being both stimulating and salutary. In the wider administrative area the high ethical standards of the civil service, the strongest day to day influence upon the behaviour of ministers, have, I hope, been buttressed by the committee's work, and its advice upon the use and control of special advisers, task forces and whistle blowers has been well received. The judges have been spared from the attentions of the committee (despite irreverent suggestions from some of my fellow committee members), but have made their own contribution towards ensuring the propriety and fairness of ministerial action through the medium of judicial review.

All of this has had its effect on public opinion. In its January 2000 report the committee found general agreement that standards had improved, and quoted Peter Preston, former Editor in Chief of *The Guardian*, as saying:

> I think that the Committee and the reports ... and the implementation of their recommendations have made a substantial difference, not only to the way in which public life in this country is perceived but to the actual practice of it.

I believe that the committee has a long and busy life ahead of it. The key requirements of openness and independent scrutiny are firmly in place to ensure, so far as possible, that ministerial misconduct is exposed and pilloried, but there are still and always will be dragons to slay. The Honours system must come high on the list. It is hard to escape the suspicion that, if only occasionally, money still talks.

This brings me to my last point. I do not believe that *personal* financial gain is the strongest motivating factor among our politicians. Most of them could find much pleasanter and easier ways to pay the bills. I do believe that many are motivated by a desire to change the world and make it better — in some cases by simple altruism or a sense of duty. Power and fame are agreeable accessories, but can hardly be pursued as an end in themselves. What we nearly all want, however, is reasonable financial security for our families and ourselves. We ask too much of our politicians if we deny them that, yet expect them to observe high ethical standards. I do not think it is a coincidence that the reputation for incorruptibility of British civil servants and judges dates from the middle of the nineteenth century, when they achieved adequate salaries and job security. Our ministers have no job security, and I do not think that we pay them nearly enough. Money is not everything, but it is much easier to be moral if you can afford it. A democracy undervalues its politicians at its peril.

Chapter 3

'Educating Devils': Theoretical Reflections on Ethics and Governance

Haig Patapan

The Problem of Rule

The enduring, apparently intractable, political problem is how to secure good government. Practically this question has been articulated in terms of rule. Who, if anyone, should rule? Is ruling an 'art' that can be acquired by instruction? Intimately connected with these concerns has been the question of justice: What are the foundations to just rule? Are there limits to justice and morality? When is it just to question legitimate rule?

From this perspective the question of how to motivate ministers to be ethical and moral is clearly of ancient lineage — it seeks to re-enter the long-standing dialogue concerning the fundamental and perennial problem of good government. But to the extent that these questions have elicited modern answers and solutions to the problem of rule they merit closer scrutiny and attention. In the USA, the UK and Canada there has been an increasing emphasis on measures to insure good government, from basic pecuniary codes and registers to more ambitious codes of conduct, ethical and integrity codes, even ethics commissioners to counsel and advise politicians.[1]

Until recently Australia appeared suspicious of attempts to 'institutionalize ethics'. Recent developments and reforms, however, suggest there may now be increasing support for such proposals (see generally Brien, 1998; Preston *et al.*, 1998; Sampford *et al.*, 1998; Uhr, 1996). These reforms, discussed throughout this book, challenge us with a range of significant and far-reaching questions. What do these changes seek to accomplish? How are we to evaluate their success? Are these changes consistent with liberal democratic constitutionalism? Clearly the reach of these questions places their adequate consideration beyond the scope of this chapter. Nevertheless, as a preliminary issue, a discussion of the role and efficacy of institutions in securing good government does provide the necessary context and background for posing and pursuing these questions. This chapter considers the various attempts to institutionalize ethics by distinguishing between the classical and modern understandings of how to secure good government.[2] For the classical perspective Aristotle's notion of ethics, politics and virtue is examined to suggest that for the ancients education to virtue was an essential means and end of good government. In contrast, the modern view first articulated and developed by Machiavelli took its bearings from the 'real' rather than the imaginary. Modernity does not seek to 'reform' human nature or educate it to virtue, it takes humans as they are; it attempts to secure good government by relying on institutions to marshal and defray human desire and ambition. Thus in the case of American constitutionalism, separation of powers is the pre-eminent modern solution to the problem of rule.

This admittedly simplified dichotomy is intended as a heuristic distinction to bring to light the contending assumptions implicit in each school of thought regarding human nature, the role of ethics and virtue and the importance of institutions. My intention in delineating these different theoretical positions is to provide a better understanding of the reasons and arguments advanced for the various proposed reforms to institutionalize ethics. Accordingly in the final part of the chapter I rely on these contending positions to examine in the context of Australian constitutionalism these new measures to 'motivate ministers' to ethical behaviour.

Education, Legislation and Virtue

The classical understanding of the problem of rule, the importance of virtue and the need for education for good government is most clearly developed by Aristotle. In his famous and influential work on ethics, the *Nicomachean Ethics*,[3] Aristotle differentiates between virtue of thought and virtue of character or *ethos*, which results from habituation and is developed by appropriate action (Aristotle, 1985, 1103b–04a). Virtue is a state, a mean between two vices, one of excess and one of deficiency (Aristotle, 1985, 1107a). For example, the liberal or generous person who takes pleasure in giving the right amount to the right person at the right time is neither wasteful nor mean (Aristotle, 1985, 1120a–22a). Thus the *Ethics* consists of a profound meditation on the virtues of courage, moderation, liberality, honesty, gentleness, politeness and magnificence as well as justice and friendship.

What is remarkable about the *Nicomachean Ethics*, however, is its emphasis on the need for a 'legislative' art. Aristotle argues that the study of virtuous action and the arguments about virtue and happiness are not by themselves sufficient to make everyone decent. Arguments influence and encourage only some people; many naturally obey fear rather than shame, avoiding what is base not because it is disgraceful but because of penalties. As they are impervious to argument (they yield to compulsion more than argument, to sanctions more than what is noble and fine), most people need to be habituated into virtue. For this reason, according to Aristotle, moral education requires legislation (Aristotle, 1985, 1179a–80a).

Because to be good requires a fine upbringing and decent practices it is necessary that human beings have moral educators. But parents' instructions, and more generally instructions by an individual, lack this influence and compulsive power. Law, on the other hand, does compel. Indeed, while people become hostile to individuals who oppose their impulses they are more inclined to accept law's prescriptions. Therefore the greatest educators in the city are its laws. Aristotle suggests that irrespective of the nature and character of law it will unavoidably exercise moral influence on individuals — it is impossible to separate law from morality. But few cities are aware of the powerful educative role of laws according to Aristotle. Moreover, this crucial nexus between ethics and legislation points to the need for a legislative science. It is for these reasons that Aristotle embarked on the work that became the foundation of political science, the *Politics* (Aristotle, 1985, 1180b–81b). Thus Aristotle's *Nicomachean Ethics* is in fact the first half of a comprehensive work on ethics, philosophy and education, the second part of which is the *Politics*.

An important aspect of Aristotle's understanding of moral education is the necessity of virtue for happiness and therefore the primacy of ethics as a practical science. Consequently, Aristotle makes the study of the legislative art, politics, subservient to the study of ethics: politics is to be guided, shaped and informed by ethics. Ethics is not something that is occasionally introduced into politics; it is the core and substance of political life. Though acknowledging the importance of compulsion in politics, Aristotle never abandons the possibility that human beings can be persuaded to be decent. In fact, the *Nicomachean Ethics* culminates in the praise of theoretical life as the happiest and most akin to the gods (Aristotle, 1985, 1178b).

But what form of legislation is conducive to virtue and a decent life? The very title of Aristotle's *Politics* (*politeia* or 'regime') points to the complexity of the problem and the fundamental inadequacy of understanding politics simply in terms of 'power'. For Aristotle the regime is the organization of offices (especially the most authoritative) in the city. It also refers to the way of life of a city as the end pursued by the city as a whole and those constituting its governing body. In Aristotle's famous formulation, the three correct regimes, those that look to the good of the ruled are monarchy or rule by one, aristocracy or rule by the few best, and polity or rule by the many. The deviations are tyranny, oligarchy and democracy (Aristotle, 1984, Bk 4, Ch. 1–2).

In practice, however, two regimes dominate: democracy, where the many free and poor have authority to rule, and oligarchy, where the few wealthy and better born have authority (Aristotle, 1984, Bk 4, Ch. 4). Though both democracy and oligarchy are based on a notion of justice, it is a partial notion according to Aristotle. Democrats hold justice to be equality but in holding this principle they disregard the possibility that equality is just for equals and not for all. Similarly, the oligarchs hold inequality to be just, but for unequals and not for all. Aristotle diagnoses the cause of these partial notions of justice as the fact that human beings are bad judges concerning their own things (Aristotle, 1985, 1280a).

All regimes tend towards extremes and therefore ultimately to revolutions (Aristotle, 1984, Bk 5). This insight determines Aristotle's twofold approach to the problem of rule. The first is to reform and moderate the inherent tendency towards excess in regimes and thereby promote stability. His discussion of the ways to reform democracies, oligarchies, even tyrannies, should be seen in this light (Aristotle, 1984,

Bks 5, 6). But the best practical regime for Aristotle is the polity, or mixed regime, which seeks to combine democratic and oligarchic principles and importantly encourage a middle group which will act as a moderator between the extremes (Aristotle, 1984, Bk 4, Ch. 12 cf. Bk 7). The pressing political problem of faction, especially the competing claims of rich and poor to rule, is overcome by Aristotle by means of the mixed regime which allows each faction a share in rule. Thus the Aristotelian or classical regime relies not on institutions but on its citizens; it attempts to cultivate certain human virtues and excellence as a means of moderating the instability that is caused by the differing demands to rule (Aristotle, 1984, 1295a 25 ff.).

Aristotle is fully aware of the different parts that make up a regime. He distinguishes, for example, between the part that deliberates about common matters, the part connected with offices and the adjudicative part (Aristotle, 1984, Bk 4, Chs 14–16). The similarity with the modern conception of separation between the legislative, executive and judicial is not accidental. But in Aristotle's formulation these different parts are not divisions in functions allotted to institutions that can in some way 'balance' each other. For example, the deliberative element that is said to have authority over war and peace, alliances and dissolutions, laws, death or exile or confiscation and the choosing of the auditing of officials is clearly not simply a 'law-making' role confined to the legislative office. That is, it encompasses some of the duties of the modern executive and the judiciary. The emphasis on deliberation shows Aristotle's acknowledgement of the need for prudence and therefore virtue in political life. The discussion of offices or the magisterial aspect of the regime (Aristotle, 1984, Bk 4, Ch. 15) notes the extent to which the character of the regime will determine the nature of the office. For example, an office of preliminary councillors that will deliberate before matters are brought before a council is considered oligarchic. Who selects the officers, from whom and in what manner they are chosen are questions that point to the primacy of the regime over the nature of the institution. The same principles decide the nature of the courts and the adjudicative functions (Aristotle, 1984, Bk 4, Ch. 16). The eight types of courts distinguished by Aristotle include political courts, demonstrating that Aristotle was aware the courts would have a significant political role in the regime — in fact he suggests that revolutions in regimes can arise from factional disputes about the courts (Aristotle, 1984, 1300b).

This necessarily brief discussion of the different aspects of the regime shows how Aristotle, indeed the classical theorists generally, did not believe that the problem of political rule, especially the problem of faction, could be overcome by allocating different functions of rule to separate institutions and allowing each to check and balance the other. Instead Aristotle sought to give each faction a part of rule, and aware of the potentially unstable nature of such arrangements suggested education as the necessary requirement for sound politics. Because there is no simple institutional solution to political problems, the principle of separation of powers or a balance of functions is not found in Aristotle or in classical political thought.[4] For this we have to turn to the modern understanding of human nature and good government.

New Modes and Orders

The break with classical thought is most clearly seen in the writings of Machiavelli. Machiavelli's observation regarding human nature, ethics and morality in *The Prince* is a succinct formulation and expression of the major change in orientation that we discern in modernity — the attempt to replace the imaginary and ideal republics and principalities of the classical political thought with the 'effectual truth' or realism (Machiavelli, 1985, Ch. xv, p. 61). In *The Prince* Machiavelli states:

> And truly it is a very natural and ordinary thing to desire to acquire, and always, when men do it who can, they will be praised or not blamed; but when they cannot, and want to anyway, here lie the error and the blame (Machiavelli, 1985, Ch. iii, pp. 14–14).

The appetite to acquire has no natural limits according to Machiavelli: 'human appetites are insatiable, for since from nature they have the ability and the wish to desire all things and from fortune the ability to achieve few of them, there continually results from this a discontent in human minds and a disgust with the things they possess' (Machiavelli, 1996, Bk ii, I, p. 125). If one starts from the 'realistic' assessment of human beings as acquisitive and dangerous creatures then it will be possible to re-order the way we evaluate their motives and actions — redefine virtues and vices or what is praised and blamed — and devise more successful means for securing what everybody agrees upon, the need for security and property.

Accordingly Machiavelli in the *Discourses* states that 'it is necessary to whoever disposes a republic and orders laws in it to presuppose that all men are bad, and that they always have to use the malignity of their spirit whenever they have a free opportunity for it'. This means that human beings are not good, they need to be made good:

> Men never work any good unless through necessity, but where choice abounds and one can make use of license, at once everything is full of confusion and disorder. Therefore it is said that hunger and poverty make men industrious, and the laws make them good (Machiavelli, 1996, Bk 1, Ch. 3, p. 15).

Thus his statement in *The Prince* that 'where there are good arms there must be good laws' (Machiavelli, 1996, Ch. xii, p. 48).

This understanding of human nature, which underlies much of modern thought, has important political consequences. The political art comes to resemble the art of war — the means for acquiring the greatest things (property and reputation). Because of the dangerousness of human beings it is better to be feared (to use cruelty well) than loved — it is safer to rely on punishment to achieve political objectives (Machiavelli, 1985, Ch. xvii, p. 65). Therefore laws and more generally institutions can be used to marshal and channel human desires (and chance), just as dykes and dams are used to control potentially violent rivers (Machiavelli, 1985, Ch. xxv, p. 98). In fact, in some cases institutions can be designed to counter each other, securing individual liberty.

The modern reliance on fear and institutions to solve the political problem of rule can be seen most clearly in the political philosophy of Hobbes. Hobbes, the theoretical architect of the modern state, defines the 'Leviathan' as an artificial entity constructed to control the 'children of pride', those individuals who threaten to return everyone to the violence of the state of nature. Without a superintending power to overwhelm and terrify human beings, their natural passions inevitably lead to partiality, pride, revenge and war (Hobbes, 1968, Ch. xvii, p. 223). But the institution of the Leviathan appears to have limited goals. No longer concerned with virtue or the best life (because there is no *Finis ultimus* or *Summum Bonum*: Hobbes, 1968, Ch. xi, p. 160), the new Commonwealth has as its goal the simple but necessary end of preservation and 'contented life' (Hobbes, 1968, Ch. xvii, p. 223). Therefore the state is not concerned with educating its citizens towards a good life; its more limited educational ambition is to remind the citizens of the power of the state (in case they forget and are tempted to break the law), to teach them about honesty (keeping one's word or contract), health and safety (universally accepted as desirable).

The major themes we discern in modernity — the limited role of the state, the need to use fear, laws and institutions as necessary to channel human passions — were subsequently taken up in the formulation of liberal constitutionalism. It is not possible in this context to examine in detail the subtle development of these ideas. For our purposes it may be sufficient to note one major aspect, the understanding of separation of powers developed by Locke and Montesquieu. Locke, the theoretical defender of liberal constitutionalism, distinguished between three powers, the Legislative, the Executive and the Federative. The Legislative power is the supreme power though it is not arbitrary, dispensing justice by promulgated standing laws and known and authorised judges. The Executive is ministerial and subordinate to the Legislative, having the duty of executing the laws, especially of the prerogative. By the Federative power Locke means the power of war and peace and all matters concerning international relations. According to Locke the Executive and Federative powers are almost always united. Consequently in Locke's formulation of separation of powers there is a separation between the Legislative and the Executive (Locke, 1992, *Second Treatise*, Chs xi, xii, xiv).

Though Blackstone mentions separation of powers to be of the essence of English constitutionalism, it is only when we come to Montesquieu that we discern clearly the modern conception of separation of powers. For Montesquieu separation of powers was an institutional solution that would not require virtue; it was an arrangement that would ensure the rule of law and thereby the liberty and security of the individual. In Montesquieu's *Spirit of the Laws*, the principles in the English Constitution are drawn out and perfected to ensure the rule of law. Montesquieu separates the legislative task from the deliberative and the magisterial. He also distributes it between the nobles and the people. Relying on the principle of representative government he distinguishes between the legislative power, the executive power and what he calls 'the power of judging'.

Separation of powers is necessary, according to Montesquieu, to ensure a balance of powers and therefore the liberty of the constitution. However, the more fundamental reason for the separation of the power of judging is the liberty of the citizen:

> Nor is there liberty if the power of judging is not separate from legislative power and from executive power. If it were joined to legislative power, the power over the life and liberty of the citizens would be arbitrary, for the judge would be the legislator. If it were joined to executive power, the judge could have the force of an oppressor (Montesquieu, 1989, Bk 11, Chs 6, 18, p. 157).

The judicial power is separated to keep it independent; it is given only enough power to defend itself from the other two powers. The separation of the judicial power is the most important part of the separation of powers because it guards the government against its own lawlessness; it prevents any deviation from the rule of law by allowing the legislative and executive powers to be checked by a judicial arm that will interpret the laws and apply them equally to everyone. Therefore for Montesquieu separation of powers is an institutional arrangement that ensures the rule of law and thereby the liberty and security of the individual (Montesquieu, 1989, Bk 11, Chs 1–4).

American Constitutionalism

It is useful to turn to American constitutionalism to see how the modern reliance on institutions to solve the problem of rule and more specifically the notion of separation of powers is appropriated and deployed.[5] Though the framers of the American Constitution were influenced by the writings of Locke and Montesquieu, the new Constitution was an innovation, based on principles derived from modern political science (*Federalist* 9).[6] It was devised to address the twofold political problem outlined in Madison's famous observation in *Federalist* 51:

> If angels were to govern men, neither external nor internal controuls on government would be necessary. In framing a government which is to be administered by men over men, the great difficulty lies in this: You must first enable the government to controul the governed; and in the next place, oblige it to controul itself. A dependence on the people is no doubt the primary controul on the government; but experience has taught mankind the necessity of auxiliary precautions.

The primary precaution is dependence on the people or representation. Separation of powers proves to be the chief of the 'auxiliary precautions', which combined with the 'double security' that arises due to the federal division of powers and the multiplicity of interests guards against majority oppression.

Two arguments for separation of powers are advanced in the *Federalist*. Separation of powers is needed as a precaution against the encroaching nature of power. As Madison puts it in the *Federalist* 47:

> The accumulation of all powers legislative, executive, and judiciary in the same hands, whether of one, a few, or many, and whether hereditary, self appointed, or elective, may justly be pronounced the very definition of tyranny.

It is based on the 'policy of supplying by opposite and rival interests, the defect of better motives' (*Federalist* 51). But the separation of powers does not mean that power should be kept in isolation from other powers in their branches (*Federalist* 47 and 48). The encroaching nature of power demands that each branch has the means to ward off such attempts; independence is secured only by means of mutual checks: 'Ambition must be made to counteract ambition'. In this way separation of powers provides a precaution against oppression by rulers (*Federalist* 51).

That ambition is to counter ambition reveals the second justification for separation of powers. In describing the three branches of government and the different qualities required for success in each, the *Federalist* speaks to the ambitious, as well as the common people, evoking better motives than mere ambition. Separation makes the powers work better because in vying with each other the ambitious are drawn to better motives, connecting private interest to virtue in carrying out one's constitutional duty. But in directing and encouraging the virtue of politicians the *Federalist* subordinates it to liberty — the distribution of power in the Constitution has as its aim liberty, achieving for all citizens security from fear as well as a share in rule through elections, and for some an opportunity to exercise their ambition (Epstein, 1984; Mansfield, 1994).

The final part of *Federalist* (78–84) is devoted to the examination of the judiciary. According to Hamilton, 'the judiciary, from the nature of its functions, will always be the least dangerous to the political rights of the constitution; because it will be least in a capacity to annoy or injure them'. It has 'neither Force nor Will, but merely judgement; and must ultimately depend upon the aid of the executive arm even for the efficacy of its judgements'. Being the weakest of the three departments of power, it is important that it has a means of defending itself. Therefore, permanency in office is essential to counter the 'natural feebleness of the judiciary' (*Federalist* 78).

Hamilton defends the need for an independent judiciary on a number of grounds. Independence is essential in a limited constitution, where specific exceptions to legislative authority are spelled out. Thus the courts are the 'bulwarks of a limited constitution against legislative encroachment'. As well, the judiciary as the 'faithful guardians of the constitution' guard it against the 'arts of designing men' and the momentary inclination of the majority. The courts will counter the 'occasional ill humors in the society' in the case of laws generally by 'mitigating the severity, and confining the operation of such laws'. By providing permanent and secure tenure the judiciary are able to protect the rights of the Constitution and the individual while acquiring skills in the law (*Federalist* 78).

According to Hamilton, 'the courts must declare the sense of the law'; judges should not be disposed 'to exercise Will instead of Judgement', to substitute 'their pleasure to that of the legislative body'. Though he seems to dismiss such a possibility, the subsequent discussion reveals his more considered views on the subject. Strict rules and precedents will avoid an arbitrary discretion in the courts according to Hamilton. And even if the will of the legislature is contravened, the nature of judicial power is such that judicial encroachments on the legislative authority is in reality a 'phantom'. In any case, the constitutional check of impeachment is in itself a 'complete security' according to Hamilton.

This general discussion of *Federalist* is intended to show the dominant themes in the modern approach to government. Here the emphasis shifts away from education and virtue to an institutional solution to the problem of ambition and pride. That the 'defect of better motives' can be remedied by the proper arrangement of interests and motives reveals the importance of institutions in modern thought. Thus checking and balancing and separation of powers in general become the modern innovations that solve the encroaching nature of power — it is 'realistically' impossible to educate or limit power, one can only channel and divert it.

Ethics and Australian Constitutionalism

Having developed a distinction between the classical and modern understanding of ethics and politics, it is instructive to see how the specific measures that have been suggested or implemented to motivate ministers can be understood within this framework. For the purposes of this discussion we will develop our argument in the context of the Westminster form of government and in particular Australian constitutionalism. In doing so, however, we are confronted with a preliminary difficulty: how are we to characterize these constitutional traditions? The attempt to answer this question is complicated by a number of factors. To the extent that the above dichotomy has not examined or emphasized the Christian and therefore scholastic and neo-platonist traditions that inform modernity, it is difficult to bring out the subtle and complex character of evolving Westminster tradition. Moreover, the evolutionary nature of this tradition makes it difficult to be precise in our assessments. Significantly, the Westminster tradition is not unambiguously modern. English constitutionalism exercised a major influence on American constitutionalism, directly through colonial practice, mediately by the reflections of political theorists such as Locke, Montesquieu and others. Accordingly, it would seem that in terms of our discussion the Westminster tradition is to be evaluated as essentially modern. The evolving Westminster system, which formed the constitutional basis for the new colonies such as Canada and

Australia, was liberal democratic — it relied on the fundamental principles of modernity we have noted above. As Montesquieu noted, though not fully articulated into a coherent theoretical thesis, the English institutions of a bicameral Parliament, the separation of the judiciary, and the jury system, pointed to institutionally fragmented sources of power that would ensure individual liberty.

But in important respects the Westminster tradition did not strictly adhere to the modern conceptions of power. General observations about the nature of these institutions will demonstrate the extent to which this tradition relied on education as an essential element of good rule. The theoretical, if not practical, primacy of parliament as a deliberative, law-making and representative institution in the Westminster system revealed a concentration rather than dispersal of power. The sovereignty of parliament, though often overstated, was an important premise that demonstrated confidence in government. Far from being a threat, parliament was seen as a check on the real danger, the executive, as well as a deliberative body that would represent the people and secure the *salus populi* or welfare of the people. Along with sovereignty of parliament, the fundamental principle at the heart of Westminster system — responsible government — revealed the extent to which the English system had a different conception of political authority. The conventional aspect of responsible government, that ministers and members were expected to act appropriately, without reference to written rules or codes, reveals much about the way authority and power was to be exercised.

At the Australian founding, parliamentary sovereignty and responsible government, present in the colonial constitutions, were incorporated into Australian constitutionalism. The founders were aware that to the extent that the Constitution appropriated from both English and American constitutionalism, parliamentary sovereignty and responsible government were at tension with the American innovation of federalism. Nevertheless parliamentary government was retained as an essential aspect of Australian polity. But the increasing power and influence of political parties in Australia, which has favoured government by the executive and bureaucracy rather than parliament, has challenged the relevance of parliamentary responsible government in Australia (Uhr, 1998b). The 'decline of parliament' thesis has prompted a 'new administrative law' — freedom of information and privacy legislation, ombudsmen, administrative tribunals and statutory consolidation of judicial review procedures (see generally Allars, 1997). It has also encouraged attempts to entrench a bill of rights, though these have proven to be singularly unsuccessful. The High Court's implied rights jurisprudence — discerning in the Constitution an implied right to political communication — is arguably another attempt to insure the efficacy of parliamentary democracy in Australia (Williams, 1999).

The recent proposals to encourage ethical ministerial behaviour should therefore be evaluated within the larger context of the decline of parliament thesis, and the view that there is a general lack of public confidence in politics and politicians. But to the extent that each of these measures — pecuniary codes, codes of ethics and codes of conduct and related advisory and supervisory institutions — seeks to address different aspects of ministerial behaviour, it is important to note the significant differences between them. Here I want to attempt to distinguish, within the constraints of this discussion, and in light of the distinction above between classical and modern notions of virtue and education, these different measures.

I would suggest that pecuniary codes and independent bodies that seek to exercise a supervisory role and monitor ministerial behaviour, such as Queensland's Criminal Justice Commission and the New South Wales Independent Commission Against Corruption, are principally modern institutional measures that seek to curb, check and control power. Arguably pecuniary codes seek to reduce to writing what was conventionally accepted as improper conflict of interest. The fundamental difficulty in defining the various manifestations of such conflict, and their crude evaluation in terms of property, reveals the limitations of codifying mores. Independent commissions, as 'checking institutions', appear to fit neatly into the modern understanding of the need to have institutional checking and balancing of power. However, being institutional innovations that are not of parliament (as a committee, for example) although ultimately accountable to it, they reveal the tension in combining parliamentarianism with modern institutionalism. They highlight in particular the problem of responsibility and accountability — how is the power now placed in the newly devised institution to be checked? *Quis custodiet ipsus custodes?*'

In contrast, it would appear that codes of conduct, ethical codes and even institutions such as the ethics or integrity commissioners seek to do more than limit power; they seek to educate with a view to a proper use of power. If liberal democracy is concerned with 'comfortable self-preservation', leaving to individuals choices about the good life (or 'life styles'), it would appear that these attempts at motivating ministers hark back to earlier traditions, introducing into the lexicon of autonomy, rights, equality and rule of law a new moral vision.

It is arguable, of course, that the ethical codes that are being implemented seek to educate to the minimal ethical standards, those that are not contestable; that is, those things we all agree are bad rather than those we agree are good. For example, not cheating, 'transparency', due process, non-discrimination, non-violence, as 'thin' rather than 'thick' notions of the good, are consistent with modern ethical codes (Rawls, 1971). An ethics commissioner who is to advise and educate on such minimal notions of virtue is arguably consistent with the modern understanding of power.

But these codes and indeed the ethics and integrity commissioners clearly cannot confine their advice and education to matters of procedure. This is because inevitably procedural matters draw upon, or are sustained by, more profound ethical and moral considerations. Before long these codes will engage serious moral dilemmas. In this light an ethics commissioner, who is presumably wiser and more prudent, will have to advise on the proper course of action to be taken. Such an institution seems to fit uneasily with the bedrock liberal notion of the equal moral dignity of all individuals (Beiner, 1992; MacIntyre, 1981; Sandel, 1982).

This raises a number of intriguing questions. Why do we feel a need to return to the older notions of ethics and virtue? Is it an honest acknowledgement that liberal democracy, with its emphasis on choice as the highest good, in fact needs and presupposes such virtues? Is it the only way religion and faith, relegated to the private sphere, can gain purchase in public deliberation in liberal democracy? Perhaps it is the only proper answer to the decline of parliament thesis. In any case it brings to mind Constant's concerns that to the extent that ancient liberty, the active and constant participation in rule, is no longer possible (replaced by modern liberty of individual rights), there are dangers in transplanting ancient ideals, expectations and institutions into modern climes (Constant, 1988) — we should not try to educate devils.

Old Virtues, New Liberty

Perhaps the best way to sum up the difference between the classical and modern conceptions of ethics and politics is to refer to the familiar story of the two children who have to share a pie. The innocuous solution that is generally proposed is that 'one cuts the pie, the other chooses the piece'. Consistent with game theory win–win solutions the child cutting the pie would be advised to cut two equal pieces — to be equitable or fair — not because the child has been brought up to behave that way (indeed the 'institutional' device works even with Kant's 'race of devils', provided they are intelligent: Kant, 1963, p. 112), but because it can be reliably assumed that the friend will behave just as inequitably given half a chance. By making the 'safe' or 'realistic' assumption that faced with a choice of a small and a large piece every person will choose the larger, the child is prepared to settle for loss minimisation. The assumption of unlimited acquisition and no real limits to individual desires results in the contractual position of equality of distribution: not because this is good, but simply because it is not as bad as the potentially risky option of satisfying one's true desires and taking it all. The pie story, apparently a charming tale of 'best practice' if not justice, covers over its Machiavellian presuppositions. It is intended to show that a quick and efficient solution to the problem of sharing and distributing good things exists — the laborious and uncertain reliance on education and virtue is no longer warranted in modern life.[8]

Of course in reality the distinction between ancient and modern is less clear cut: modernity is arguably perceived in the context of, and sustained by, the past; all institutions inevitably educate at some level; education is simply inadequate for some purposes. Nevertheless I have suggested that the distinction between the ancient and modern understanding of how to secure good government is a useful starting point for asking how we can motivate ministers. The attempts to institutionalize ethics is a welcome reminder of the central place that ethics and morals occupy in all states, even those that seek to return such contentious issues to the private sphere. In making possible a more profound engagement with the question of what is justice, these measures sustain and justify a necessary return to debate and deliberation about the nature of politics, ethics and morality and their place in our lives.

Notes

1 For the US experience see Mancuso (1998); regarding the UK see Nolan (1995); for Canada see Wilson (1998), House of Commons, Canada (1995).
2 For an earlier discussion of the difference between classical republican and modern or liberal republican perspectives see Uhr (1998a).
3 Aristotle wrote two works on ethics, the *Nicomachean Ethics* and the less well known *Eudemian Ethics*. This discussion focuses on the *Nicomachean Ethics* (Aristotle, 1985).
4 Polybius also attempts to rely on an institutional solution to counteract the natural cycles of political revolution whereby constitutions change, disappear and finally return to the starting point (1979, Fragments of Book VI, 3–18, pp. 271–311). The Roman Constitution is his model where power is distributed between the institutions of the consuls, the senate and the commons, enabling them to cooperate in times of necessity, while countering and thwarting excessive ambition in times of prosperity. Polybius' institutional solution relies less on virtue, allocating to each faction a share in power to preserve unity and stability in the regime. (For Polybius Lycurgus is the first one to reason about the natural changes in constitutions. His solution was to neutralize the different aspects of governments to encourage a sort of equilibrium: 1979, VI, 10 5–8, p. 291).
5 For an earlier discussion of the theoretical and constitutional understanding of separation of powers in Australia see Patapan (1999).
6 For references to *Federalist Papers* see Hamilton *et al.* (1982).
7 Who is to guard the guards themselves?
8 Compare this with the social contract theories of Hobbes (1968), Locke (1992) and Rousseau (1968) as well as Rawls' (1971) 'veil of ignorance' which, not surprisingly, also yield equal slices of pie for everyone.

PART II:
LESSONS FROM WESTMINSTER: CODES AND CONVENTIONS

Chapter 4

The Role of Ministerial Responsibility in Motivating Ministers to Morality

Diana Woodhouse

This chapter examines the way in which the Westminster convention of individual ministerial responsibility motivates ministers to morality, in both their personal behaviour and their departmental roles. The convention provides the mechanism by which ministers account to parliament for their own actions and for those of their departments and, in extreme circumstances, it may impose the requirement of resignation. It can therefore be seen as containing the rules by which 'the political actors *ought* to feel obliged' (Marshall, 1986, p. 12) and, by so doing, providing a critical or constitutional morality against which a minister's behaviour and performance can be assessed. This morality is not, of course, absolute but is determined by the mores of the time. Moreover, the judgement as to whether it has been infringed is a political judgement and will depend on a number of factors, not least the effect on party and prime minister of a resignation. The effectiveness of the convention in imposing a constitutional morality may therefore be questioned, particularly given changes in the structure and culture of government and the seeming inability of modern parliaments to hold ministers to account. Nevertheless, it continues to provide some ground rules, even if ministers seek to avoid their consequences, and, by providing those rules, it would seem to be a motivating force.

Resignation as a Moral Imperative

Personal Fault

Resignation as a moral imperative is most obvious when there is 'causal responsibility' (Hart, 1968, p. 212). This may concern an error of political judgement, such as that made in 1988 by Britain's Minister for Health, Edwina Currie, whose statement that most of the egg production in the UK was infected with salmonella resulted in a dramatic drop in egg sales (see Woodhouse, 1994, pp. 53–65). However, usually it relates to personal indiscretion, most obviously of a sexual or financial nature. Whether sexual impropriety or indiscretion provides sufficient grounds on its own for demands for resignation is doubtful. The evidence suggests that, in the absence of a minister choosing to relinquish office for personal reasons, there needs to be another factor which undermines the minister's reputation or embarrasses the government. Thus the resignations of Parkinson and Mellor from the UK government in 1983 and 1992, respectively, were necessary because of sustained media coverage of their infidelity, coupled with concern about Parkinson's reliability and criticism of Mellor's handling of the press, for which he was the responsible minister, and his acceptance of a holiday from a friend who had connections with the Palestinian Liberation Organization (Woodhouse, 1994, pp. 72–86). Similarly, the resignations of Yeo, Brown, Hughes and Richards from the Major government (1992–97) were less a reflection of the seriousness of their indiscretions and more about their failure to live up to the standards of personal behaviour they and their colleagues publicly proclaimed, the government having made private morality a political issue (Woodhouse, 1999, p. 105). This was a mistake the Blair government was at pains not to repeat and in 1997 the prime minister stated that he had no intention of imposing a code of proper sexual behaviour upon ministers. As a consequence, the Foreign Secretary, Robin Cook, remained in office despite extensive media reporting of his decision to leave his wife for his constituency secretary. The prime minister having redrawn the boundaries, there was no other factor to trigger Cook's resignation.

Where errors of judgement of a pecuniary nature are concerned, there may not be the need for an additional offence before resignation is required. Ministers who accept gifts and hospitality, fail to declare financial and business interests or use their political position for personal gain or to benefit family or friends are unlikely to remain in office, hence the resignations from the Australian federal government of Treasury ministers, Jim Short and Brian Gibson (in 1996), who had made decisions concerning companies in which they had shares, and of Geoff Prosser, Minister for Small Business (in 1997), who had breached the requirement that ministers 'must not engage in any professional practice or in the daily work of any business' (Thompson and Tillotsen, 1999, p. 53). The resignations of David Jull, John Sharp and Peter McGauran, who had misused travel allowances, were also forthcoming in 1997 (see Tiernan, Chapter 8).

Similarly in the UK, Neil Hamilton and Tim Smith resigned in 1994 after allegations that they had accepted cash for asking questions in parliament, and a year later Jonathan Aitkin relinquished office following revelations of financial impropriety. Peter Mandelson had the dubious distinction of resigning twice. The first time was in 1998 when he resigned from his position as Secretary of State for Trade and Industry after it was revealed that he had borrowed money to buy a house from a ministerial colleague, Geoffrey Robinson, one of whose companies then came under investigation by Mandelson's department. There was no suggestion of financial impropriety, Mandelson having distanced himself from the inquiry, but he had failed to tell his permanent secretary of the loan, as required, or to declare it in his mortgage application. Robinson, who had previously survived accusations of a conflict of interest, was also a casualty of the incident. They had no place in a government seeking to portray an ultra-clean image. However, Mandelson's offence was sufficiently minor to allow him to return to office some 10 months later, as Secretary of State for Northern Ireland, only to resign for the second time in January 2001 over a telephone call made to a Home Office minister to check on the progress of an application for citizenship by an Indian businessman. Again, there was no suggestion of impropriety but it seems Mandelson misled the prime minister and parliament about the phone call — a capital offence.

Instances of financial impropriety and the improper use of office cast doubt on an individual's suitability and trustworthiness as a minister and on the prime minister's judgement in selecting a ministerial team. In sufficient numbers, they may also suggest that a government is unfit to govern, thereby damaging its chances of being returned to office after an election, the perception of 'sleaze' undoubtedly playing a part in the defeat of the UK Conservative government in 1997.

Where personal behaviour is concerned, there is a clear link between responsibility for that behaviour and control over it and it is not surprising, therefore, that the vast majority of resignations fall within this category. The removal of such ministers, or at least those who have been involved in financial misjudgement, is of utmost importance to good government. However, 'such resignations have very little to do with ensuring an ongoing system of sound and accountable administration' (Thompson and Tillotsen, 1999, p. 57). This requires there to be mechanisms for dealing with departmental error and here the link between responsibility and control is less evident, the size and complexity of government making it impossible for a minister to have more than a supervisory or overseeing role. It is therefore in relation to departmental fault that the resignation requirement is least clear.

Departmental Fault

Notions that ministers should accept consequential or vicarious responsibility and resign for the errors of their officials (Anson, 1935; Jennings, 1959), regardless of their distance, geographically or hierarchically, from the minister, are unsupported by precedent (Marshall, 1986; Finn, 1990; Woodhouse, 1993). However, the convention may require resignation for serious departmental fault in which the minister was involved or of which he/she knew, hence the resignation of Ros Kelly from the Australian government in 1994, after reports from the Auditor-General and House of Representatives Standing Committee on Environment, Recreation and the Arts found that the way in which she had personally administered the sports facilities programme was seriously inadequate (Thompson and Tillotsen, 1999, p. 52).

Ministerial involvement is not always so evident. Nevertheless, it was sufficient in the UK to require the resignation of Sir Thomas Dugdale in 1954, Lord Carrington in 1982 and Leon Brittan in 1986. Dugdale resigned following criticism of the way in which his department disposed of land at Crichel Down which had been requisitioned during World War II. His resignation statement suggested that he was accepting vicarious liability for errors by his officials. In fact, although there had been maladministration within the department, he was paying the price for pursuing a policy which was unpopular with government backbenchers, and for being inefficient in the running of his department (Nicholson, 1986). For his part, Lord Carrington forfeited office after he and his department failed to foresee the invasion of the Falklands by Argentina and for his misjudgement in not initiating a review of policy on the islands (Franks, 1983; Woodhouse, 1994). Brittan was a casualty of the Westland affair, resigning after it was revealed that he had authorized his officials to disclose extracts of a confidential letter from the Solicitor General to Heseltine, another government minister, with the aim of discrediting Heseltine's policy (Oliver and Austin, 1987).

In addition to ministers being responsible for their own actions and decisions, the convention of ministerial responsibility also imposes a 'negative responsibility' (Lucas, 1995, p. 182), such that ministers are responsible for failing to act when they should have done so. This arises from the minister's role or 'distinctive place or office' (Hart, 1968, p. 212). This lays upon him/her certain duties, both personal and organizational, and the responsibility for ensuring that these are fulfilled. Failing to exert the appropriate level of supervisory authority is a breach of these duties. Thus not knowing that something is happening may not be a good defence if it is felt that the minister should have known. This was evident after 14 people died when a viewing platform collapsed at Cave Creek, New Zealand, in 1995. The pressure on the minister to resign arose not from his personal involvement but from feelings that he had failed to exercise a supervisory role through at least ensuring that the department had adequate resources to fulfil its safety obligations (Gregory, 1998).

How much ministerial involvement is necessary to trigger demands for resignation depends on the circumstances. Where the consequences are very serious even the tenuous involvement of the minister may be sufficient for resignation to be required, as it was when the Falkland Islands were invaded by Argentina. Similarly, a hint of ministerial negligence may be enough for the resignation requirement to operate, as after the Cave Creek tragedy. In such circumstances resignation is necessary not only to restore the government's political reputation but also to restore confidence in the system. Political requirements in such instances therefore work to reinforce constitutional morality. Indeed, if ministers are to be motivated to act in accordance with constitutional morality, political and constitutional requirements need to coincide. It is a rare minister who resigns while retaining political support.

The Effectiveness of the Convention

The Policy/Operations Division

Where departmental fault is concerned, it is a rare minister who resigns at all. Indeed, it would seem that rather than being motivated to morality, ministers are motivated to distance themselves from any culpability and hence from the requirement of resignation. This has been most evident in the use of the policy/operations division. In the UK it was first imported into the departmental context by James Prior, who, as Secretary of State for Northern Ireland, sought to limit his responsibility for the break out of 38 IRA prisoners from the Maze Prison in 1983 by arguing that he was under no obligation to resign for administrative errors (House of Commons Debates (HC), 24 October 1983, cols 23-4). To an extent he was correct. Most administrative errors are too remote from ministers to be within their knowledge or control. However, this does not mean that ministers can abdicate responsibility for all administrative mistakes. Much depends on the nature and scale of the errors, their centrality to policy, and the extent to which the minister had been involved or should have been involved in overseeing the operation of the department. Yet the division, which was contested by parliament at the time (HC, 9 February 1984, col. 106) and about which a host of authorities have expressed reservations before and since (e.g. Royal Commission on Australian Government Administration, 1976; Treasury and Civil Service Committee (TCSC), 1988-89), has become part of the constitutional landscape. Indeed, with the management reforms in New Zealand, Australia and the UK, whereby operational responsibilities are delegated to officials through contracts and framework documents, it has become an essential feature of government.

Such delegation may provide greater clarity and transparency, as well as improving efficiency (Efficiency Unit, 1988; New Zealand Treasury, 1987). However, there may still be difficulty in determining, first, 'what is an operational matter and what is policy' (Woodcock, 1994, para. 9.2.9) and precisely who has taken a particular decision; second, whether the minister has interfered; and, third, whether the minister should have interfered but failed to do so. Even when the division is clearly made, so-called 'operational errors' may be the result of poor policy or erratic changes in policy direction, with policy success or failure frequently only becoming apparent at the operational level. They may also be the result of inadequate resourcing. Such confusion provides ministers with the opportunity of distancing themselves from anything that goes wrong and thus escaping the constitutional and political consequences of ministerial responsibility. In such instances, responsibility is transferred to officials.

This was evident in the UK context in the cases of the Child Support and Prison Service Agencies. In 1994 the chief executive of the Child Support Agency resigned after the agency had been blamed for widespread maladministration and a failure to meet targets, although it was apparent that the ability of the agency to operate effectively had been directly affected by the failure of ministers to provide sufficient resources (Social Security Committee, 1993-94) and by the priority they gave to saving money rather than providing a quality service (Select Committee on the Parliamentary Commissioner for Administration, 1994-95). Similarly, the Director General of the Prison Service Agency, Derek Lewis, was dismissed in 1996 after the Home Secretary blamed his management of the agency for two prison breakouts. The minister claimed the errors were operational and thus the responsibility of the Director General, a claim disputed by Lewis, who contended that the agency had been subject to extensive interference from the Home Secretary and to changes in policy which had been unaccompanied by increased resources (Barker, 1998; Lewis, 1996).

The ministerial focus on 'causal responsibility', with the cause always being cited as operational error and thus the responsibility of officials, rather than on 'role responsibility', which resides with ministers, confuses managerial and constitutional responsibility and ignores the principle that only ministers can accept constitutional responsibility (Cabinet Office, 1996). Thus while the public blaming of officials may be seen as forwarding the accountability process (Mulgan, 1997, p. 31), providing blame is appropriately apportioned and those blamed have the opportunity of defending themselves, it should be additional to, rather than instead of, the constitutional responsibility of ministers.

Problems relating to the policy/operations divide are not confined to the UK. In New Zealand similar issues have arisen, most notably in the aftermath of the Creek Cave tragedy, when the subsequent Commission of Inquiry found that that the 'proximate or dominant' cause was that the platform had not been built in accordance with sound building practice but that the 'most significant secondary cause' was the Department of Conservation's failure to maintain an adequate project management system (Gregory, 1998, pp. 520–3). The inquiry's report was also critical of the way in which responsibility had been transferred to the department, of management failures at head office and the lack of resources. Thus although the division between policy and operations, which formed the basis for the contractual relationship between the minister and the department's chief executive, suggested that responsibility lay with the latter, the lack of funding, which had undermined the ability of the department to operate effectively, together with the lack of oversight of the department, required the minister also to accept responsibility (Gregory, 1998, pp. 520–3). In the event, while the chief executive remained in office for a further two years to take corrective action, the minister resigned his Conservation portfolio 'as an indication of his sorrow' (Gregory, 1998, p. 531). There was therefore some acceptance of constitutional responsibility, albeit tempered by the minister retaining a cabinet position.

'Accountability' and 'Responsibility'

The problems surrounding the policy/operations division have been compounded by the distinction made by the UK government between 'responsibility' and 'accountability'. While the meaning of responsibility in the context of ministerial responsibility has been subject to considerable discussion (Johnson, 1977; Marshall and Moodie, 1959), it has tended to be used interchangeably with accountability or answerability. Where different meanings have been attributed, it has been to the extent that the responsibility of ministers to parliament is described as requiring them to account or answer for their responsibilities. However, in 1993 the UK government sought to distinguish between the two words, arguing that while accountability related to the constitutional obligation of ministers to account to parliament for their departments and agencies, responsibility 'implies personal involvement in an action or decision, in a sense that implies personal credit or blame for that action or decision'. It therefore follows that 'a Minister is *accountable* for all the actions and activities of his department, but not *responsible* for all the actions in the sense of being blameworthy' (Cabinet Office, 1993).

The use of such a distinction to protect ministers from being seen as personally responsible for minor failings or for actions of their officials, of which they had no knowledge and could be expected to have none, is uncontroversial, although it would seem to serve little constitutional purpose, merely restating the position as understood since Crichel Down (Maxwell Fyfe, 1954). However, the premise that ministerial responsibility is composed of two separate elements, rather than being part of the same process and inextricably linked, enables ministers to escape responsibility (in the sense of blame) for a series of operational errors, which amount to mismanagement or negligence on the minister's part, on the basis that no individual mistake was his/her own (Public Service Committee (PSC), 1995–96, para. 13). Moreover, the apparent separation of the two concepts presents a danger of there being a surfeit of ministerial 'accountability', that is, of ministers giving explanations and justifications which protect their positions and deflect blame, and little acceptance of ministerial 'responsibility' (Gregory, 1998, p. 527).

There has always been a reluctance by ministers to accept such responsibility, hence the infrequency of resignations for departmental fault.[1] However, the distinctions made between policy/operations and responsibility/accountability suggest that, more than ever, the convention of ministerial responsibility is dependent for its operation on ministerial integrity.

This dependence is exacerbated by the failure of modern parliaments to fulfil one of their constitutional functions, that is, to hold government to account.

The Failure of Parliament

Parliament is the most obvious mechanism for motivating ministers to comply with the morality of the constitution. However, majority governments and party discipline mean that parliament's ability and will to motivate ministers to conform to the requirements of ministerial responsibility is in doubt. Nowhere was this more evident than in the failure in 1996 of the UK House of Commons to extract the ultimate penalty from William Waldegrave and Sir Nicholas Lyell for their part in the Arms to Iraq (Matrix Churchill) affair. Waldegrave had given misleading information to parliament about government policy on the sale of arms and Lyell, the Attorney General, was criticized by the subsequent inquiry, chaired by Sir Richard Scott, for failing adequately to oversee the work of some of the officials in his department (Scott, 1996a). The continuation in office of these ministers represented a low point in British politics and in constitutional morality and suggested that the convention of ministerial responsibility was failing to motivate ministerial behaviour.

Parliament did subsequently pass a Resolution, which includes the provision 'If Ministers knowingly mislead the House, the House will expect them to offer their resignation to the Prime Minister' (HC, 19 March 1997, cols 1046–7). However, although this statement was constitutionally significant and its status was enhanced by inclusion in the *Ministerial Code* (Cabinet Office, 1997), it would be wrong to see it as an act of parliamentary independence. It was negotiated with the government and the inclusion of the word 'knowingly', which had been employed by the prime minister to save Waldegrave, would seem to remove instances where the minister has been negligent or incompetent in what was said (Bogdanor, 1997, p. 74). Thus ministers are protected from the requirement to resign unless they are found to have actively plotted to deceive.

Moreover, while the resolution provides parliament with some authority to which appeals can be made, in practice it may make little difference given that a minister who has prime ministerial support is also likely to retain the support of government backbenchers and thus be able to resist any call for resignation. The same backbench support will also be forthcoming where departmental errors are concerned, and it was in recognition of parliamentary impotence that the PSC in the UK attempted to transfer the responsibility for ministerial behaviour from the House of Commons to the prime minister. Nolan had sought to make the prime minister responsible for ensuring that 'ministers live up to the standards required of them' (PSC, 1995–96, para. 52). The committee went further, stating:

> A Minister has to conduct himself and direct the work of his department in a manner likely to ensure that he retains the confidence both of his own party and of the House. It is for the Prime Minister to decide whom he chooses for Ministers; but the Prime Minister is unlikely to keep in office a Minister who does not retain the confidence of his Parliamentary colleagues (PSC, 1995–96, para. 32).

This suggested that it foresaw a situation in which a minister loses the support of parliament, but, contrary to the conventional understanding, remains in office with the prime minister's support. The government rejected the committee's recommendation (PSC, 1996–97, p. vi). Thus both parliament and the prime minister disclaimed responsibility for ministerial standards and thus for motivating morality. Moreover, a subsequent attempt by the Public Administration Committee to secure 'prime ministerial ownership' of the Code (Public Administration Committee, 2001, para. 20) and his/her accountability to parliament for it likewise meet with a negative response.

Supporting Mechanisms for Motivating Morality

There have, however, been developments, namely the establishment of codes of conduct and regulatory regimes, which work to support the operation of ministerial responsibility. A particular concern during the 1980s and early 1990s, especially in Australia, was financial impropriety. Instances such as the Marshall Islands affair in

1992[2] made the regulation of ministerial conduct a political issue and resulted in the publication of codes of conduct for both ministers and officials, including *Ethical Standards and Values in the Australian Public Service* (1996), *Guidelines in Official Conduct of Commonwealth Public Servants* (1995) and a *Guide to Key Elements of Ministerial Responsibility* (1996). Much of this material had been contained in previous documents, for instance, the *Australian Cabinet Handbook*, or simply gave written form to existing conventions. Nevertheless, the publication of codes was a recognition of public concern about ministerial behaviour (see Weller, Chapter 5). In a similar way, the UK government of John Major published the ministerial guide, *Questions of Procedure* (Cabinet Office, 1992), subsequently renamed the *Ministerial Code: A Code of Conduct and Guidance on Procedures for Ministers* (Cabinet Office, 1997) by Tony Blair. Major also instigated the publication of the *Civil Service Code* (Cabinet Office, 1996).

Codes of conduct provide base-line standards against which behaviour can be measured, and in supporting the convention of ministerial responsibility provide a basis for calls for resignation. Yet not all ministers whose activities appear to infringe the code have relinquished office. Both John Moore and Warwick Parer remained in the Australian government despite Moore's refusal in 1996 to sell a share trading company and Parer's apparent use in 1998 of a ministerial visit to Japan to further his business interests (Thompson and Tillotsen, 1999). In both cases the ministers retained the prime minister's support, thereby demonstrating that, unless ministers break the law, motivating ministers to morality in instances of financial impropriety will depend largely on the prime minister's interpretation of the rules and a political judgement of the situation.

In addition to instigating codes of conduct, governments have also responded to public concern about standards by establishing regulatory bodies, such as, in the UK, the Committee on Standards in Public Life and the Parliamentary Standards Commissioner and, in Australia, the NSW Independent Commission against Corruption, the Queensland Criminal Justice Commission and the Western Australian Commissioner for Public Sector Standards and Commission on Government. These represent real attempts 'to get accountability out of the swamp of politics' (Evans, 1999, p. 88), but their effectiveness can be limited by their insulation from, and lack of understanding of, the political process and their dependence on government to give effect to their conclusions (see Fleming, Chapter 11). This was evident in the refusal of John Major's government to implement the recommendation of the Committee on Standards in Public Life, chaired by Lord Nolan, that *Questions of Procedure* should stipulate that it was for the prime minister to determine whether or not ministers had upheld the highest standards (Nolan, 1995). The government's refusal was on the grounds that it went 'too far towards suggesting that the Prime Minister's relationship with his ministerial colleagues is that of invigilator and judge. And it would not reflect the responsibility that ministers should have to justify their conduct to Parliament' (Cabinet Office, 1995).

Thus while codes of conduct and regulatory bodies are important in the maintenance of standards, ultimately, the fate of a minister will depend upon his/her integrity and the judgement of the prime minister as to whether resignation is required and whether it is more politically damaging to lose a minister than to keep him/her in office. Regulatory bodies, as so far established, are in any case only concerned with ministerial responsibility as it relates to financial conduct. Although the codes of ministerial conduct also relate to the responsibility of ministers to parliament for their departments, they fail to articulate the conventional requirement for resignation.

Conclusion

The protection afforded to ministers by the prime minister and the party means that they are seldom motivated to comply with the morality of the constitution. This suggests that the effectiveness of ministerial responsibility, as a constitutional and political check, is limited. Indeed, in the main, it is the prime minister who keeps ministers in check through ministerial reshuffles. These 'reveal the valuation placed on ministers' day-to-day performance' (Blick, 1999, p. 59). However, important though reshuffles are as a regulatory mechanism, they leave too much in the gift of the prime minister and do not have the symbolic quality of resignation.

Resignations represent a political apology and/or a punishment for the violation of public trust, their style and speed determining which category is dominant. A resignation, such as Lord Carrington's after the invasion of the Falklands in 1983, which was a swift acceptance of responsibility, or at least an acceptance of the belief of others that he was responsible, can be classified as an apology. The same cannot be said of the resignation of Leon Brittan over the Westland affair in 1986. He did not accept responsibility until the Head of the Home Civil Service had undertaken an inquiry and three officials from his department had been publicly named. Moreover, his acceptance carried no explanation and his resignation was reluctant. It can therefore best be seen as punishment, or alternatively as protecting the then prime minister, Margaret Thatcher, whose bidding some believed Brittan was doing.

Reshuffles represent neither an apology nor obviously a punishment. Yet 'at base, accountability is a form of control designed to force those holding power to own up for their conduct. To be made accountable is to be made to pay and this theme of punishment is essential to the core meaning of accountability' (Uhr, 1999b, p. 99) and to any interpretation of ministerial responsibility. The threat of resignation therefore 'remains an essential component of the control of government. It is, in effect, the final stage in the process of accountability' (PSC, 1995–96, para. 33).

However, the domination of parliament by the executive and party means that it is seldom able to extract the accountability required. Moreover, imposing a legal requirement on ministers to resign should they lose its support is unlikely to provide a solution. The experience in Denmark, where the Constitution contains such a provision, indicates that the parliament is 'most reluctant to enforce theoretical political responsibility through serious criticism or a demand for the resignation of a minister'. Rather, it 'has taken up a political position that places decisive emphasis on whether or not a minister has broken any law, and on whether, if this is in fact the case, the minister knew or should have known what he or she was doing' (Christensen, 1999, p. 2). Thus the political judgement of what constitutes a 'serious error' is even modified to limit a written constitutional requirement for resignation.

Similarly, the effect of censure motions may be modified. Votes of confidence or censure were a feature of the nineteenth century Westminster parliament and have remained so in Australia, where, during the period 1976–89, there were 41 censure motions, although all but one of these were lost (Page, 1990). In the UK the advent of majority governments and strong party discipline resulted in a decline in the practice of formally censuring ministers. However, the establishment of the Scottish parliament and the Welsh Assembly in 1998, together with the election of minority governments, raised the prospect of the practice being resurrected to force resignation. In October 1999 it was, when a censure motion was passed against the Agriculture Secretary in the Welsh Assembly. Yet, despite this formal expression of a lack of confidence in her abilities, the minister did not resign. Moreover, Opposition members took no further action, preferring to focus their attention on a bigger prize, the First Secretary, who resigned from office some four months later. It seems therefore that while censure motions may be an important political weapon, the loss of such a motion will not necessarily motivate a minister to resign.

This suggests the need for other mechanisms which will support parliament in upholding the requirements of ministerial responsibility, such as independent commissions of inquiry, which could be automatically established to investigate and report on serious incidents of departmental error, on the lines of Scott's inquiry into the Arms to Iraq affair, or perhaps a standing commission, similar to the Committee on Standards of Public Life, which goes beyond looking at financial impropriety and corruption. In addition, as the Public Administration Committee recommended, 'the parliamentary ombudsman could be empowered to conduct independent investigations of alleged breaches of the Ministerial Code and to report to the Prime Minister and the House' (2001, para. 30). There is, of course, the danger that the conclusions of these bodies will be contested, misinterpreted and ultimately ignored, as those of Sir Richard Scott were. But an effective system of inquiry would seem an important addition and one that might give substance to the ideal of the constitutional state that 'power walks hand in hand with responsibility' (Christensen, 1999, p. 2).

However, ultimately the key to motivating ministers to comply with the requirement of the convention is the fear of the consequences of not doing so (Jennings, 1959). The worst consequence is losing the support of the electorate. If ministers believe that their failure to act in accordance with the morality of the constitution could mean being returned to the Opposition benches, or worse not being returned at all, their motivation might increase. They might also be much less likely to protect their errant colleagues. Such a development requires the education of the electorate in civic responsibility, so that constituents will put pressure on their elected representatives. It also necessitates the education of the elected members of parliament, who:

> ... need to be reminded again and again that our chosen form of liberal democracy, the 'Westminster model' ... is highly vulnerable to abuse and distortion — because of its heavy reliance on conventions or unwritten rules which means dependence on the good faith and integrity of political practitioners (Boyce, 1994).

Such integrity can only be assured if politicians believe that if they fail to abide by the unwritten rules they will be punished by the electorate. There needs to be a public expectation that ministers will resign not only when their personal behaviour falls below the accepted standard but also when they are implicated in serious departmental fault or have failed to supervise their departments adequately. The resignation or the dismissal of an official in such circumstances should not be seen as a substitute for ministerial responsibility.

Resignations lie at the extreme end of the accountability spectrum and because of this occasions on which they are forthcoming will, by their nature, always be infrequent. Some argue that the emphasis on resignation detracts from the requirement that ministers should give information and explanation to parliament, and, by so doing encourages a culture of secrecy (Scott, 1996b). There is substance to that argument. Indeed, there is substance to the view that accountability is better achieved away from parliament, for example through citizens' charters and user groups and even through the courts. These are important mechanisms of accountability. They are, however, of a different nature to the convention of ministerial responsibility, which, through the threat of resignation, remains a symbol of the morality of the constitution. The problem lies in motivating ministers to accept that, on rare occasions, resignation needs to be a reality.

Notes

1   The only resignations in the UK that can be categorized as departmental fault with any degree of certainty are those of Wydham (1904), Dugdale (1954), Carrington (1982) and Brittan (1986).
2   Senator Graham Richardson resigned from the Australian parliament in 1992 following controversy surrounding what came to be known as the 'Marshall Islands Affair'. In this, the senator had improperly mixed his private and ministerial roles in his efforts to assist a friend. He was, however, reinstated the following year (Tiffin, 1999, p. 166).

Chapter 5

Ministerial Codes, Cabinet Rules and the Power of Prime Ministers

Patrick Weller

Once it seemed easy to determine proper behaviour for ministers. Rules of behaviour were determined by the same principles as in a man's club: they were what decent and honourable men would do. Ministers were to be judged at the bar of public opinion, tried by election and sentenced by the votes of their supporters. That might have worked once. There was no need to write everything down. Those who mattered knew what should be done. Those who did not, did not need to know. Political life was enclosed and élitist.

But as government became more complex so the need for some guidelines for new ministers grew, if only to make it easier for them to find their way through the thickets of government. Guidelines started as letters from the secretary of cabinet, telling the ministers how cabinet worked, with perhaps a few hints on the expectations the prime minister had of them, or even to help in the understanding of ministerial responsibility. But they were intended to be no more than guidelines: prime ministers telling their ministers what their expectations were. There was a difference between the 'lore' of the guidelines and the 'law' which ministers as citizens were bound to uphold (Butler, 2000, p. vii). Since the guidelines were promulgated by prime ministers, they were also the interpreters. They determined how rigidly they should be applied, when ministers had transgressed and what the penalties should be. Unsurprisingly those decisions were heavily coloured by political and partisan calculations. But then, they were just guidelines.

Over the years those guidelines have expanded, often as a reaction to some crisis where the best response was unclear and where it might be useful to ministers to have better guidance in the future. But they were still secret and prime ministers chose not to release them, defending the secrecy on the grounds that there was no need for people outside to know them. Since they were not legally binding and could be amended, ignored or applied as the prime minister wished, there was no point in making them public. It might indeed create problems by raising expectations of more rigour than they were designed to carry. But item by item, country by country, that veil of secrecy has been lifted. Sometimes new governments have agreed to publish the internal rules, occasionally as part of an election promise, sometimes because they saw no reason not to. Rules for cabinet have been followed by demands that codes of ethics or guidelines for good behaviour be developed, in the belief either that they will provide good publicity in a climate where cynicism about politicians' motives reaches new heights or in response to the occasional illustration of venality and greed.

This chapter provides a brief account of the process by which the guidelines became public documents as a prelude to asking whether these developments have had an impact on the way political life is organized and run. Does their publication change the attitude of ministers in order to make then think more explicitly about good behaviour for fear of public exposure? Is it a vehicle for motivating them to think more carefully about decisions that may be potentially in breach of those guidelines? Has it altered the influence of the prime minister? Any such assessments must have a caveat; there are difficulties with trying to develop easy notions of cause and effect in any discussion of the impact of codes of behaviour. If there are no casualties of an ethical code, is it because ministers are now being careful, because they are not caught or because no one wishes to apply it? All these interpretations are possible, so any analysis of consequences must be treated with care. But we do not need to ask only if there are casualties. It is legitimate to argue that the growing bureaucratisation of cabinet and ministerial codes, public accessibility to them and the public debate which occurs when they are, or appear to be, breached has changed the dynamic of public scrutiny of ministers. It has also made harder the prime minister's role as judge, jury and executioner of ministers in trouble.

The Australian Experience

In 1969 following the general election, the secretary of the Department of Prime Minister and Cabinet wrote to the ministers after the first cabinet meeting. He explained on behalf of the prime minister what was required in the submission of documents for cabinet consideration, and the need for ministers to abide by the three-day rule and a variety of procedural issues. But that is what the circular was concerned to explain: how the cabinet system was meant to work (see Weller and Grattan, 1981, pp. 217–19).

By 1981 these rules had been codified into a loose-leafed folder that provided more detail about the way that cabinet was meant to work. The *Cabinet Handbook* opened with a statement of cabinet principles, including a definition of collective responsibility and a demand for complete confidentiality. It provided far more detail about the form of the submissions and the procedures required for consultation, announcement and follow-up. It contained a statement that background briefings of the press were a legitimate way of explaining the government's point of view, and warned that care should be exercised to avoid any indication of the personal views of the minister or other members of cabinet. The only exhortation on personal behaviour was the requirement for declarations of interests of a minister if ministers or their immediate family had interests that could conflict with their public duty. The handbook was a confidential document. It was subsequently published in the May 1982 edition of *Politics* (now the *Australian Journal of Political Science*). The decision to publish was taken in the knowledge that it was in breach of copyright, but it did mean that, for the first time, the rules of cabinet were in the public arena. No one cared or even seemed to notice.

One consequence of this publication was that, since the handbook was already public, the Cabinet Office decided, after revising the text, that it might as well publish it officially. Consequently an official version was published by the Australian Government Printing Service in 1983 and revised in 1988 (Cabinet Handbook, 1988). These publications provided yet more detail on the way cabinet business should be undertaken, designed of course for the requirements of the Labor government then in power. The handbook again expressed the need for the confidentiality of cabinet discussions and gave a unique definition of collective responsibility carefully designed to take account of the peculiar factional demands of the then Labor government.

The section entitled the Declaration of Interests was expanded. Ministers were required to give the prime minister an annual return of their private interests and, 'as far as ministers are aware of them, the interests of their immediate family'. That was to be tabled. A confidential form gave the prime minister more detailed information, including the monetary value of their interests. Ministers were also required to declare at meetings any matter that might give rise to a conflict of interest. They were encouraged to take a broad view. 'Generally, declarations should be made in all cases where an interest exists which could not be said to be shared with the rest of the community' (Cabinet Handbook, 1988, p. 6, para. 2.17).

On conflict of interest, the *Handbook* (1988, p. 6) was now much more explicit:

> Ministers are also obliged not to engage in professional practice or in the daily work of any business and to resign any directorships in public companies. Directorships in private companies must also be resigned unless, for example, such companies operate a family farm, business or investments and the retention of a directorship is not likely to conflict with the public duty of the Minister. Ministers are to derive no income through personal exertion other than as ministers or members of parliament, to divest themselves of shares or similar interests in any company or business involved in their portfolio responsibilities and, should any particular conflict between duty and interest arise during the course of their administration of their departments, to inform the Prime Minister so that it can be decided how the particular matter is to be handled.
>
> In short, if Ministers have any concern about a conflict or a potential conflict of interest in any area of their responsibilities they should advise the Prime Minister (paras 2.17, 2.18).

The prime minister was to be the judge, but there was clearly a concern to ensure that the onus was on the ministers to report any possible problem.

After John Howard won office in 1996 he released a *Guide to Ministerial Conduct*, intended as a quick reference for ministers and their staff:

> [t]o the main principles, conventions and rules by which government at the Commonwealth level is conducted. The emphasis in the Guide is on the necessity of adherence to high standards by people occupying positions of public trust. The Australian people have this as their entitlement ... (Howard, 1996a, p. 1).

The section entitled Ministerial Conduct is part exhortation:

> Ministers must be honest in their public dealings and should not intentionally mislead the parliament or the public ...
> Ministers should ensure that their conduct is defensible and should consult the Prime Minister when in doubt about the propriety of any course of action (Howard, 1996a, s. 4).

The guide also provides some additional details. For example, 'the transfer of interests to a family member or to a nominee or trust is not an acceptable form of divestment (Howard, 1996a, s. 4). This was doubtless designed to close a loophole that someone had tried to utilize. But much of it repeats the demands included in earlier handbooks.

A few new, and rather obvious, caveats were added to section four of the *Guide to Ministerial Conduct*:

> Ministers should perform their duties uninfluenced by fear or favour,
>
> Ministers should not accept any benefit where acceptance might give an appearance that they may be subject to improper influence,
>
> Ministers should not exercise the influence obtained from their public office, or use official information, to obtain any improper benefit for themselves or another,
>
> Ministers are provided with facilities at public expense in order that public business may be conducted effectively. Their use of these facilities should be in accordance with this principle. It should not be wasteful or extravagant. As a general rule, official facilities should be used for official purposes (Howard, 1996a, s. 4).

All of these comments should be taken as given. Just to ask who would be prepared to argue the opposite is to illustrate how unexceptional they are.

It would be grossly ahistorical to regard Howard's *Guide to Ministerial Conduct* as a great break with tradition. It was written within the department and in effect is a combination of a series of statements that would once have been taken for granted and expansions of the practices already set out in the earlier cabinet handbooks. There is little there that is new. Indeed it reflects the whole process which has seen a gradual expansion of the rules, often making them more explicit, often in response to individual cases. What started as rules of procedure became in part a catalogue of good behaviour. Almost all the detail that can be found in the *Guide* can be implied from general comments in earlier documents. The exhortations would once have been assumed as good practice and it would have been regarded as unnecessary to state them so obviously. What was new was that the *Guide* was released in an easily accessible form that made it a useful source of reference not only for the ministers and staffers for whom it was designed but also for the media and critics looking for grist with which to criticise the government's practices.

That was illustrated in the resignation of a number of Australian ministers in 1996 when their private interests clashed with their public responsibilities. Initially Howard accepted the resignations. But eventually he dug in when Senator Parer, minister and friend, was accused of breaching the guidelines about his share holdings: a former mining executive, his family still held shares in the areas for which he had ministerial responsibility. The press and the Opposition cited sections of the *Guide* to demand that Parer resign but Howard denied he was in breach and refused to ask for his resignation. He had earlier argued that:

> At the end of the day, every individual is the ultimate judge of his or her own propriety, and no document, no Minister, no senior bureaucrat, no adviser can really, at the end of the day, define what is wrong in any given situation and it is always at the end of the day a matter of individual conscience and a matter of individual judgment as to what is the right and proper thing to do (Howard, 1996b).

Howard accepted Parer's word that no breach had occurred and was criticized for his failure to insist on proper standards. Of course it is not simply the individual who decides; the prime minister is the custodian of the behaviour and morality of the government and in allowing Parer to determine he had done nothing wrong, Howard's judgement was also in the dock. Prime ministers can and do decide who stays or goes. But Howard had made the judgement that the damage to his government from another resignation would be greater than toughing it out. Normalcy returned, but with a twist. Howard had to defend his interpretation of the guidelines in a way that none of his predecessors had been required to do. None of them had had so explicit a set of guidelines to defend.

The United Kingdom

The UK was, as might be expected, far more cautious about releasing details on how their government was run. Requests that details of the existence of cabinet committees be made public were rejected on the grounds that any publicity would detract from collective responsibility if it were known that decisions were made in committee rather than by the full cabinet. It was also feared that publicity might leave ministers on committees open to lobbying. The process of governance was a secret and should remain so.

That secrecy was certainly extended to the document *Questions of Procedure for Ministers* (*QPM*, Cabinet Office, 1992) that was given to new ministers in the Blair government as a guide to their behaviour (for a history of the development of *QPM*, see Baker, 2000). In 1989 Peter Hennessy, political correspondent for *The Independent*, wrote to the British prime minister, Margaret Thatcher, and asked that Britain follow the Australian example and publish the *QPM*. He enclosed with his letter a copy of the Australian *Cabinet Handbook* and an annual report from the Department of Prime Minister and Cabinet that included details of cabinet committees and statistics of the numbers of meetings and cabinet submissions. Hennessy was told: 'The Prime Minister asks me to say that there are no plans for publishing *Questions of Procedure for Ministers*'. No reasons were given (*The Independent*, 1 May 1989).

When John Major took office, Hennessy tried again. This time he was told that the prime minister 'was interested in the degree of publication by the Australian government' (Baker, 2000, pp. 68–9). He took the proposal to publish *QPM* to cabinet. That was surprising as the rules were still essentially those desired by the prime minister. But it was an unusual step but Major wanted, and got, cabinet support. During the 1992 election campaign, Major promised that he would publish the *QPM*. He kept that promise in May when the Cabinet Office officially released the *QPM*. It has been the subject of some debate since.

Much of the document describes how the cabinet system works, what procedures should be followed when there are parliamentary statements to be made and how visits should be organized. Like the Australian document, it was essentially about the way government was run, a guide through the thickets of government. One section dealt with ministers' private interests, including partnerships, investment and membership of Lloyd's.

After the change of government in 1997, *QPM* became the *Ministerial Code: A Code of Conduct and Guidance on Procedure for Ministers*. The Foreword from the prime minister, Tony Blair, states:

> In issuing this code, I should like to reaffirm my strong personal commitment to restoring the bond of trust between the British people and their Government. We are all here to serve and we must try to serve honestly and in the interests of those who gave us our positions of trust. I will expect all ministers to work within the letter and spirit of the Code (cited in Baker, 2000, p. 149).

The code followed the same lines as the *QPM*, with details of requirements for the preparation of documents for cabinet sitting beside the rules for relations with party and parliament and a section on ministers' private interests.

Since the publication of *QPM* there has been a continuing debate on the best way these rules should be enforced. The Committee on Standards in Public Life, established in 1995 as a response to public disquiet about political standards (see Nolan, Chapter 2) argued that the *QPM* was inadequate. According to the committee it did not provide a coherent series of principles of practical guidance to ministers. It recommended that the ethical principles be drawn out of *QPM* and either put in a separate section or form a free-standing code of conduct. In its original proposal the Committee had recommend that a new ministerial code should read:

> It will be for individual Ministers to judge how best to act in order to uphold the highest standards. It will be for the Prime Minister to determine whether or not they have done so in any particular circumstance (Neill, 2000, p. 53).

When the ministerial code was published, the wording was different:

> It will be for individual Ministers to judge how best to act in order to uphold the highest standards. They are responsible for justifying their conduct to Parliament. And they can only remain in office for so long as they retain the Prime Minister's confidence (Neill, 2000, p. 54).

The committee's formulation was rejected because, in the government's view, it went 'too far towards suggesting that the Prime Minister's relationship with his Ministerial colleagues is that of invigilator and judge'. The committee felt that if a minister failed to meet the required standards, then the prime minister would still have to make a judgement, and was therefore, as custodian of the code, the ultimate judge of its requirements and the consequences of any breaches (see Woodhouse, Chapter 3). The committee recommended the following wording:

> It will be for individual Ministers to judge how best to act in order to uphold the highest standards. They are responsible for justifying their conduct to Parliament and retaining its confidence. The Prime Minister remains the ultimate judge of the requirements of the Code and the appropriate consequences of breaches of it (Neill, 2000, p. 54).

It is now in the hands of government. Both codes raise the same question: is it up to the individual to determine when good behaviour has been breached, or is the prime minister to be the final arbiter?

Is Open Government Beneficial?

There is an assumption that openness is desirable and that the rules of procedure ought to be available for all to see. Certainly this assumption has been the basis of the argument for the publication of documents such as the *Cabinet Handbook* and *QPM*. Everyone should know the rules by which we are governed. But what was the status of these rules? The Australian *Cabinet Handbook* is essentially the prime minister's guide to the ministers; it codifies practice as much as it sets that practice.

Take one example: in Australia in 1984 a left-wing member of the Hawke Labor cabinet objected to a government decision on the export of uranium. He wanted to oppose the government's decision in caucus (the meeting of the Labor parliamentary party). So he resigned from the cabinet but not from the government. He remained a minister in the outer ministry; it was just that he was no longer a member of cabinet. The prime minister allowed that stratagem, contrary to all practical interpretations of collective responsibility, to stand because it let him off a politically inconvenient hook and kept the peace within the government. The cabinet secretary then carefully changed the wording in the handbook to state that a non-cabinet minister who did not attend the relevant cabinet meeting could oppose a cabinet decision in caucus, but not in public (Cabinet Handbook, 1988, p. 4, para. 2:3).

Such an interpretation runs contrary to all previous tradition, except in the Whitlam government, where ministers constantly re-fought cabinet losses in caucus. It was precisely that practice that the Hawke government wanted to avoid, but it then decided to allow the odd exception where political expediency required a degree of flexibility. This example is a clear indication of the extent to which the handbook was seen as the prime minister's document, to be amended as necessary to allow the smooth running of cabinet on his terms.

In this case the rules followed practice and political convenience, as also occurred when Howard published his code of ministerial conduct. It was perhaps an odd decision for him to make. A month or so later, in launching a paper, 'Ethical Standards and Values in the Australian Public Service', Howard commented that he was 'a little surprised to find myself launching a document of this kind, being a person who normally eschews the notion that you write down, in a detailed descriptive way, codes of behaviour' (Howard, 1996b). He explained why he was making an exception in the particular case. However, as several ministers fell victim to the fine detail in his *Guide,* he might have had regrets about launching it in the first place. A guide is not law. But it provides hooks on which opponents can hang their criticisms. Oppositions are absolute in their analysis. Many cases are more uncertain, more ambiguous and need judgment.

The same could be said of *QPM*. Hennessy was told that his description of *QPM* as 'the nearest thing we have to a written constitution for the proper conduct of cabinet government' was overdoing it. It was, said former Cabinet Secretary Burke Trend, 'not a constitution, merely some tips for beginners — a book of etiquette' (*The Independent*, 1 May 1989). Another cabinet secretary claimed it was 'never intended to be part of the constitution. It is lore, not law — a compendium of good practice, not a set of rules' (Butler, 2000, p. vii). They are in fact the prime minister's rules. At least, even if written in both cases by the cabinet offices, they are presented officially as the requirements set by prime ministers. That means of course that they can be amended by prime ministers too. If they did not appear when published as a 'coherent series of principles', that was because both documents grew like Topsy, with the addition of clauses and rules designed to meet problems as they occurred, and examples here, caveats there, as a means of meeting the developing conditions. Neither was started from scratch as a means of establishing a set of rules.

Publication has meant that the two documents are now political weapons in their own right. Perhaps *QPM* is the more controversial because of the idea that it somehow represents the 'written Constitution'. According to one comment, it 'may now be taken as *the* defining document on Prime Minister and Cabinet' (cited in Baker, 2000, p. 101, emphasis added). That is somewhat bizarre, even given the British notion of constitution as the accepted conventions and rules of procedure. Rules and conventions are malleable: they do not have the constitutional force of a legally binding constitution as most people understand the word. By contrast, in Australia there is no doubt where the Constitution is found and that the *Handbook* and the *Guide to Ministerial Conduct* are mere non-binding add-ons to the formal document.

What is certain is that publication creates public standards to which ministers may be held to account and the appearance of formal rules that prime ministers are meant to apply. That makes prime ministers more accountable too. Once they could assert that they had declined to accept, or demand, the resignation of a minister for some reason or other. They could often not explain what the reason was but implied that since they had the advantage of 'all the facts' they were in a better position to make a judgement. When the rules are implicit or secret, then the standards too are left to the discretion of the prime minister. And it might benefit ministers too, in argument with the prime minister: they can point out that what they are accused of is not in breach of the published code of conduct and therefore assert they see no reason to go.

However interpreted, publication has made the application of the rules the clear responsibility of the prime minister. Failure to apply them can be a matter of comment. In 1976 a former minister could say that a minister:

> Will only resign if the Prime Minister believes it is for the good of the government but in most cases that simply admits error and, party conflict being what it is, admission of error is more serious than the error itself (Garland, 1976, p. 24).

With the publication of the codes anyone can make an assessment of whether the ministers are meeting the rules and a judgement of what should happen. The idea that ministers are all people who can be trusted is dead.

Sanction and Motivation

Ministers must satisfy three different worlds:

1. In personal behaviour they are bound to answer to the prime minister who is satisfied that they should continue to be members of the government. Unethical

behaviour, even disloyalty, may be as a good reason to remove a minister as ineffectiveness. It is essentially a personal relationship.
2. They are collectively responsible to their cabinet colleagues for upholding the unity of the government in parliament and in public.
3. They are administratively responsible for the activities of their departments.

Thus they have links upwards, sideways and down (Weller, 1999, pp. 62–3).

For survival the first remains vital. If the prime minister is not satisfied then survival is not an option. The hands of prime ministers may be forced by outside opinion when there is doubt. Eventually they will decide as much for political as for any other reason whether a minister stays or goes. What information they seek in advance will differ from case to case. Cabinet secretaries are able to make some inquiries but are not in a position to undertake an investigation that might prove ministers guilty of some offence. In effect they can not go behind the back of a minister to test their propositions because they are not the independent guardians of the codes but the agent of the prime minister in their actions. Outsiders want a more formal presence, with the appointment of an individual who has a capacity to run proper investigations; they feel that civil servants have to accept the word of their ministers when issues of conflict of interest arise. Ministers are, according to one observer, 'judge and jury in their own case'. But such an appointment is unlikely to be made. In the end prime ministers have to protect the reputation of their governments and they alone can make the final decision on the interpretation of their own codes.

The need for a working relationship with a prime minister is certainly useful. Ministers know that if a crisis occurs the prime minister is the one person who can determine whether they have a career. One eye on the prime minister's office, with an awareness of the rules of procedure, is good advice for ministers. They can no longer plead ignorance, even if, as Tiernan shows (Chapter 8), they still get it wrong.

The sideways commitment to cabinet is covered by the need for collective responsibility. When crises in the behaviour of ministers develop, cabinet may discuss the possible responses. The atmosphere is likely to be tough and political, rather than moral. If survival of the government depends on the outcome, anyone is expendable.

Ministers as departmental heads provide a different arena; there they are recognized as the source of authority. Their word is final. But there are also circumstances where their decisions may be unwise, potentially ineffective or even unethical. Who advises them then? If the question is one of legality, there should be no doubt. The secretaries of the departments have an obligation to inform the ministers that their proposed action is not possible. Departments can of course monitor the ministers' pecuniary interests and indicate if they see a conflict of interest; but if the ministers do not agree when such a case is brought to their attention, there is little more that can be done. As Howard comments, the final judgement in many cases is likely to be an individual one. But what if it is closer to the line, legal but dubious: using, for instance, government information for improper purposes. Then there are two alternatives: one is to suggest that there are better ways of achieving the government's objectives, ways that may be more acceptable. The second is to advise against such actions.

In Britain, Lord Nolan has suggested that the quality of the British civil service has been responsible in part for the lack of corruption in Britain and for ensuring that British ministers receive fearless advice, particularly where there may be issues of questionable practice. But then the heads of departments are still largely permanent and do not depend for their positions on the goodwill of their minister. In Australia the department heads can effectively be removed at the whim of the minister if he/she can get the agreement of the prime minister. In theory that may make the job of departmental secretaries more difficult if the minister wants to undertake actions that are legally permissible but morally harder to defend. In these cases, after all, the morality of an issue may be a matter of judgment. Secretaries of departments have been known to tell the secretary of the Department of Prime Minister and Cabinet if they think the minister is out of line, but there are limited avenues if the minister will not listen and there is no incentive to adopt the departmental secretaries' recommendations if the issue is not one of major import. Contractual differences may make a departmental secretary think carefully before advising a minister not to adopt a path of action (see Weller, 2001).

Finally there is the traditional remedy: electoral defeat, whenever the next election comes along. Prime ministers who preside over a long list of scandals, whether the ministers resign or are protected, will face electoral justice. It is an old solution, but still a good one. In the main it works: governments tainted with reputations for scandal often do not survive. But it is unlikely that the fate of the government will rest on the behaviour of a single minister, so fear that an action might destroy the government is unlikely to be a strong motivating factor in determining the action of an individual. Rather a broader impression of incompetence and impropriety will leave a poor taste in electors' mouths at election time. If the codes are to work it will be because they affect the immediate future of ministers.

Whither the Rules?

Prime ministers have a harder job than their predecessors. First, their rules are now public. Everyone knows what is expected and can make a judgement about whether a minister has or has not breached them. In obvious cases there may be no doubt; there never was. But many of the cases are not obvious. Should private life intrude on ministerial tenure? These are not matters of law but of judgement. Even if a prime minister does know more of the detail than the public, everyone else will have an opinion about the connection between the action, the rules and the subsequent reaction.

Second, any change to the rules may become a matter of debate, often with ulterior motives assumed if they are not given. The guidelines used to be flexible and adaptable. Now they are likely to be firmly set and rigidity has its problems.

Third, the prime ministers' actions will be under greater scrutiny. The exercise of power and the application of discretion will always be a matter of opinion. Whereas in the past the prime ministers decided on the basis of information that they had and on the rules that they had promulgated, now the rules are in the public domain and the use of discretion will be scrutinized keenly. Any decision not to apply the guidelines becomes a failure of the prime ministers' will.

Consequently the drama is played out in public where once it was a private debate hidden behind the shroud of government secrecy. It may make the exercise of power harder; that should not be a matter of public concern. Publicity and debate can only make ministers more aware of the roles. Even if they are confident that the prime minister will not sack them, the public debate that follows a known breach of the rules can only cause caution and a sense of care. That is a benefit. Protection of their reputation is the key to their future; that may be the most significant means by which the codes will motivate ministers to behave morally.

Chapter 6

Lessons from Westminster: The Scottish Executive and New Improved Codes of Conduct?

Mark Shephard

> ... there are weaknesses in the procedures for maintaining and enforcing those standards. As a result people in public life are not always as clear as they should be about where the boundaries of acceptable conduct lie. This we regard as the principal reason for public disquiet. It calls for urgent remedial action (UK Parliament, 1998).

Prompted by widespread allegations of improper financial and commercial conduct by all holders of public office, Prime Minister John Major established the Committee on Standards in Public Life in October 1994. Chaired by Lord Nolan, the committee published its first report in May 1995. The report contained a number of recommendations that included the revision of the ministerial code of conduct (then entitled *Questions of Procedure for Ministers*) to provide a clearer set of principles of practical guidance to ministers. Timescales for achieving changes were established according to the difficulty of implementation. At Westminster, the ministerial code (MC) was revised in July 1997 following the victory of the Labour Party. Several years on and the MC is still subject to examination and further recommendations by the committee. The latest report by the committee (Neill, 2000), now chaired by Lord Neill, provides a number of new recommendations on ministerial conduct. However, despite much of the evidence that called for quite radical changes such as the introduction of an external adjudicator on conduct, the Committee has recommended that 'No new office for the investigation of allegations of ministerial misconduct should be established' (Neill, 2000).

Instead, the committee has urged ministers to take full responsibility for decisions taken after advice given by permanent secretaries; clarified the role of the prime minister as the ultimate judge of the MC and its breaches; and strengthen of the opening section on ethical principles governing ministerial conduct. Since the oral evidence for the report was taken in June and July 1999, the committee was unable to include the codes of the devolved administrations (Scotland, Wales and Northern Ireland) within its scope. Now that the devolved codes have been produced, this chapter compares and contrasts the Westminster and Holyrood (Scottish) codes to see whether differences in the wording of the two codes has an impact on ministerial conduct in the UK today.

Comparisons and contrasts between the theory of the codes in the UK and theory of the Scottish Ministerial Code (SMC) are then assessed. The purposes behind this exercise are twofold. First, by analysing the differences between both the theory and the practice in both contexts this chapter suggests ways in which the codes could be improved to better address requirements of 'best practice' advocated by the Cabinet Office. Second, by analysing what has gone wrong in practice, consideration is given to the question of how we should go about motivating ministers to do the right thing.

A comparative approach allows us to assess the extent to which the Scottish Executive has devised a new improved code of conduct for ministers. Excluding the obvious differences in the codes that reflect clear variations in working practices and areas of competence, this chapter investigates those differences where there are no immediately apparent obligations for the Scottish Executive to differ from the MC at Westminster. Contrasting theory with practice, assessments are made concerning the extent to which the SMC has addressed problems with the MC and the reasons why this may be the case. The chapter suggests that changes have more to do with the logistics of coalition government than with addressing problems at Westminster.

Theory and Practice of the UK and Scottish Ministerial Codes

At first glance, the SMC appears to be a carbon copy of the MC. Both codes have the same number of sections, and each of these sections appears to be similarly worded. However, on closer inspection the SMC contains a number of important differences from the MC used at Westminster. Some of those differences reflect the specific institutional arrangements of the UK government compared with the Scottish Executive. These differences include minor variations such as titles, for example 'prime minister' (Westminster) instead of 'first minister' (Scotland) and 'Speaker' (Westminster) instead of 'Presiding Officer' (Scotland). However, they also reflect the very different institutional arrangements that exist. In the case of Westminster, for example, additional subsections exist within the MC on ministerial committees, parliamentary private secretaries, and Commonwealth and Foreign ministers. In each case, these subsections are missing from the SMC because they do not apply to the Scottish Executive. Subsections on Commonwealth and Foreign ministers do not apply because foreign policy is not a devolved matter. Also, subsections on ministerial Committees and parliamentary private secretaries are absent because these institutions do not exist in Scotland. These differences between the two codes are to be expected. They reflect fundamental differences between the structures and competencies of the Westminster government and the Scottish Executive. Meanwhile the SMC contains one additional subsection on visits by ministers from foreign or Commonwealth countries. This subsection exists to remind the Scottish Executive that foreign policy is a reserved matter and that all 'major visits' by ministers from overseas first require consultation with the Foreign and Commonwealth Office.

A final difference of some note includes greater emphasis in the SMC on the need for ministers to cooperate with the parliament in scheduling appropriate times for the announcement of statements. Part of this difference can be explained by the fact that the Scottish Executive is limited to making parliamentary statements on plenary days (more of a time constraint than Westminster). However, the main reason for the difference is that the Parliamentary Bureau (on which all the main political parties are represented) is responsible for the scheduling of business in the Scottish parliament (and not the government as in the case of Westminster). Consequently, ministers in Scotland have to work more closely with the parliament over the scheduling of statements (personal communication).

More interesting from the perspective of comparative ministerial ethics are those differences in the codes for which there is no apparent reason. For example, the main duty of both the Scottish parliament and the Westminster parliament is to hold the executive accountable, and yet the corresponding sections in each of the codes are very different from each other. This leads us to the second category of differences and the focus of this chapter — substantive differences with no apparent institutional cause.

Substantive Differences with No Apparent Institutional Cause

A number of substantive differences exist between the SMC and MC that appear to have little immediate connection to institutional differences. The first and most notable of the differences appears in the sections on 'ministers and parliament'.

Ministers and Parliament

Several core differences exist between the two codes. First, unlike the Westminster version, the SMC establishes from the outset a set of 'key principles' which ministers are asked to 'uphold and promote'. These principles reflect the main concerns of the Consultative Steering Group on the Scottish parliament. These principles are:

- The Scottish parliament should 'embody and reflect the sharing of power between the people of Scotland, the legislators and the Scottish Executive'.
- The Scottish Executive should be accountable to the Scottish parliament and the parliament and the executive should be accountable to the people of Scotland.
- The Scottish parliament should be accessible, open, responsive and develop procedures which make possible a participative approach to the development, consideration and scrutiny of policy and legislation.
- The Scottish parliament in its operations and its appointments should recognize the need to promote equal opportunities for all.

By contrast, the MC does not mention key principles. These differences between the codes are important because the SMC reminds ministers from the outset of the pivotal position of parliament in the political system and of their need to be accountable to the parliament. While this point is implicit in most understandings of the Westminster model, failure to state this explicitly in the MC provides a context in which the British government can down play the primacy of parliament.

The SMC also provides greater detail on the specific duties expected of ministers in relation to the introduction of Bills in parliament. An additional subsection on the introduction of Bills states that:

> ministers responsible for Bills being introduced in the parliament should ensure that the Bill is accompanied by clear, informative and comprehensive explanatory notes and by an appropriate policy memorandum detailing, *inter alia*, the policy objectives of the Bill and the consultation which has been undertaken on it (Scottish Executive, 1999, para. 3.3).

The difference in the SMC exists because Rule 9.3 of the Parliament's Standing Orders require that a Bill being introduced by a member of the Scottish Executive must be accompanied by an Explanatory Memorandum and a Policy Memorandum. By comparison, no such requirement is placed on ministers at Westminster. Consequently, the requirements facing Scottish ministers go further than those facing ministers at Westminster (personal communication).

Compounding the above points are important differences in the semantics of seemingly similar ministerial duties. In particular, according to the wording of the current MC, there is ambiguity over whether ministers should make parliament their first forum for the announcement of the most important government policies:

> When parliament is in session, ministers will want *to bear in mind the desire of parliament* that the most important announcements of Government policy should be made, in the first instance, in parliament (Cabinet Office, 1997, para. 27, italics added).

By contrast, the SMC states:

> When parliament is in session, ministers will want *to ensure* that the most important announcements of Government policy should be made, in the first instance, in parliament (Scottish Executive, 1999, para. 3.4, italics added).

Unlike the MC, the SMC provides its ministers with a clearer understanding that they should make the most important announcements of government policy in parliament in the first instance. The wording of the MC provides greater latitude for interpretation by ministers. According to this part of the code, the minister in Westminster only has 'to bear in mind the desire of parliament', he/she does not have 'to ensure' that parliament is the first port of call for major announcements.

In terms of governance theory this difference is important because the SMC clearly identifies the Scottish parliament as the first institution responsible for the scrutiny of Scottish Executive policy. In stark contrast, while much of the literature portrays the Westminster parliament in this light (see, for example, Verney, 1992; Norton, 1993), the wording of the MC questions the validity of theories that locate parliament as the focus of power in the political system.

Indeed, this part of the MC provides a clear example of the ambiguity that Nolan sought to rectify. To recall, Nolan advocated 'urgent remedial action' to address the 'weaknesses in the procedures' which means 'people in public life are not always as clear as they should be about where the boundaries of acceptable conduct lie' (UK Parliament, 1998). In the case of Westminster, it appears that there are still clear ambiguities in the wording of the MC that could be corrected if it is going to ensure ministers are clear about the boundaries of acceptable conduct.

To what extent is this difference more than just academic semantics? The real test of any ambiguity is in the practice. Is there any evidence to suggest that this part of the code is causing ministers confusion in Westminster compared with Scotland? The evidence to date suggests that this part of the code is causing interpretation problems at Westminster, most noticeably, although not exclusively, in the case of the recent Labour administration. Between May 1997 and her retirement in October 2000, the Speaker of the House of Commons, Betty Boothroyd, made a point of rebuking ministers for failing to make sure that policy announcements were made in parliament in the first instance. Prominent examples included Gordon Brown over the single currency in 1997, Harriet Harman over the reform of the Child Support Agency in 1998, and John Reid over the 1998 Strategic Defence Review. Continued allegations of leaks to the media prior to statements in the House of Commons were reiterated recently in Boothroyd's farewell retirement speech in which she stated:

> Let's make a start by remembering that the function of parliament is to hold the executive to account. It is in parliament in the first instance that ministers must explain and justify their policies (*Daily Telegraph*, 27 July 2000).

Boothroyd has argued that the parliament needs 'to win the war' against external announcements. One way of helping to achieve this objective could be the tightening of the MC on ministerial responsibilities to parliament in much the same way as the SMC has done.

By comparison, the practice in Scotland to date suggests that ministers are more attentive in ensuring that parliament is the first forum for major policy announcements. In contrast to Boothroyd at Westminster, the Presiding Officer in the Scottish parliament, David Steel, has drawn less attention to this part of the code. Indeed, it does appear that the primacy of key principles, the addition of further duties and the greater clarity in the wording of the SMC is having a positive effect on the behaviour of the executive *vis-à-vis* parliament. While part of this difference is no doubt explained by differences in Speaker styles, comparisons of media coverage on this issue suggest that the Holyrood model has made some difference to the behaviour of ministers towards parliament.[1]

The problems associated with the wording of the MC have not gone unnoticed by parliamentarians. In his report *Strengthening Parliament*, Lord Norton of Louth advocated changing the current wording of the code to 'impose a requirement on ministers to make the most important announcements to parliament' (Norton, 2000, p. 50).

While the most notable differences between the two codes exist in the sections on 'ministers and parliament', a number of other substantive differences in some of the other sections are worthy of comparison. Additional sections of most note include 'ministers and the government/executive', 'ministers and responsibility', 'ministers and civil servants' and 'ministers' visits'.

Ministers and the Government/Executive

Notable differences also exist between the Westminster and Holyrood codes in relation to the subsections on collective responsibility. Unlike the MC, collective responsibility is more clearly defined in the SMC, especially in relation to the individuals to whom the doctrine applies. In the Holyrood model collective responsibility applies to 'the executive' and 'any junior Scottish ministers who are appointed by the First Minister ... even though they are not members of the executive' (Scottish Executive, 1999, para. 2.4). The comparable section in the MC makes no specific mention of the role of junior ministers in relation to collective responsibility. In the MC, collective responsibility applies at various times to the 'Cabinet', to 'ministers' and to 'all members of the government' (Cabinet Office, 1997, paras 16 and 17). Comparing it with the SMC, it is not clear whether 'ministers' refers exclusively to cabinet ministers or also includes junior ministers. Moreover, what is meant by 'all members of the government'? Indeed, the wording in the Westminster code is so vague that collective responsibility is effectively open to the interpretation of the prime minister.

This is not just a question of academic semantics. Unless codes are clear, it becomes easier for the executive to abuse interpretations of the rules, and this will ultimately occur at the expense of parliament. Past experience suggests that failure to have a clear understanding of a code has meant that the groups included under collective responsibility have grown over time. David Ellis's (1989) analysis of the changing interpretations and application of collective responsibility in Britain provides evidence for this. Ellis states that the requirement that collective responsibility be made to apply to junior ministers is largely a twentieth century phenomenon that post-1945 has been applied more rigidly to junior ministers than it has to cabinet ministers. Under the current Labour administration, Peter Kilfoyle's resignation speech as a junior Defence minister provides evidence for the continuation of this practice: 'As a minister, even a junior minister, I feel my hands are tied ... I do not have the freedom to speak out about the issues I feel are most important' (Kilfoyle, 2000).

Ellis (1989) charts the further widening of the definition since the 1970s as new groups such as private parliamentary secretaries (PPSs) (unpaid aides to individual ministers) have been included under the application of collective responsibility. Although much ambiguity remains in the case of PPSs, the MC clearly warns 'no PPS who votes against the government may retain his or her position', and that 'they should avoid associating themselves with recommendations critical of or embarrassing to the government' (Cabinet Office, 1997, para. 46). However, PPSs are 'private members' — they are not part of the cabinet, are not ministers and are not members of the government. Yet the practice of the MC suggests that collective responsibility applies to PPSs as well.

While on first inspection it looks as though the SMC provides a broader definition of the groups expected to uphold collective responsibility, at least this code provides parliament with a clear set of boundaries. Under the SMC, if the Scottish Executive wants to extend the groups included under collective responsibility, it will first have to change the code itself. Practice will have to follow theory. In contrast, the ambiguity of the MC allows the prime minister latitude for interpretation. As Ellis (1989, p. 56) contends:

> ... collective responsibility ... is seeking to thrust itself, almost without justification, into other developing areas of the constitution.

Consequently the position of the Westminster parliament *vis-à-vis* the executive is made weaker than it is in Scotland. Practice does not have to follow theory because the theory is open to interpretation. And if experience over time is instructive, could we predict a time when 'all members of the government' came to apply to the entire number of MPs of the party in office?

Another difference of note under the section on ministers and the government/executive includes the subsections entitled, for example, 'Cabinet Documents' (Westminster) and 'Confidentiality of Documents' (Scotland). According to the Holyrood model, 'official documents' that are 'required for current administration' should be 'handed over to their successors'[2] (Scottish Executive, 1999, para. 2.14). Although very similarly worded, the MC refers instead not to 'official documents' but to 'Cabinet documents' (Cabinet Office, 1997, para. 19). The distinction is important because the MC restricts the definition of materials that 'should' be passed onto the successive administration. As one official in Scotland commented:

> ... our wording simply reflects the fact that we thought it appropriate that the guidance should cover *all* types of official papers rather than deal with only a relatively small sub-set of official papers — i.e. Cabinet papers (personal communication).

While in practice successors normally receive all relevant documents from officials rather than from their predecessors (personal communication), the SMC nonetheless provides ministers with more extensive guidance on the range of documents that they should consider passing on to the successor administration. Excluding sensitive papers (those bearing a protective marking), which must either be returned or destroyed in both Scotland and Westminster, the wording of the MC provides greater latitude for the retention of documents by ministers than the SMC. In the interests of good governance, it is surely in the best interests of the MC to cover all types of official documents rather than refer to cabinet documents only. However, in both cases there is still latitude for ministerial interpretation and both codes need to reflect this in future if documents that would allow better governance are not to be retained by ministers.

Meanwhile, comparisons between the sections on 'ministers and their departments' (Westminster) and 'ministers and their responsibilities' (Scotland) point to a pertinent difference in terms of the subsections on 'special advisers'. Special advisers are individuals who are appointed to provide ministers with expert technical and/or political advice. Although subject to the same terms and conditions as civil servants, their tenure is subject to the term of the minister(s) and/or government, and in the case of Scotland at the discretion of the first minister. According to the Westminster code, 'Cabinet ministers may each appoint up to two Special Advisers ("political" or "expert")' subject to the 'approval of the PM' (Cabinet Office, 1997, para. 48). This contrasts with the Holyrood model, which states:

> Up to 12 special advisers may be appointed to assist ministers. The First Minister is responsible for deciding on the distribution of special adviser posts within the executive, whether in support of the individual ministers or as a collective resource' (Scottish Executive, 1999, para. 4.6).

Given the number of cabinet ministers in the UK (20 excluding the prime minister), the MC allows for there to be 40 special advisers. As of December 1999, cabinet ministers (excluding the prime minister) employed 58 special advisers. Five cabinet ministers[3] had breached the code by employing more than two special advisers. When the prime minister is included in the analysis, the number of special advisers rises to 74. Indeed, Downing Street (the home of the prime minister) employed 25 special advisers in December 1999. Whether one distinguishes between part-time and full-time advisers, and whether one includes the prime minister in the rules or not, practice under Labour exceeds the limits prescribed by the code. Moreover, comparisons with earlier administrations suggest that this has become a burgeoning issue for Labour. When John Major left office, for example, Downing Street employed only eight special advisers and the total number employed was 38. Either the code has to be amended to reflect changed circumstances and expectations, or the cabinet needs to ensure that it adheres to the code that it sets for itself. At a time when leaks have become rife within the government the number of advisers per minister must surely have become an issue in the quest for good governance and 'best practice'.

By comparison with Westminster, the number of special advisers employed by the Scottish Executive stood at nine in December 1999. One could argue that it is early days yet in Scotland and that the Scottish Executive may subsequently exceed the limits prescribed by their code.

More important than the numbers debate is the issue of patronage — who decides on the appointments? According to the MC, the minister decides on his/her advisers and the prime minister approves the selection. This is very different from the Scottish practice where the first minister not only approves the selection of advisers but also decides on their allocation. The first minister can decide to make any or all of the special advisers available to the collective, or can allocate advisers to specific ministers. Initial practice suggested that First Minister Donald Dewar had opted to make most special advisers available for the collective ministerial team. Allegations that the initial preferences for adviser 'pooling' were giving way to more specific appointments arose in February 2000 after attempts were made to hire a trade unionist and education specialist for the specific purposes of advising Health Minister Susan Deacon and Education Minister Sam Galbraith. However, the appointments were not made and the current situation suggests that while a few of the advisers have specific connections with ministers based on the nature of their expertise, most have been hired to provide broader assistance to the executive as a collective entity.

From the nine special advisers in place at the end of 1999, eight had previous connections with the Labour Party and one had links with the Liberal Democrats — a slightly skewed distribution given that four out of the 22 ministers are Liberal Democrats. Since the electoral system used in Scotland is likely to produce coalition government for the foreseeable future, it does seem odd from the perspective of executive 'power sharing' that the SMC *vis-à-vis* the MC should extend the powers of the first minister in this area. In the interests of 'power sharing' one might have expected to see the code reflect this in a division of powers between the first minister and the deputy first minister. However, compared with the MC, as the SMC currently stands the reverse is the case.

Ministers and Civil Servants

A further difference of note between the two codes can be found in the sections on ministers and civil servants. Unlike the MC, in the SMC restrictions are placed on the materials that civil servants can provide ministers for 'party political occasions'. In the Westminster code the subsection on 'Civil Servants and Party Conferences' reads as follows:

> If a minister wishes to have a brief for a party political occasion to explain executive policies or actions, there is no reason why this should not be provided (Cabinet Office, 1997, para. 61).

This contrasts with the subsection in the Scottish code:

> If a minister wishes to have a brief for a party political occasion to explain executive policies or actions, there is no reason why this should not be provided. It cannot however contain material which could be construed as

designed to promote one Party's line or to anticipate criticisms from other Parties (Scottish Executive, 1999, para. 5.6).

The difference between the two codes points to an obvious distinction between the systems of government in Westminster and Scotland. Compared with Westminster, Scotland has two parties comprising the executive — there is coalition government. Consequently, it appears that conditions have been added to this subsection of the code that clearly reflect the need for the Scottish Executive to present a united front in public. The fact that ministers should not be provided with materials 'designed to promote one Party's line' suggests that this part of the code has been amended to suit the requirements of collective responsibility under coalition government. However, the additional wording in the SMC on anticipation of criticism from other parties takes the code beyond the requirements of collective responsibility and into the realms of farce. Indeed, the 'anticipation of criticism' creates a near impossible situation for civil servants and ministers since the Opposition could always tailor its subsequent message to show that the minister had anticipated criticism. In turn, although the SMC tends to be more detailed than the MC, the case above provides an interesting example of the difficulties facing those responsible for drafting codes. While codes should provide more detail on what constitutes ethical behaviour, additional detail should not be included if it compounds confusion and/or is patently impracticable.

Explaining Differences

Apart from the obvious differences in the codes, why are they substantively different in other ways? Two explanations seem likely. First, the SMC could represent a genuine attempt by the administration to provide further details on the duties of the executive. In terms of parliament, for example, the SMC (unlike the MC) makes it clear that parliament's primary duty is to hold the executive accountable. The SMC also makes it clearer than the MC that the executive should 'ensure' that parliament hears about major announcements first. Written in the wake of prominent criticisms over the workings of the code on this point at Westminster, the Scottish administration could have wanted to clarify problem areas in order to avoid similar tensions arising in Scotland. As one official argued:

> where we saw opportunities to do so, we adjusted the wording in order to remove potential ambiguities or re-ordered the provisions in order to make the Code easier to use as a source of reference by ministers and their private offices. It would be wrong therefore to read too much into minor differences in wording between the SMC and the MC — it may be simply that we thought our wording read better or that we adjusted the wording to try to clarify the scope or meaning of the relevant provision (personal communication).

However, this begs the question of why the clearer and more detailed wording used in the SMC has not yet been mirrored at Westminster. Moreover, it also begs the question of why differences such as those pertaining to the allocation of special advisers do more than 'clarify the scope or meaning of the relevant provision'. This prompts a second explanation for the variance that focuses on the differences that exist between the Scottish and Westminster administrations. Leaving aside the instances where wording differences are patently the product of divergent administrative arrangements, there do appear to be examples where wording differences are motivated by reasons of a more political nature.

At Westminster, the government has for many decades comprised members from a single political party. Constraints and tensions from a coalition partner have been absent. Consequently, it is in the interests of the Westminster government to adopt a code that grants the members of that government the greatest degree of freedom that the system can tolerate. Meanwhile, in Scotland the executive comprises members from two political parties, Labour and the Liberal Democrats. Unlike Westminster, in the Scottish context there will be constraints and tensions from the coalition partner. One way to exercise control over the potentially divisive behaviour that could originate from a coalition partner would be to tighten the wording of ministerial duties. By stating more clearly the role of the executive *vis-à-vis* the parliament, for example, both coalition partners would have a greater sense of security that they would not be undermined by the non-parliamentary dealings of the other, most notably in the case of media leaks. Similar arguments can be put for other differences of note. For instance, the tighter restrictions in Scotland in relation to special advisers and civil servants both point to the need to check insecurities of coalition government. In the case of special advisers in particular, the first minister not only has powers of approval (like the prime minister at Westminster) but also powers of allocation. In Westminster, ministers can theoretically have up to two advisers each. In Scotland, the first minister has absolute discretion over which ministers get what assistance from special advisers. The degree of control is greater in Scotland and one explanation for this difference is that the leading coalition partner requires a greater degree of control over the advice that the junior partner receives.

Irrespective of the civil servants, politicians and advisers involved in drafting the codes, it is ultimately up to the prime minister and the first minister to approve their own respective codes. The fact that anomalies between the two codes remain suggests that both administrations have adopted codes that are best suited to their own particular working environments. In the case of Scotland, a tighter ministerial code *vis-à-vis* parliament, for example, provides the main coalition partner with a greater degree of control over the actions of ministers from the junior coalition partner and vice versa. This contrasts with Westminster where the absence of coalition government provides little incentive to entrench further the scrutiny rights of the parliament *vis-à-vis* the government.

While the SMC does provide a number of improvements on the Westminster code, both codes are nonetheless commendable in that they are publicly available. While the public circulation of a ministerial code has never been an issue for the Scottish parliament (both came into existence in 1999), the MC has only been available in the public domain since John Major agreed to publish the then entitled *Questions of Procedure for Ministers* in 1992 (see Weller, Chapter 5). The importance of publication is that both codes provide the respective parliaments with tangible standards against which the activities of the respective executives can now be scrutinized. Given that one of the main functions of a legislature is the effective scrutiny and oversight of the executive (Packenham, 1970), this function can only be enhanced if both parliaments are able to compare the actual conduct of ministers alongside the norms of conduct outlined in the codes.

Remaining Problems?

Although publication of the codes does enhance the capacity for legislative oversight of the respective executives, oversight is nonetheless limited by the elastic nature of both codes. A common theme in the reports produced by the Westminster Standards Committee is the need to 'tighten principles'. Some of the biggest problems to do with ministerial conduct arise because codes of conduct are not clear about the behaviour that can be expected — there is too much elasticity. In the MC, for example, the most pertinent example of this is provided in the section on ministers and parliament. Phrases such as 'ministers will want to bear in mind the desire of parliament' are open to interpretation. While the SMC has tightened this and other sections of the comparatively weaker MC, many of the subsections in both codes still need further clarification. For example, in the opening sections on ministers, both codes are so elastic on the principle of the disclosure of information that the requirements placed on ministers *vis-à-vis* parliament are made almost meaningless. In one sub-section ministers are expected to 'give accurate and truthful information to the parliament', and yet in the very next subsection ministers 'should refuse to provide information only when disclosure would not be in the public interest'. While some elasticity is a necessary criterion for any workable code, interpretative problems remain. Every effort needs to be made to ensure that 'best practice' is not made a casualty of gratuitous elasticity.

However, having a clearly defined code is only one-half of the equation. The other half of the equation is to have a code that works in practice. While a code may provide clear, high standards these are meaningless if the means of ensuring compliance are weak. How can we motivate ministers to live up to the requirements of the code and do the right thing? As both codes currently stand, ministers are expected to do the right thing through self-regulation, ultimate enforcement being decided by the prime minister/first minister. In the opening section on ministers both codes state:

> It is for individual ministers to judge how best to act in order to uphold the highest standards. They are responsible for justifying their conduct to the parliament. And they can only remain in office for so long as they retain the Prime Minister's/First Minister's confidence (Cabinet Office, 1997, para. 1; Scottish Executive, 1999, para. 1.2).

While both codes represent a welcome addition to the capacities of both legislatures to scrutinize the activities of the executives, ultimately both executives remain responsible for enforcing their respective codes. Following the recommendations of Lord Nolan, the UK parliament appointed an independent parliamentary Commissioner for Standards. The commissioner is responsible for maintaining the Register of Members' Interests, advising Westminster MPs on their own code of conduct and, most importantly, for investigating allegations of misconduct. If the parliament is subject to oversight by an independent commissioner then perhaps the executive should also be subject to something similar. This problem is particularly acute because prime ministers have been reluctant to act as invigilators and judges (see Woodhouse, Chapter 4).

Apart from the lessons that can be learned from the differences between the theory and practice of the Westminster and Scottish ministerial codes, it may well be that the biggest problem facing both codes in the future is their lack of independent oversight, whether in terms of independent advice and/or independent enforcement. Given the breaching of the code by the government at Westminster, it is likely that this issue will not recede and that eventually the government will face the same scrutiny in relation to its code as ordinary members face in relation to the members' code of conduct. Meanwhile, compared with Westminster the Scottish members' code is also lacking in independent oversight. At Westminster, the conduct of members is subject to review by fellow parliamentarians sitting on the standards committee. Again the same problem applies with self-regulation — how can we ensure that ethics are properly upheld if no external adjudicator is in place?

In addition, what penalties, if any, exist to better facilitate compliance? Current practice and the current recommendations by the standards committee allow the prime minister or first minister a free hand in deciding the nature of penalties. Yet experience suggests that prime ministers have been reluctant to make these decisions. While publication of the codes has enhanced the scrutiny and influence capabilities of both parliaments, without further clarification and openness regarding adjudication, criteria and their associated penalties, this in-built elasticity will ultimately weaken the impact of the codes in motivating ministers to morality.

Just as Lord Nolan realized that we needed an independent parliamentary commissioner to oversee and enforce parliamentary codes of behaviour, so it may not be long before breaches of the ministerial codes make us realize that we need independent oversight of the executive as well. If self-regulation did not work for the parliament, why do we have a system in place that assumes it will work for the executive? Current problems with lack of independent advice and/or independent enforcement of the codes suggest that it might be time to consider the case for an independent ethics commissioner.

Finally, given that both codes are meant to be 'evolutionary' and not static, it will be interesting to see how the wording of the codes might change over time. Will the MC be modified after the next election to reflect many of the substantive refinements of the SMC? Or will the governing dynamics at Westminster (a Labour/Liberal coalition for example) have to change first?

Notes

1. However, on 18 January 2001 Deputy Presiding Officer George Reid refused to let Finance Minister Angus MacKay make a statement on executive plans for quangos as many of the details had been reported in the press first (Shephard, 2001, p. 8). Consequently, it may be too early to tell if the stronger wording in the SMC makes a comparative difference to ministerial behaviour.
2. In both the Scottish and UK cases, 'successors' only applies if there is no party change to the executive/government.
3. Deputy prime Minister; Chancellor of the Exchequer; Secretary of State for Education and Employment; the Minister for the Cabinet Office; and the Secretary of State for Scotland.

PART III:
WALKING THE TIGHTROPE:
SERVING THE PARTY

Chapter 7

Institutional Weaknesses, Ethical Misjudgement: German Christian Democrats and the Kohl Scandal

Wolfgang Seibel

Private Morality and Political Ethics

The success of the constitutional state is founded on its ability to separate the exercise of power from the moral character of the power holders. The modern state represents such an enormous concentration of power that personal morals would be a far too unreliable mechanism for the control of that power. It is the constitution and the rule of law that enables us to maintain a vast machinery of state for the pursuit of collective ends and still sleep peacefully at night: constitution and law are the basis of our confidence that the power of the state will not be misused. The creativity and productivity of societies in capitalist democracies is supported by this confidence.

Compliance with the standards of political ethics by the representatives of the political order is of fundamental significance in creating trust in the constitution and the rule of law. The more important and visible these representatives are, the greater is the signal effect of their political behaviour. We can compile various catalogues of standards of political ethics, but the core of these standards must include respect for the constitution and law (Goodin, 1992, pp. 100–23; Thompson, 1987, pp. 79–87). Politicians in democracies must respect these fundamental standards, and if necessary they must publicly demonstrate this respect. Compliance with the norms of the constitution and law (despite negative effects on personal political interests) is always a good test of the validity of the principles of political ethics. Politicians who satisfy this test need not be moral persons *per se*. They can be egoistic, bully their children or commit adultery and yet be politicians who do much good for society.

This has two important implications. First, constitutions and the rule of the law do not reproduce themselves automatically, they do so through the actions of persons and only if these persons respect constitution and law. Of course the constitutional state with its norms and institutions is the best but not an absolute guarantee against the misuse of power. Ultimately the enduring stability of a democratic constitutional order depends on the willingness of the bearers of the political order to respect its norms and obey its institutions. Second, if political ethics in democracy is more than mere compliance with norms motivated by fear of sanctions, that is, if it is not merely a logic of calculation but rather internalized norms of appropriate behaviour, then it must be grounded in the political culture of a society. The strength of the democratic political culture determines whether a society will or will not tolerate the unethical political behaviour of representatives of the political order.

Political ethics in a democratic constitutional state requires a fairly high ability to make political judgements (Berlin, 1996b). It requires an understanding that respect for the constitution and laws are more important than personal moral qualities. It also requires an understanding of the fundamental meaning of the democratic constitutional order, namely effective control of power. It requires an understanding that all participants in the political process are obligated to respect the constitution and law. And, finally, that the norms and institutions of the democratic state can be *more* or *less* suitable for controlling power.

We have no validated theory of the causes of unethical political behaviour. The theoretical foundations and the empirical evidence are limited by the specific nature of the phenomenon. Studies based on survey data are practically impossible because of the limited access to empirical information. Case studies are the main source of empirical evidence. It is the logic of the democratic constitutional state that provides a yardstick for 'measuring' unethical political behaviour and gives us a starting point for investigating the *possible* causes of unethical political behaviour.

Late in the autumn of 1999 the most successful democratic party in Germany, the Christian Democratic Union (CDU), was plunged into the worst crisis of its history by the unethical political behaviour of some of the most prominent of the party leaders, including the former federal chancellor, Helmut Kohl. The technical core of this scandal consists of illegal party financing, but there are also signs that bribery may have been involved. In this chapter the scandal will be presented, explained and interpreted. My central thesis is that the origin and development of the scandal involving the CDU can be explained in terms of a confusion of private morality and political ethics.

Framework: Financing Political Parties in Germany

The German Constitution, the so-called Basic Law (*Grundgesetz*), refers to parties in Article 21. This states: 'The parties shall help form the political will of the people. They may be freely established. They shall publicly account for the source and use of their funds and for their assets.'

Article 21 represents a good compromise between two democratic principles. On the one hand, it is designed to strengthen the parties as core institutions of political participation. On the other hand, the power of the parties is controlled by the regulation of their internal order and their finances. A special law, the party law, specifies these provisions of the German Constitution.

In the international arena German political parties are relatively powerful. This is largely due to Germany's electoral system and the federal governmental system.

Only half of the representatives in the German federal parliament, the *Deutscher Bundestag*, are directly elected. The other half are elected according to the order of candidates on electoral lists which the parties present for national elections at the level of each *Bundesland* (state). This system gives functionaries and oligarchs in the parties considerable influence on the selection of candidates for the various parliaments. Moreover, the parties provide a counterweight to the strong decentralization and fragmentation of the federal state. The regular career patterns of politicians are characterized by a vertical climb from the local to the regional and then to the federal level. This is possible due to the unified federal structure that all parties in Germany have adopted. The power of the parties is thus not only a consequence of, but also a prerequisite for, the successful functioning of the German governmental system.

A central dilemma in the control of party power is that it is contingent on sound legislation while the legislators themselves belong to those to be controlled. Characteristically, the legal regulation of German political parties is realized above all by the rulings of the Federal Constitutional Court (*Bundesverfassungsgericht*) rather than by the federal parliament. The last major decision of the Federal Constitutional Court on party financing was passed in 1992. This decision required a change in the party law, which went into effect in 1994 (Boyken, 1998).

According to the 1994 revision of the party law, the German parties have three key sources of financing: member contributions, state subsidies and donations. An annual ceiling of 230 million deutschmarks (DM) is set for state subsidies. Each party receives as a subsidy a specific amount of money for each vote it obtains at the ballots and a specific amount of matching funds for member contributions (currently the parties receive 0.50 DM in state subsidies for each deutschmark received as contributions up to 6 000 DM for an individual contributor). This regulation is intended to provide political parties with an incentive to mobilize public support. A so-called public disclosure limit of 20 000 DM annually is set for contributions. Only contributions above that level must be publicly disclosed. Both individual and corporate donations are permitted. Individual contributors may deduct contributions of up to 6 000 DM annually from their tax debt. Corporate donors are not entitled to this particular tax exemption.

German political parties are required to present an annual report on the sources of their funds to the president of the Federal Diet, the *Bundestag*. This report forms a basis for setting and paying state subsidies.

The monitoring of German party assets is weak. Parties can offset debts on assets with income from assets before reporting their sources of funds in the annual report to the president of the *Bundestag*. This is quite different from the regulations for government budgets. In German government budgets all income and expenditures must be documented to ensure complete transparency. By contrast, parties are entitled to limit their disclosures to the 'tip of the iceberg'.

A low degree of transparency and a limited range of sanctions for violations of legal requirements are characteristic of the regulation of party financing in Germany. In principle individual or corporate contributions do not have to be publicly disclosed, except when they exceed 20 000 DM annually. This regulation represents an incentive to break up larger donations into smaller amounts of less than 20 000 DM (although this is illegal), which is precisely what has happened in many instances. Party assets need not be disclosed in full. Violations of the constitutional regulations and party law are not punishable as far as individual violators are concerned. Parties themselves, however, are subject to a fine if acceptance of illegal donations is detected. In particular, punishments are not prescribed for illegal donations, for contributors or individual recipients. Contributions to parties can be given to intermediates, including members of parliament.

Thus there are only weak institutional incentives to comply with the constitution and the laws in regard to the power of parties and influence exerted on parties. The addressees of the legal sanctions are only parties themselves, not individual violators. Politicians have strong incentives to solicit personal contributions. Using bribes to influence political decisions is thus not greatly discouraged, to put it mildly. Existing law only weakly fulfils the actual intention of Article 21 of the Constitution. The non-institutional factor of political ethics is thus particularly important.

The Scandal Over the Illegal Financing of German Christian Democrats 1999-2000[1]

On 4 November 1999 the public prosecutor in the city of Augsburg issued an arrest warrant against a former treasurer of the CDU,[2] Walter Kiep, for suspected tax fraud. The object of the investigation was a sum of one million DM for which taxes were not paid. On 5 November 1999 Kiep surrendered himself to the public prosecutor. He explained that together with the CDU's financial consultant Horst Weyrauch, he had received the sum of one million DM in cash from a lobbyist, Karlheinz Schreiber. The million DM was declared to be a contribution to the CDU.

Schreiber, the lobbyist named by Kiep, is active in the German weapons industry. The public prosecutors were also investigating him for tax evasion in Germany. Schreiber was then residing in Montreal, however, where in the following weeks he was repeatedly interviewed by the German media. In an interview on 12 November 1999 Schreiber stated that he had given former CDU treasurer Kiep one million DM to influence the CDU with regard to his weapons industry employer. This was linked by the media with the delivery of reconnaissance tanks manufactured by a major German weapons manufacturer Thyssen-Henschel to Saudi Arabia in 1991. This prompted former Federal Chancellor Helmut Kohl to make a public statement for the first time on 21 November 1999. Kohl denied the allegation that the federal government's approval of the 1991 delivery of reconnaissance tanks to Saudi Arabia had been influenced by illegal contributions to his party, the CDU. In the *Bundestag* Kohl expressed outrage at this allegation and demanded an immediate investigation.

On 26 November 1999 the former General Secretary of the CDU, Heiner Geißler, disclosed that during the Kohl era[3] the party had maintained a system of irregular bank accounts. Kohl admitted the existence of these irregular accounts and conceded that this violated the party law. Kohl again denied, however, that his or the government's political decisions had been influenced by illegal donations. On 30 November 1999 Kohl also revealed that in his role as chairman of the CDU he had on several occasions provided regional party organizations with money from illegal accounts for campaign funding or to cover debts. In December the *Bundestag* set up an investigative committee to examine the financial practices of the CDU and the possible link between political decisions and illegal funds.

On 16 December 1999 Kohl publicly revealed that he had personally received contributions amounting to approximately two million DM in cash in the 1990s and that these contributions had not been disclosed in the CDU's annual reports, as required by party law. While admitting to violating the law Kohl nevertheless refused to disclose the sources of the contributions. According to party law, the CDU must turn illegally received donations over to the public treasury and pay a fine twice as large as the illegally accepted contributions.[4] On 3 January 2000 the Bonn public prosecutor's office initiated an investigation into Kohl's activities on suspicion of a breach of trust.

On 18 December 1999 it became known for the first time that records had disappeared from the federal chancellor's office, records which concerned the privatization of the former East German chemical industry after German national unification in 1990. The French, Swiss and German press reported assertions by French managers that Elf-Aquitaine had in the 1990s transferred 70 million DM to illegal CDU accounts in Switzerland in an attempt to influence the decisions of the German government on the privatization of the former East German chemical industry (articles in *Le Parisien*, 11 July 2000, *Der Spiegel*, 11 July 2000, and *Die Welt*, 13 July 2000).

On 18 January 2000 the CDU Executive Board demanded that Kohl either reveal the sources of the donations he had illegally accepted or resign his honorary CDU party chairmanship. Kohl immediately resigned, stubbornly refusing to name the anonymous donors.

By mid-January 2000 the scandal over the illegal financing of the CDU in the state of Hessia had become a big news story. Already in November the German news magazine *Der Spiegel* had noted a dramatic increase in 'miscellaneous income' reported by the Hessian CDU between 1989 and 1991.[5] The General Secretary of the Hessian CDU, Herbert Müller, declared in December that between 1989 and 1991 the Hessian regional organization of the CDU had in fact received 'bequests' (*Vermächtnisse*) from anonymous foreign sources amounting to 6 million DM and that the donors of the gifts desired to remain anonymous. Müller claimed that the treasurer of the Hessian CDU, Casimir Prinz zu Sayn-Wittgenstein, suspected that German emigrants of Jewish ancestry had made the anonymous bequests. At a meeting of the *Landtag* (state parliament) held on 16 December 1999, the Minister-President of Hessia, Roland Koch, who was also the chairman of the Hessian CDU, was confronted by Opposition questions about the anonymous 'bequests'.[6] The Opposition argued that the 'bequests' were actually illegal contributions. On 3 January 2000 the

German press covered the 1999 financial report released on 30 December 1999 by the Hessian CDU. In the report a personal credit amounting to 1.5 million DM was listed which the party treasurer, Prinz Wittgenstein, had allegedly donated to the CDU.

On 14 January 2000 a press conference was held in the Hessian capital city of Wiesbaden with Minister-President Koch and a former chairman of the CDU, Manfred Kanther. Kanther, a former Minister of the Interior of the Kohl government, revealed that the Hessian CDU had maintained illegal accounts in Switzerland and Liechtenstein. Since the 1980s several million deutschmarks had flowed from these accounts to the Hessian CDU and been disguised as 'bequests' or as campaign loans. The reference to German emigrants of Jewish ancestry was nothing but a legend intended to disguise the illegal financing. The Opposition demanded the resignation of the state government.

On 8 February the chairman of the Hessian CDU, Minister-President Koch, confessed that he had lied to the public. He had known that in the Hessian CDU's financial report for 1998 party treasurer Wittgenstein had disguised a transfer of 796 000 DM from an illegal account in Switzerland as a personal loan to the party. A fictitious loan offer by Wittgenstein, backdated with Koch's knowledge to February 1998, had served as camouflage. Nevertheless, a month previously Koch had publicly declared the statements in the 1998 CDU financial report to be correct.

After these new revelations, severe tensions surfaced in the Free Democratic Party (FDP), the CDU's Hessian coalition partner. On 10 February 2000 the Federal Executive Board of the FDP demanded that the Hessian FDP withdraw from its coalition with the CDU. The executive board of the Hessian FDP, however, voted unanimously to continue the coalition with the CDU. At a regular party conference of the Hessian CDU on 19 February 2000 Minister-President Koch was confirmed as state chairman of the CDU with 97 per cent of the votes. At a party conference two weeks later, the Hessian FDP voted with a bare majority to continue its coalition with the CDU. This guaranteed that despite the manipulated financial report and the attempted concealment of this manipulation with lies, CDU Minister-President Koch would not lose office.

At the national level the scandal over the illegal financing caused a severe crisis in the CDU because of the special role played by Kohl. Already in December 1999 the CDU General Secretary, Angela Merkel, had publicly distanced herself from Kohl in an article in the *Frankfurter Allgemeine Zeitung*, the leading German daily newspaper. Kohl aggravated the problems of the party leadership and the CDU chairman, Wolfgang Schäuble, with his refusal to reveal the sources of the illegal contributions. This refusal to obey the constitution and the law resulted in severe criticism of Kohl within the CDU. Kohl's resignation as honorary chairman of the party was a consequence of this. Early in the new year, evidence began to accumulate that Kohl was putting pressure on CDU members investigating the scandal. Kohl's successor as CDU chairman, Schäuble, confessed in January that he had also received a cash donation amounting to some 100 000 DM from lobbyist Schreiber. Schäuble had previously denied this in parliament. Another treasurer of the federal CDU and a

Kohl confidant, Brigitte Baumeister, denied that Schäuble had given her the 100,000 DM as a donation thus weakening Schäuble's position.

An important issue was that in two states, North-Rhine Westphalia and Schleswig-Holstein, regional parliamentary elections were in the offing. Initiatives to remove Schäuble from the office of party chairman were immediately initiated by CDU regional organizations in these states. On 16 February Schäuble announced that he did not wish to be considered for the position of party chairman at the national party convention to be held in April 2000. Schäuble also resigned from his office as chairman of the CDU/CSU faction in the *Bundestag*. Schäuble, who was more of a peripheral figure among the 'perpetrators' of the scandal, thereby became its first prominent victim.[7] Schäuble's successor as parliamentary leader was Friedrich Merz; his successor as the chair of the party was Angela Merkel who had until then been General Secretary of the CDU.

In the following months there were scattered press announcements relating to lobbyist fees paid to CDU politicians by the German weapons industry. When questioned by the parliamentary investigative committee, a former state secretary in the federal Defence Ministry, Agnes Hürland-Büning, admitted that after her service as state secretary she had received a 'consulting fee' amounting to 8.5 million DM from the Thyssen concern. In early July the weekly newspaper *Welt am Sonntag* reported that after receiving a contribution of 100 000 DM from lobbyist Schreiber, former CDU treasurer Baumeister had approached Kohl concerning an export permit which would have enabled the Thyssen concern to deliver reconnaissance tanks to Taiwan (*Welt am Sonntag*, 9 July 2000). The French daily newspaper *Le Monde* reported at the same time that the Elf-Aquitaine mineral oil concern had transferred millions of deutschmarks to the CDU via illegal accounts in Liechtenstein (*Le Monde*, 11 July 2000).[8]

In late June 2000 a report by special investigator Burkhard Hirsch revealed that in October 1998, directly after the defeat of the CDU/CSU and Kohl in the *Bundestag* elections, large quantities of data and records had been systematically destroyed in the federal chancellor's office. This also included documents on the privatization of the former East German chemical industry in the 1990s (*Die Welt*, 26 and 29 June 2000; *Der Spiegel*, 3 July 2000).

In March Kohl announced that he had again solicited donations. He wanted to make up for the financial damage to the CDU caused by the party law fine. He also wanted to contribute a large sum from his personal funds. On 9 March Kohl announced the results of this fundraising effort. At that point he had collected about 6 million DM. Among the contributors were several prominent personalities, including Helmut Maucher, president of the Swiss food concern Nestlé, and Leo Kirch, president of the second largest German media group.[9] Kohl and his wife Hannelore themselves donated 700 000 DM of their own.

On 29 June and 6 July the parliamentary investigative committee questioned Kohl. Kohl admitted that between 1993 and 1998 he had received 'between 1.5 and 2 million DM' in cash contributions which, in violation of the legal requirements, were not disclosed in CDU financial reports. Kohl emphasized, however, that he would continue his refusal to name the anonymous contributors. He justified this with his alleged promise to protect the contributors' anonymity. Kohl had already expressed his resolve to persist in disregarding the stipulations of the constitution and the law in December 1999, immediately after his receipt of illegal contributions became known, and had repeated this on several occasions (*Der Spiegel*, 10 July 2000).

Kohl used the hearing by the parliamentary investigative committee to attack the governing parties, the Social Democratic Party (SPD) and Green coalition, and above all, the media. The aim of the governing parties and part of the media, Kohl alleged, was to discredit his very successful 16 years as German chancellor — especially his contribution to German unification and European integration. Furthermore, according to Kohl, the sums he had collected in violation of the stipulations of the party law amounted to less than 0.5 per cent of the CDU's total income in the relevant time period.

Kohl also used the negative reaction to the donations raised by himself (to offset the CDU financial losses resulting from the fines imposed on the party) as further justification for his refusal to reveal the sources of the donations he had received and to name the contributors.

Why Motivation to Political Ethics Failed

There are many reasons for assuming that the facts reported above are only a small share of all illegal actions and violations of the standards of political ethics. It is not known whether a connection exists between illegal donations to the CDU and policy decisions of the CDU-led German government between 1982 and 1998 and those of Federal Chancellor Kohl himself. It is certain that a German weapons firm paid large 'consulting fees' to at least one former member of the CDU-led federal government, state secretary in the federal Defence Ministry Agnes Hürland-Büning. It is certain that several CDU politicians accepted large donations in cash on several occasions and that these were not disclosed in partial violation of legal stipulations. It is certain that immediately after the 1998 national elections records were systematically destroyed in the federal chancellery (*Bundeskanzleramt*) and that these records concerned actions undertaken by several persons in connection with illegal contributions to the CDU (especially the privatization of the former East German chemical industry in the 1990s). It is not known, however, what the specific reasons were for the payment by the Thyssen firm of an enormous 'consulting fee' to a former state secretary. It is not known why the records were destroyed in the chancellery. Nor do we know who gave Kohl cash donations for the CDU, because, in clear violation of the constitution and law, Kohl still refuses to name the donors. It is certain that Kohl illegally obtained funds for the CDU and that he had arranged this illegal action with another person. Finally, beyond doubt, Kohl continues to violate the constitution and law by refusing to reveal the anonymous donors.

The fact that Kohl violated the law — in this case s. 25 of the party finance law — and was not under investigation by the public prosecutor because of his violation of the party law has irritated many observers in Germany and beyond. This was the first time that the inconsistencies of the German party law became subject to broader public awareness. The party law indeed defines illegal actions without providing for a means of prosecuting them.

There are two phenomena which demand explanation, the unethical behaviour of Kohl and the other CDU representatives, and the course of the scandal which developed around this. Why have Kohl and others violated the law? Why does Kohl justify his illegal actions the way he does? Why was Kohl *relatively* successful with this justification?

The manner in which power is acquired and controlled in Germany and in which abuse of power is sanctioned necessarily provides important explanations here. The most powerful office in the political system is the office of federal chancellor, which Kohl occupied for 16 years (1982–98). Because of the crucial role of parties in the political systems of the former West Germany and reunited Germany, the power of the chancellor chiefly depends on the support of his/her own party. This fact shaped Kohl's political socialization. Several times in his career before 1990 Kohl had to fight hard for his candidacy for the office of chancellor and his power as chancellor.[10] Kohl had also seen how Helmut Schmidt (SPD) had failed as chancellor because he could not control his own party.

Furthermore, the CDU had thoroughly modernized its party organization in the 1970s. The new, professional party machinery required far greater financial resources. Still, at the parliamentary investigative committee in June 2000 Kohl stated that the CDU was at a disadvantage compared with the SPD, because the SPD had considerably greater assets than the CDU at its disposal (the core of the SPD funds stems from compensation for the confiscation of SPD assets by the Nazi regime, 1933–45). It was not surprising that the good contacts with the business world maintained by the CDU as a conservative middle-class party were used intensively by Kohl, under whose chairmanship the modernization of the party began, to mobilize needed financial resources. Already, then, in the 1970s and early 1980s the acceptance by Kohl personally of important cash donations had become standard CDU financing practice. This was revealed by the first party contributions scandal of the former West Germany, the so-called Flick Affair (Seibel, 1997).

The mobilization of funds through personal power and for the increase in personal power could under these circumstances have easily become an established practice in the CDU. In justifying his illegal action since late 1999 Kohl has repeatedly claimed that he only wanted to help his party. This is credible if we interpret it as evidence of a symbiosis. Kohl certainly wanted to help his party by increasing his personal power and vice versa (cf. Clemens, 2000). At any rate, we can assume that Kohl's illegal action was not motivated by personal corruptibility.

Kohl's illegal action was furthermore also encouraged by the fact that control of legal party power is relatively weak. The most important control mechanism is the competition between the parties themselves (Lehmbruch, 2000). Whenever the parties have common interests, this control mechanism is necessarily ineffective. This is typically the case in regard to party financing. It is thus not surprising that the parties have only half-heartedly realized through the party law the stipulations of Article 21 of the constitution (that parties 'shall publicly account for the source and use of their funds and for their assets').

The German party law contains at least as many counter-incentives as incentives to comply with the standards of transparency and control in the financing of parties. The most important counter-incentive is the lack of sanctions for violations of the law. It is the parties as corporate actors, rather than the individual perpetrators, that are punished. This is obviously an absurd construction, because it makes the parties defenceless against individual violations of the law. The individual perpetrators themselves are only 'punished' if the parties enforce compensation for financial harm through the courts. It is obvious that the principle of controlling power is turned on its head. The more powerful the violator of the law, the less chance there is that an injured party can successfully assert a claim to compensation. Kohl, who had solidified his power in the CDU by means of financial resources, was able to mobilize these resources again in early 2000 in order to compensate the CDU for the financial losses he himself had caused. It appears that beyond a certain threshold present legal framework conditions tend more to reward than punish the accumulation of power through the illegal mobilization of funds.

Beyond these unfavourable structural framework conditions, however, there is an ethical core of political behaviour. After all, it makes little sense to assume that Kohl had no choice but to engage in illegal behaviour. He made a wrong decision and chose illegal instead of legal means in his efforts to mobilize funds for his party. Sound theoretical reasons suggest that deviations from norms cannot be attributed solely to the weighing of costs and benefits[11] but rather to the successful coping with tensions between personal normative ideals and actual behaviour (the well-known concept of *cognitive dissonances* (Festinger, 1957)). In his public rhetoric after the disclosure of his illegal action in 1999, Kohl tried hard to reconcile his own behaviour and the standards of political ethics. This could succeed only if his own behaviour and the standards of political ethics were reinterpreted. This reinterpretation has led to a characteristic confusion of personal morals and political ethics.

Kohl alleged that he could not reveal the source of the illegal funding because he had *promised* to protect the identities of the anonymous donors. The core of Kohl's self-justifying rhetoric lies in his appeal to the credibility of his own moral integrity. His 'credible' reference to his personal incorruptibility supported this style of rhetoric. A further important rhetorical component which Kohl extensively used in what was entitled his 'diary' for the years of 1998–2000 (Kohl, 2000) was his appeal to his personal trustworthiness.

For the distanced observer the confusion may be obvious; for the participant in political discourse in Germany it is not necessarily so. Kohl's rhetoric follows a logic which Richard Sennett (1977) has described as an erosion of the separation between the private and the public spheres. In Kohl's rhetoric the public office which he held as chancellor and chairman of the CDU disappears. Thereby the actual problem of his illegal action also disappears, namely the violation of standards for the control of power. Kohl attempts to suggest a different standard for the judgement of his action, the standard of personal morals and he thereby confirms Sennett's thesis. Kohl would not use this rhetorical pattern if he did not believe that the separation between the private and public spheres, and thereby the separation between personal morals and political ethics, had been eroded in German political consciousness. How far this erosion has gone is an empirical question, but obviously it can be rewarding for a politician to confuse implicitly the private and the public spheres as a starting point for the justification of unethical political behaviour. The accusation of unethical *political* behaviour is supposed to be waived precisely through confrontation with obvious *personal* moral integrity.

Kohl's public rhetoric demonstrates not just a confusion of morals and political ethics, but also the danger that this confusion poses. Kohl tried — relatively successfully — to mobilize the moral sensitivities of the public to support his violation of constitution and law. The 'unethical' character of Kohl's behaviour is thus threefold. First, Kohl violated the constitution and law by accepting cash donations for the CDU and planning together with the alleged donors to break the law, that is, illegally to withhold the donors' names. Second, after admitting his illegal action, Kohl expressed his resolve to continue breaking the law by refusing to name his donors. Third, he employed a specific demagogic argument to conceal his disrespect for the constitution and law, that is, he claimed he could not break a personal *promise* he had made.

The allusion to this promise contained an appeal to the moral sentiment in support of unethical behaviour. In a constitutional democracy political leaders are obligated to help strengthen public respect for the constitution and the law. The core of Kohl's unethical behaviour consists in his doing just the opposite. The gravity of this unethical behaviour lies in the fact that he attempted to mobilize good motives — virtues like integrity, trustworthiness, honour, loyalty — to justify wrongful behaviour and disregard the constitution and his violation of the law.

Conclusion: Institutions and Ethical Judgement

In approaching the question of what motivates politicians to ethical or unethical behaviour, the scandal over the illegal financing of German Christian Democrats reveals two crucial factors of more general significance, namely institutional weaknesses and weaknesses in ethical judgement. The institutional weaknesses lie in the counter-incentives to compliance with the stipulations of the constitution and law. The weaknesses in ethical judgement exist in the confusion of personal morals and political ethics.

Unethical political behaviour is embedded in a setting consisting of institutional and cultural incentives and counter-incentives. The actual motivation for ethical political behaviour thus depends on the quality of institutions, on the will to improve poorer institutions and the willingness to act when political ethical standards are violated. Institutions and political ethics are mutually interdependent. Weak ethical standards do not produce sound political institutions and unsound institutions are a weak stimulus for political ethics.

The road to hell is paved with good intentions. Sometimes, even this irony is blunted by reality. German legislators have combined a good constitutional article — Article 21 of the Basic Law — with a bad law — the party law of 1967, last revised in 1994. Article 21 of the Basic Law states clearly and simply that political parties 'shall publicly account for the source and use of their funds and for their assets'. The party law repeats this regulation, but contains no sanctions against individual violators. Nor does German criminal law specify any punishment for representatives who accept cash from third parties. Furthermore, the party law encourages concealment of party assets instead of transparency. Those who should have changed this bad law are simultaneously those who profit from its current version, namely the parties. The limitation of party power can in the end be realized only through the power of public opinion. Therefore the question of how deeply the standards of political ethics are anchored in public opinion itself is of crucial importance.

The case of Kohl suggests that standards of political ethics in Germany are too weak to serve as a counterweight to the power of the parties. The principle that the powerful should not put in question the laws intended to limit their power could not be upheld in the Kohl case. The principle itself played only a peripheral role in public opinion and public discourse during the scandal outlined here. Kohl himself has strongly influenced this discourse. He placed his moral integrity in the foreground and did not shy away from playing the principles of personal morality and political ethics off against each other. The credible claim that he was incorruptible distracted from the fact that the harm done by persistent disrespect for the law was far greater than the potential harm of corruption. Behind the veil of this confusion, Kohl was able to continue abusing his power well after the beginning of the scandal. He also resisted the efforts of his successor as party chairman, Schäuble, to investigate the affair. He conspired with the representatives of the CDU in the parliamentary investigative committee, and these representatives conspired with Kohl, even though the committee was set up to uncover the truth Kohl himself was actively concealing. Kohl furthermore employed what prestige he retained to collect several million deutschmarks in additional contributions with which finally to buy himself free from the public prosecutors.[12]

The institutional order of constitutional democracy is designed to make the control of power relatively independent of the quality of the personal morals of the powerful. The standards of political ethics are thereby all the more important. If they are to be effective they must themselves assist in distinguishing between personal morals and political ethics. The foundation of this distinction is a specific sense of reality (Berlin, 1996a), of constitutional democracy. Constitutional democracy represents the promise of effective control of power. The basis of this is the institutionalization of control and thereby its emancipation from the moral character of the powerful.

Notes

1. The most important information on and chronologies of the scandal over illegal financing of Christian Democrats are available on the Internet under www.spiegel.de and www.welt.de.
2. German Christian Democrats are organized into two independent parties which form a single group or 'faction' in the *Bundestag* (federal parliament). These are the *Christian Democratic Union* (CDU) and the *Christian Social Union* (CSU). The CSU is active only in Bavaria (after the union of the two German states in 1990 there was a brief, failed attempt to found an equivalent of the CSU in the former East Germany). Only the CDU is affected by the scandal concerning illegal party financing. The CDU/CSU and the Liberal Party (Free Democratic Party) have formed the Opposition in the federal parliament since elections held in the autumn of 1998, in which Gerhard Schröder of the Social Democratic Party (SPD) replaced Helmut Kohl (CDU) as German chancellor.
3. Kohl was the chairman (*Vorsitzender*) of the CDU from 1974 to 1999 and federal chancellor from 1982 to 1998. At the CDU Federal Party Convention in 1999 Helmut Kohl was named honorary chairman of the CDU. Appointed to serve as Kohl's successor as party chairman in November 1998 was the then chairman of the CDU/CSU faction in the German *Bundestag*, Wolfgang Schäuble. Formerly a close confidant of Kohl in his days as Minister-President of Rhineland Palatinate (1969–76), Heiner Geißler served as General Secretary of the CDU in the 1980s. In 1989 he took part in a plot to remove Helmut Kohl as chairman of the CDU. Geißler has since then repeatedly criticized Kohl within the CDU.
4. The administrative responsibility for these matters rests with the president of the *Bundestag* and his/her administration. The president of the German *Bundestag* reached a decision on the monetary penalty amounting to 6.5 million DM on 19 July 2000.
5. 'Miscellaneous income' or 'other income' (*sonstige Einnahmen*) is, in a technical sense, income which does not consist of state subsidies, membership dues or donations.
6. Koch is the Minister-President of a coalition government with the Liberal Party (FDP). The Opposition in the Hesssian *Landtag* consists of the Social Democrats and Green Party.
7. In March 2000 a lengthy television interview was broadcast in which Schäuble expressed great bitterness toward Helmut Kohl. Schäuble's comments in this interview were interpreted by the press as implying that Kohl had neutralized the most charismatic CDU leader in order to prevent the CDU from undertaking a thorough investigation of the scandal and distancing itself from Kohl himself (*Frankfurter Allgemeine Zeitung*).
8. In its 11 July 2000 edition, *Le Monde* quoted former Elf-Aquitaine manager André Tarallo. Tarallo allegedly told *Le Monde* that, with the authorization of then French President Mitterand, former Elf-Aquitaine chief Loic Le Floch-Prigent had arranged for the payment of 256 million French francs as a 'commission' to various recipients in connection with the privatization of the former East German chemical industry and the construction of a new mineral oil refinery.
9. Maucher donated 500 000 DM, Kirch 1 000 000 DM. The Social Democratic Minister-President of Schleswig-Holstein, Heide Simonis, then called for a boycott of Nestlé products.
10. Kohl was chairman of the CDU from 1973 on. In the 1976 *Bundestag* election he campaigned for the first time for the chancellorship. In this election he obtained 48 per cent of the vote cast. This was a result which, except for Konrad Adenauer in 1957, only Kohl himself has outdone, in 1983. Nevertheless, in 1979 Kohl's candidacy for the chancellorship was opposed within his party and by the Bavarian CSU and its chairman, Franz Josef Strauß. In the 1980 national elections Strauß campaigned for the CDU/CSU for the chancellorship

but was decisively defeated by Helmut Schmidt (SPD). In 1982 Kohl did become chancellor, because the small Liberal Party (FDP) under Foreign Minister Hans-Dietrich Genscher left its coalition with the SPD and formed a new coalition with the CDU/CSU, which lasted until 1998. However, Kohl was definitely not the undisputed number one person in the CDU/CSU until 1989. His most important rival, Franz Josef Strauß, died unexpectedly in 1988. In September 1989, a few weeks before the fall of the Berlin Wall, a group supporting Lothar Späth, the Minister-President of Baden-Württemberg, and Heiner Geißler, the General Secretary of the CDU, unsuccessfully attempted to oust Kohl as party chairman. With the fall of the Berlin Wall on 9 November 1989 events were set in motion in which Kohl displayed uncontested statesmanship. After his election victory in the first all-German elections in December 1990, his position in the CDU/CSU was completely unchallenged.

11 This is the variant which Gary Becker (1968) presents and which, to some extent at least, may explain Kohl's illegal action up to 1999.

12 On 23 July 2000 several German newspapers reported that Bonn public prosecutors were willing to terminate their investigation of Kohl for breach of trust because Kohl had compensated for the financial damage to the CDU and thereby contributed a considerable share of his personal assets.

Chapter 8

Problem or Solution? The Role of Ministerial Staff

Anne Tiernan

Personal advisers, those partisans selected to work within a minister's office, form an important part of the system of support for ministers, yet are subject to vastly different employment arrangements and accountability requirements than politicians or public servants. Known as 'ministerial staff' in Australia and 'special advisers' in the UK, advisers, as they are described throughout this chapter, work in close personal contact with ministers, and under their direct supervision. Their positions are contingent upon the strength of this relationship, and their fortunes are inextricably linked to those of their minister.

This chapter outlines the changes that advisers have wrought on the system of advice and support to ministers in Australia and Britain. Using an Australian case study, the 1997 'Travel Rorts' affair, key questions about the role advisers play in the ethical conduct of ministers are explored. In focusing on the institutional and individual factors which condition the conduct of advisers, and of their ministers, the chapter considers whether advisers are 'part of the problem' or 'part of the solution' in motivating ministers to behave ethically.

Support to Ministers: The Role of Personal Staff

Ministers in Westminster systems of government perform a wide variety of functions and have a raft of responsibilities conferred upon them through both statute and convention (Headey, 1974; Weller and Grattan, 1981; White, 1988). The pace and complexity of the minister's job has increased significantly over recent decades, reflecting pressures on policy making more generally. These factors, together with a desire by ministers to assert greater policy control, are driving important changes in the structure of support at the summit of the core executive (Peters *et al.*, 2000).

Personal advisers have long been a feature of executive politics (Jones, 1984; Plowden, 1987; Walter, 1986, 1989). For example, the Committee on Standards in Public Life (the Neill Committee) noted recently that special advisers have been a feature of British political life since 1916 (Neill, 2000). It is generally agreed, however, that the systematic recruitment of advisers from outside the bureaucracy began under Prime Minister Harold Wilson in the 1970s (Gay, 2000; Hennessy, 1989). In Australia the Whitlam government was the catalyst for the growth in both the size and influence of ministerial staff (Forward, 1977; Smith, 1977, 1989; Walter, 1986, 1989, 1992; Waterford, 1996). Prior to the Whitlam government there was no impetus to seek alternatives to public service advice (Smith, 1977). Personal staffing capacity was sourced from the bureaucracy, and mainly comprised secretarial and limited media functions (Sinclair, 1996; Walter, 1986, 1989, 1992).

In Australia the expansion of ministerial staff, and especially prime ministerial staff capacity, has continued under successive governments. The Members of Parliament Staff Act 1984 (MoPS Act) institutionalized this practice. This legislation also enables ministers to seek highly specialized and/or expert advice through the use of consultants (see, for example, Halligan and Campbell, 1992; Weller, 2001). There is now substantial evidence that policy advising is highly competitive, and that the former dominance of the public service over this function is eroding (FitzGerald, 1996; Weller, 2001). Ministers are demonstrating a preference for 'personalized' appointments, both in their private offices and more broadly across the system of advice and support, including at senior levels of the bureaucracy (FitzGerald, 1996; Weller, 2001). Within ministers' offices there has been a discernible increase in the recruitment of 'political types' (Dunn, 1995; Walter, 1986) and a corresponding reduction in bureaucratic recruits. Fewer of those now supporting ministers have their ethical outlook conditioned by public sector norms. Increasingly, serving as an adviser is a stepping-stone to a political career (Abbott, 1997; Waterford, 1996).

In Britain the number of special advisers has expanded, with the most significant increases occurring under the Blair government. Tony Blair assumed the British prime ministership determined to exert strong central leadership and control (Cockerell, 2000; Hennessy, 1999a, b; Wintour, 2000). Accordingly, the staff resources available to the prime minister have been augmented to suit Blair's priorities and operating style (see Burch and Holliday, 1999; Gay, 2000; Hennessy, 1999a; Wintour, 2000). Since the election of the Blair government in 1997, the total number of special advisers has grown from 38 to 72 (Gay, 2000, p. 18), and government expenditure on personal staff has increased from £1.5m to £3.5m per annum (Gay, 2000, p. 20).

In Australia advisers provide political, policy, administrative and personal support to the minister (Dunn, 1995; Hollway, 1996; Walter, 1986). This is what former Fraser staffer Dennis White (1988) has termed 'backup' for the minister. In both Australia and the UK ministers' need for 'backup', which it would be either impossible or inappropriate for public servants to provide, has been a key justification for the development of personal staff capacity. It is generally recognized that advisers and bureaucrats provide different and complementary forms of support to ministers based on their respective skills and expertise (Gay, 2000; Hennessy, 1989; Hollway, 1996; Howard, 1996a, 1998; Neill, 2000; Waterford, 1996; White, 1988; Wilenski, 1979).

Unlike bureaucrats, whose employment arrangements and accountabilities are prescribed in legislation and other formal mechanisms, advisers are recruited, deployed and supervised by the minister and are accountable to the minister. Their positions are explicitly political and contingent upon the fortunes of the minister. Their job is to serve, support and seek to advance the minister's interests. It is based on personal loyalty, trust and patronage as well as on specific skills. There are thus important differences between bureaucrats and advisers. One career is based on a long-term outlook, which values neutrality and expertise; the other is generalist, partisan and often brief.

Advisers and Ministerial Ethics

Advisers are an important source of advice to ministers, including advice on issues requiring ethical judgement. However, a variety of institutional factors influence their ability and willingness to provide positive guidance to ministers on ethical issues. A first problem is that the institutional arrangements which might be expected to support ethical behaviour, such as legislation, codes, guidelines, administrative law mechanisms, auditing and monitoring regimes, training and systemic support of ethical standards (see Neill, 2000; Sherman, 1998), are rudimentary or absent in the case of ministerial staff and special advisers (Select Committee on Public Administration, 2000; Hollway, 1996; Warn, 1996; Waterford, 1996). Advisers receive very limited training or induction when they arrive to begin work in the minister's office; what they do receive depends on their minister's initiative. Advisers work in secrecy. They are exempt from the established accountability mechanisms which apply to politicians and public servants. They are not required to appear before parliamentary committees, their actions are not reported in departmental annual reports, and they are not subject to auditing or other forms of public scrutiny (Select Committee on Public Administration, 2000; Gay, 2000; Hollway, 1996; Howard, 1996a; Neill, 2000; Sherman, 1998). In noting these concerns, the Neill Committee has recommended the development of a separate code of conduct for special advisers in its most recent report (Neill, 2000) In Australia, Hollway (1996, p. 142) notes:

> There may now be no group of people in the contemporary system of government in Canberra who in fact have such a high ratio of power (considerable) to accountability (limited) as ministerial staff.

Employment arrangements are a second source of influence on the ability and willingness of advisers to support their ministers to behave ethically. It can be argued that these are inherently problematic. The general conditions of employment for ministerial staff are outlined in the MoPS Act, while in the UK broad parameters for the employment of special advisers are outlined in the 1997 'Model Contract'.[1] In both countries ministers enjoy a good deal of discretion over the hiring and firing of personal staff, although prime ministers may determine the boundaries within which this can be exercised. Employment terminates automatically in the event that the minister should die or otherwise cease to hold office, but a minister may terminate an adviser's employment at any time. This, together with intense competition among ministers for favour with the prime minister, may produce an environment that encourages rather than inhibits unethical conduct. In this context, there is a powerful self-interest motive for advisers to encourage their minister to make unethical choices, especially if these are perceived to be politically advantageous. Their minister's career, and by extension their own, may be advanced by such a course. This dilemma is highlighted in the comments of Tony Abbott (1997) (emphasis added):

> To work extremely hard for someone else to get the credit, to be completely frank with your boss, but utterly discreet with everyone else, to be deeply involved in politics without becoming a political player oneself and *constantly to judge not what's right so much as what's right for the boss* takes a special kind of vocation.

The ethical culture which surrounds ministers and their staff, itself framed from the perspective of political insiders, is a third constraint on the ability and willingness of advisers to advise their ministers on ethical matters. Political insiders have a different ethical logic to those outside of politics (Jackson and Smith, 1996; McAllister, 2000; Smith, 1998, 1999). Their sense of what is right is conditioned by circumstances as well as their appreciation of the practicalities of power. McAllister (2000) and Smith (1998, 1999) argue that political parties exert significant influence on ethical outlook. As both ambitious insiders and partisan zealots, these findings raise important questions about the potential of advisers to support ministers to make ethical choices.

In the absence of a substantial literature, practitioner perspectives found in articles, interviews and biographies offer useful insights into the operation of ministers' offices. Here the pace and workload intensity of life within a minister's office is a recurrent theme (for example, Burch and Holliday, 1999; Hollway, 1996; Kerin, 1996). This is a fourth source of influence on advisers in motivating ministers to ethical conduct. The frantic pace and complex demands of the office may place both ministers and their staff in positions that limit their capacity to recognize potential ethical problems and to weigh them appropriately.

In summary, there have been important changes in the system of advice and support to ministers. Increasingly ministers are supported by an active and loyal personal staff whose *raison d'être* is to protect and advance the minister's interests. Their ambiguous operating environment may constrain the ability and willingness of advisers to motivate their ministers to make ethical choices. An unintended consequence of changes to the advisory system is that the early warning system to ministers has been fragmented and diluted. Ministers may now be exposed to a greater risk of making choices that are, or could be, perceived to be unethical. This raises the question of whether advisers are a problem or the solution in motivating the ethical conduct of ministers. The 1997 Travel Rorts affair in Australia provides a useful case study through which this question can be explored.

The Travel Rorts Affair

The travel allowance and parliamentary entitlements of Australian politicians are highly sensitive issues, prompting many efforts over the years to devise effective systems for their administration and payment. The rates and conditions of payment for travel allowance entitlements for ministers and other members of parliament are established by government decisions, by determinations of the Remuneration Tribunal, and are codified in legislation.

During the period under consideration in this case, a complex set of administrative arrangements supported the payment of travel allowances to senators and members of the House of Representatives as well as to ministers and other office holders. For ministers, responsibility was divided between the minister's portfolio department and the Ministerial and Parliamentary Services (MAPS) division of the then Department of Administrative Services (DAS). MAPS had primary responsibility for the travel arrangements of ministers, including the payment of travel allowances.[2] The entitlements of senators and members of the House of Representatives other than ministers and office holders were administered by the parliamentary departments.

The Colston Affair: A Prelude to the Travel Rorts

In early 1997 controversy erupted over the misuse of parliamentary entitlements by federal politicians. Between December 1996 and July 1997 the Australian Federal Police (AFP) brought fraud charges against two Coalition parliamentarians and the parliamentary secretary to the Minister for Health. Against this backdrop of scandal and growing community cynicism, a series of allegations were raised by a former staff member against Senate Deputy President Mal Colston over his use of travel allowance and other parliamentary entitlements (Evans, 2000; Australia, Senate, 24 March 1997, pp. 2235, 2241). Under investigation about the use of his travel allowance, Colston successfully moved that the payments received by all senators should be tabled in parliament (Australia, Senate, 4 March 1997, p. 1198). Details of travel allowance claims by senators during the period 1 January 1992 to 3 March 1997 were tabled on 24 March 1997. During the ensuing debate, the Senate requested that 'details in respect of all members of the House of Representatives be tabled in that House at the earliest opportunity' (Australia, Senate, 24 March 1997, p. 2230).

The House of Representatives Travel Allowances Report

Responding to the Senate's request, Administrative Services Minister David Jull asked his department to extract the travel allowance details of members of the House of

Representatives who were or had been ministers, parliamentary secretaries or office holders during the specified period. The information, summarized in the form of a draft schedule (hereafter 'the schedule'), was provided to the minister's office on 13 May 1997. Additional information provided by DAS Deputy Secretary Brendan Godfrey noted that:

> ... There are three areas of possible concern/criticism from the figures provided in respect of all travelling allowance by Ministers and Office Holders (including former Members) in the House of Representatives for the period 1 January 1992 to 3 March 1997. These are:
>
> - Travel that is not within entitlement;
> - Excessive travel;
> - Travel during election periods.
>
> (Minute from DAS to Jull's office, quoted in Kennedy, 1998, p. 40)

Later events would reveal that greater attention to the first issue — travel that was not within entitlement — was probably warranted. However, the third area of potential criticism — travel during election periods — became the government's focus. A long-standing convention of all major parties was that ministers did not claim travelling allowance during the election campaign — that is, from the day of the prime minister's campaign launch to the day after polling day (ANAO, 1997). Ministers would claim travelling allowance during this 'convention period' only if they were required to travel for cabinet meetings or in connection with their ministerial duties. Godfrey's briefing identified 23 former Labor Party ministers and parliamentary secretaries who had potentially broken the convention by claiming travelling allowance during the 1993 and 1996 election campaigns. Minister Jull wrote to them indicating their travel allowance details would be tabled in parliament the following week, and invited them to consider reimbursing any claims which might have breached the convention.

On 16 May 1997 Jull's Senior Adviser, John Sutherland, advised MAPS that a response had been received from a former parliamentary secretary. Sutherland suggested that where former ministers or parliamentary secretaries had offered explanations for their travel during the election period, or indicated an intention to repay monies, this should be annotated on the schedule to be tabled by the minister. Sutherland confirmed this instruction by facsimile, and the text of the various annotations that were incorporated into the schedule was agreed over the following week. In all, annotations were recorded against the records of nine former Labor ministers was tabled in parliament and was entitled *Ministers and Office Holders in the House of Representatives Travelling Allowance — Claim Details, 1997.*

At the request of the minister's office, all Coalition ministers, parliamentary secretaries and other office holders in the House of Representatives were asked to review the details of their travel allowance claims, and to notify MAPS immediately if any corrections were required. The office of John Sharp, National Party Minister for Transport and Regional Development, contacted MAPS on 27 May 1997, identifying certain inaccuracies in his original travel claim. Sharp had initially claimed travel allowance for 144 nights, for which he was paid a total of $29 205. In his revised claim submitted on 27 May 1997, he claimed a total of 97 nights, for which his amended entitlement was $20 465. Sharp indicated he would immediately repay an amount of $8 740.

Jull tabled the report entitled *Travelling Allowance Paid to Various Office Holders in the House of Representatives — 1 January 1992 to 3 March 1997* on 29 May 1997. In his tabling statement Jull drew particular attention to the convention issue. However despite Jull's knowledge that his colleague John Sharp had been overpaid, the amount cited in the schedule was the amount of Sharp's travel allowance entitlement ($20 465) rather than the actual payment he had received ($29 205). In contrast to the records of former Labor ministers, there was no annotation showing that Sharp was required to reimburse the overpayment. Jull's office was also aware of errors in the travelling allowance claims of National Party Veterans' Affairs Minister Bruce Scott, but these were also not identified in the tabled report.

DAS bureaucrats were concerned about the annotations to the schedule proposed by the minister's office. Throughout subsequent investigations into the matter, senior officials maintained they had cautioned the minister's office about the potential for criticism over inconsistencies in the way travel during the convention period was reported (ANAO, 1997, Section 4). According to a key MAPS bureaucrat:

> The matter of annotations and the implications for amendments to Ministers' travelling allowance schedules was raised by me [and others] on 26 May … They had advice from Minister Sharp's office that he had some amendments involving repayment.
>
> I then raised with John Sutherland whether these amendments and any received from other Ministers would be handled by footnote, i.e. consistent with the advice he had previously given in relation to former Ministers who had repaid travelling allowance claimed during the last two election campaigns.
>
> John Sutherland advised (I cannot recall whether it was then or a subsequent call) that the amendments would be incorporated and not annotated. I strongly counselled that this course would raise the criticism of inconsistency from the Opposition and that the Minister would need a defence for this eventuality. John Sutherland was politely testy about my caution. I reiterated the risk involved in this course, but he confirmed that the annotations were to stay.
>
> John Sutherland considered that the defence lay in the Ministers [Sharp, and Scott in due course] having identified and volunteered the changes and repayment and that this distinguished them from the other cases (quoted in Kennedy, 1998, p. 71).

This suggests that the efforts of DAS bureaucrats to discourage selective annotation of the schedule went unheeded by the minister's office, although it is unclear who within Jull's office determined this course of action. However, the ANAO report (1997, Section 4) noted that 'a statement by Jull's senior adviser [Sutherland] advised that the MAPS officer had "thought the approach to be right. No contrary view was expressed by him"'. In response, the MAPS officer stated, 'I believe that I added that it would constitute a voluntary repayment, etc. but not that the amended schedule should be used. That was his advice' (quoted in ANAO, 1997, Section 3). While ultimately unable to reconcile the conflicting claims of bureaucrats and advisers, the ANAO was highly critical of DAS for its failure to maintain adequate records of important advice provided to the minister's office.

There were significant differences between the reports tabled in the Senate and those later tabled in the House of Representatives. No tabling statement accompanied the Senate report, while Jull's tabling statement drew attention to annotations on the records of former Labor ministers. Political considerations were thus a decisive influence on the reporting of travel allowance payments in the House of Representatives. Jull attempted to use the report tabled in May for partisan advantage, highlighting repayments made by former Labor ministers while leaving those of his Coalition colleagues unidentified and unexplained. According to the Auditor-General:

> ... The annotation in the report also contrasts with a lack of annotation and footnotes in the earlier report which was tabled in the Senate on 24 March 1997. The report to the Senate does not identify or distinguish any payments claimed for the 'convention period'(ANAO, 1997, Section 3).

Labor Senator Robert Ray laid the blame for this strategy squarely on ministerial staffers (Australia, Senate, 17 November 1997, p. 8939). He questioned the ethics of Jull's conduct, noting that the Minister for Administrative Services:

> ... does have a slightly higher ethical responsibility to parliament because he is given a whole range of confidential material to do with all of us, and therefore he should try to be a little more impartial than he has been (Australia, Senate, 23 September 1997, pp. 6782–3).

Labor also claimed that prior to tabling the report, Jull's office had prepared and circulated to journalists a one-page document drawing attention to the annotations on the records of former Labor ministers. Senator Ray told the Senate:

> ... When he [Jull] published ministerial and office holder travel allowance and other expenses in the House of Representatives, he had his office draw up a one-page anonymous document and send it round the gallery trying to highlight what he saw was any [sic] embarrassment to the opposition. He did that. He started the war on this. He did it, but he did it anonymously through his office... (Australia, Senate, 23 September 1997, p. 6782).[3]

John Sharp's Repayment and the Alleged Cover-up

Although both Jull's office and MAPS believed the repayment from John Sharp would be made before the tabling, it subsequently emerged that the cheque was in fact not received until several weeks later. Jull had thus technically misled the parliament by tabling a document that contained incorrect information. At the time of its tabling, the report attracted only modest media coverage. Controversy arose in September 1997 when journalist Laurie Oakes, acting on leaked information from DAS, contacted Jull's office raising questions about the accuracy of the May report, particularly the details of certain Coalition ministers. Oakes' story was broadcast on 23 September 1997. In it Oakes revealed that John Sharp had 'secretly' repaid $8 740 in wrongly claimed travel expenses. He suggested that Jull had 'covered up' his colleague's repayment by failing to reveal it either in the May report or subsequently. Immediately following the broadcast, Jull made a statement in the House of Representatives in which he confirmed that repayments were received from Coalition ministers after the May tabling.

'Septem dies Horribilis' — Howard's Seven Days of Horror

Sensing a crisis for the government, especially considering the prime minister's claims of higher parliamentary standards, the Opposition was scathing in its response. Opposition Senate leader John Faulkner accused Minister Jull of involvement in a 'most blatant and underhand cover-up of Mr Sharp's travel claims' (Australia, Senate, 23 September 1997, p. 6779). By 24 September, desperate to maintain the credibility of his ministerial code of conduct, Prime Minister John Howard demanded and received the resignations of both Sharp and Jull. On 26 September, the Minister for Science and Technology, Peter McGauran, became the third minister to resign over what had become known as the Travel Rorts affair, after it was revealed he had misled the House over the details of his travel allowance claims (see Barton, 1997).

Attention then turned to finding the source of the leak to Laurie Oakes. The DAS secretary, John Mellors, called in the AFP to investigate, noting that the culprit(s) would face action under the Crimes Act (*Canberra Times*, 26 September 1997). Later in a move widely interpreted as Jull taking revenge on the prime minister for his forced resignation, Jull handed Howard a letter from John Sutherland. In it Sutherland claimed that he had advised the prime minister's chief of staff (Grahame Morris) and office manager (Fiona McKenna) about John Sharp's repayment in May.[4] In a dramatic statement to parliament, Howard raised the allegations, noting as incongruous that they had not been discussed with him previously in the many meetings between himself and the former minister. He strenuously denied any prior personal knowledge of the Sharp repayment. Both Morris and McKenna initially denied any memory of the conversations. Anxious to retain the services of two loyal staff, the prime minister sought to refer the inconsistencies in the accounts provided by Sutherland and Morris to the Auditor-General for investigation. However, the Auditor-General refused, noting that it would be beyond his statutory powers to investigate the actions of ministers or their staff (see *The Australian*, 30 September 1997).

Documents tabled in the House of Representatives by the prime minister lent support to Sutherland's claims to have earlier informed the prime minister's office (PMO) about Sharp's repayment. On 26 September 1997 middle-ranking Department of Prime Minister and Cabinet (PM&C) bureaucrat, Philomena Bisshop, recalled a conversation with MAPS officer Carolyn Hughes prior to the May tabling in which it was suggested the decision to suppress the Sharp repayment was the decision of the Minister for Administrative Services with the support of the PMO. Bisshop resigned over her 'lapse of memory' in failing to advise her superiors that Jull may have misled the parliament.

Fiona McKenna subsequently advised the prime minister that she had a vague recollection of the discussion with Sutherland, which she indicated was of a brief and general nature. Grahame Morris continued to deny any memory of the discussion, but nonetheless offered his resignation. At the end of a week he described as *septem dies horribilis*, a visibly emotional John Howard announced he had terminated the services of both Morris and McKenna. Morris rejected press speculation that his demise was the result of an act of revenge by Sutherland, saying 'John Sutherland is not like that, he's a good operator'. Notwithstanding these denials, Barton (1997) noted that 'the Prime Minister's press secretary rang around the press gallery last night in a furious bid to let it be known that Jull's senior private secretary [Sutherland] had an axe to grind about how his boss had been chopped'.

The Travel Rorts Affair and Ministerial Staff

The Travel Rorts case study exposes an important ethical dilemma in which ministerial staff played a significant role. Minister Jull's decision to use the May travelling allowances report for partisan advantage, which ultimately forced his resignation from the ministry, was facilitated by his personal staff against the advice of the public service. The remainder of this chapter draws conclusions from the Travel Rorts affair, with particular reference to the role that ministerial staff may have played. It considers whether Jull's advisers were 'part of the problem' or 'part of the solution' in motivating the behaviour of their minister.

David Jull's resignation over the Travel Rorts affair was necessary because he made an unethical choice. He sought to use the travel allowance report, an essentially administrative process, politically. The evidence suggests that advisers were influential in this choice. Instead of heeding the warnings of public service advisers, the minister and/or his staff treated the report as an opportunity to achieve political capital over Labor. We can speculate on their motives for doing so. If successful, it would improve the minister's stocks (and by extension those of his staff) with the prime minister and his office. Perhaps reflecting a lack of experience and expertise, or merely judgement on the run, there does not seem to have been a contingency in the event the strategy backfired. Partisan zealots focusing on the here and now were perhaps unable to look past the opportunity of political gain to assess properly the potential risks for their minister.

The Travel Rorts case confirms that there have been important changes in the system of advice and support to ministers. In this case, a minister relied upon his personal staff to provide administrative as well as political advice, blurring the conventional demarcation of roles between advisers and bureaucrats. Clearly this practice is fraught with dangers. In disregarding the cautions of the public service about the potential risks of the approach to travel allowance reporting, and relying on advisers whose primary concern was political, the minister was exposed to risks which cost him his portfolio. An important conclusion from the case is that problems arise when the proper demarcation of roles based on experience and expertise is not respected.

Working with competing demands and under time pressures, ministers may be tempted to make decisions too quickly. They may, for reasons suggested earlier, find among their advisers sycophants too willing to affirm the minister's views. A minister may be more circumspect about what he/she decides to ask when soliciting a public service view. The time it takes to receive this advice may provide additional opportunity for reflection and a more considered judgement. The bureaucracy is well placed to offer counsel to ministers about how a desired outcome can safely be achieved. Indeed departmental secretaries formerly fulfilled the function of managing highly sensitive issues expertly and confidentially (Weller, 2001). In the Travel Rorts case political operators usurped this role, and the secretary of the DAS was consulted too late. The immediacy and proximity of staffers, often cited as a key benefit of the personal staffing system, is a potential risk when ministers are required to make ethical judgements.

Other interesting observations can be drawn from the Travel Rorts case. The logic of a political insider was clearly at work when a distinction was drawn between the actions of Coalition minister John Sharp and those of former Labor ministers. From an insider's perspective, there was nothing problematic about the selective annotation of travel allowance records. Similarly from the insider's perspective, former minister David Jull consistently maintained he had done nothing wrong; he simply followed the advice he was given (Australia, House of Representatives, 24 September 1997, p. 8321).

Perversely, although the Travel Rorts case exposes the inherent dangers of the new advisory system for ministers, it has probably intensified the commitment of both major political parties to even greater reliance on personal advisers. Although the clear lesson of this case is that it is safer to rely on the public service for advice on issues of administration, the leaks that sparked the affair have further reinforced the suspicion and distrust of the bureaucracy that has fuelled the growth of personalized staff internationally. Loyalty and trust are of paramount importance to ministers. In Australia at least, the Travel Rorts affair is likely to have confirmed that this is attainable only through the engagement of personal advisers — regardless of the risks.

Conclusion

Since the 1970s, in both Australia and Britain, personal advisers have emerged as influential actors at the summit of the core executive. While the drivers of the search by ministers for advisers from outside the bureaucracy are increasingly well documented, the significance and impact of changes in the structure of advice and support to ministers remain largely unexplored. Recent controversies about special advisers in the UK and ongoing debates about politicization of the public service in Australia suggest there is some unease about the new arrangements. There is concern that the growth in numbers and influence of advisers may have supplanted the permanent bureaucracy as the primary providers of advice and support to ministers. In addition to the concerns inherent in the close and interdependent relationship between ministers and advisers, problems include the lack of accountability of advisers and fears that they might exercise 'undue influence' and/or act beyond the scope of their delegated authority. In Britain debate has focused on the role and influence of advisers; their conduct and accountability; the quality of their advice; and whether they are engaged in overtly partisan activity at public expense.

Advisers are an important source of advice to ministers. In some cases that advice might entail an ethical judgement. The Travel Rorts case demonstrates that their ability and willingness to encourage ministers to behave ethically is questionable. Without institutional arrangements to regulate their conduct, and in an operating environment which encourages and rewards partisan zealotry, advisers may be more problem than solution in motivating ministers to ethical conduct. These are tentative conclusions based on a currently limited body of empirical material; however, the issues raised by the Travel Rorts case clearly warrant further investigation and analysis. There is a need to examine the nature of the advisory arrangements that are now supporting ministers, and to assess their implications for key aspects of Westminster governance.

Notes

1. For the duration of their employment, special advisers work as temporary civil servants. To account for the explicitly political dimensions of their work, special advisers are exempted from certain provisions of the Civil Service Code. These are outlined in the Model Contract for Special Advisers issued by the Cabinet Office in May 1997. The Model Contract contains provisions which limit the tenure of special advisers to the life of the government. It also exempts them from the civil service obligation to provide impartial and objective advice. A copy of the Model Contract is reproduced in Neill (2000, pp. 155–6). The Model Contract is discussed in detail in Chapter 6 of the Neill Committee Report, and also in Gay (2000).
2. The division of responsibilities for ministerial services and facilities between MAPS, the minister's home department and the parliamentary departments is detailed in Appendix 1 of ANAO (1997). In the wake of the Travel Rorts affair, responsibility for entitlement

processing and reporting for all parliamentarians and their staff was shifted to the Department of Finance and Administration.

3   Support for this assertion would seem to be provided by newspaper headlines that appeared the following day. For example, on 30 May 1997 *The Australian* newspaper carried a story with the headline 'Keating Cabinet Members Forced to Repay Expenses'.

4   The letter was given to Howard five minutes before Question Time. According to the *Canberra Times* (27 September 1997) 'Jull might as well have delivered a hand grenade with the pin removed'. The same article reported comments by Workplace Relations Minister Peter Reith rejecting Jull and Sutherland's version of events: 'I think it's bizarre ... The minister could have walked down the corridor to the Prime Minister and said, "We have got a hell of a problem here. $9 000 or thereabouts having been repaid and needing to be explained". Now that did not happen. Let's not mince words about this. Grahame Morris has no memory whatsoever of being told ... I have no doubt he was not told.'

PART IV:
ETHICAL VIGILANCE:
WATCHDOGS AND GUARD DOGS

Chapter 9

Honesty and Corruption in the Canadian Federal Government: Regulating Ethics

Robert J. Jackson[1]

Canada has had some difficulties motivating ministers, members of the high executive and politicians generally to adhere to standards of honesty and ethical behaviour. If the essence of integrity for those in public office is to place public responsibilities ahead of their personal interests, then Canadian politicians have often proved woefully inadequate. In view of this, governments have commissioned research by scholars, judges and even a special Commission (Canada, 1987) in attempts to reform both attitudes and political institutions.

This chapter examines the range of federal governmental misconduct and efforts that have been taken to curtail such behaviour through legal and institutional means. It surveys the legal requirements (Criminal Code, Parliament Act, Canadian Elections Act, Lobbyist Registration Act), judicial hearings, conflict of interest rules, codes of conduct and institutions set up to monitor and control ministerial actions. In particular, it analyses the role and effectiveness of the office of the Ethics Counsellor (EC) and the prime minister's Ethics Advisor (EA) in this respect.

Canada, like all democracies, requires a high degree of integrity from its public leaders. Conflicts of interest, patronage, acceptance of inappropriate gifts and other forms of unethical conduct all create situations in which officials may be beholden to private interests and not adhere to the basic principle of the rule of law which states that all citizens are equal and deserve unbiased treatment. The relationship between ministers, members of parliament (MPs), senators and the public is fiduciary, that is, one in which the politicians are trustees of public confidence.

In Canada a plethora of laws, rules and regulations have been designed to ensure the ethical conduct of politicians and public servants. On the whole, these regulations are what Isaiah Berlin might have termed 'messy compromises' because they have emerged haphazardly and, with few exceptions, as a direct result of particular scandals and crises. Even today there is very little desire on the part of either cabinet or parliament to draw up a new, more coherent set of guidelines or ethical principles, and none at all for writing the various rules into legislation.

Over time, rules, codes, laws and even administrative norms were created to enforce what was considered appropriate. The result is that the configuration of

Canadian regulations is incoherent and sometimes even unworkable. But as we shall see, public expectations and opinions concerning what is ethical or unethical behaviour also vary. This indicates that one should be cautious about moralizing about political ethics and moral behaviour because the commentator, too, is trapped in the cultural mores and attitudinal beliefs of his/her historical period (Mancuso *et al.*, 1998). The simple fact is that the ethical landscape is fluid and changes over time.

Politicians in democratic societies share a unique circumstance. They have no security of employment, no tenure and often no specialized skills to ensure themselves a lifetime of continuous work and income. If politicians must be mindful of their special role in guarding 'the public interest', the public, in turn, must be sensitive to any quest to set up rules and norms to restrict these government officials. Efforts to make politicians' activities transparent and adhere to public standards and to ensure that they act within the rule of law should not disrupt the democratic process itself (a process which demands a significant relationship between electors and their representatives). After all, the final and most important test in a democracy is not the rules governing politicians but the electoral process itself. Politicians must be allowed to plead a case before their constituents and electors.

Scandals and Crises as Catalysts

Public attitudes about situations that constitute unethical behaviour have changed considerably over the years. Behaviour that was considered normal a few decades ago now engenders cynicism, suspicion and moral condemnation. Until the 1960s, MPs routinely carried on with their private businesses after they became ministers, and conflict of interest queries were raised only when ministerial decisions clearly and publicly produced private advantage. In those years, politics was still a part-time, rather poorly paid occupation, and ministers and prime ministers openly and frequently engaged in potentially conflicting activities. They sat on boards of directors, carried on legal practices and accepted private trust funds. It is alleged that C.D. Howe, a minister of highest repute, would routinely check his stock listings before going to cabinet to make an important economic decision for the country.

After several mini-scandals in the Lester Pearson government, public tolerance of such practices began to wane. The first tentative ministerial guidelines emerged in 1964 when Pearson wrote to his ministers about the need to be ethical. In 1972, Prime Minister Trudeau continued the process further by issuing formal guidelines for cabinet ministers. Like Pearson, he chose to rely on guidelines rather than legislation to handle the problem. These guidelines provided somewhat undefined and ambiguous instructions for ministers about how to arrange their personal affairs to avoid the possibility of conflict of interest.

Yet the possible disclosure of conflict situations was considered to be a sufficient deterrent to misconduct. The resulting political embarrassment and negative publicity was considered sufficient to make a cabinet minister feel it necessary to resign in order to protect the government's integrity. However, the lack of sanctions did not deter potential conflicts, and there were no appropriate mechanisms to determine whether such violations were taking place.

Prime Minister Mulroney introduced new conflict of interest guidelines for cabinet ministers (also guidelines for civil servants) in 1985. Like the earlier version, it stopped short of full, mandatory disclosure of private interests in order to strike a balance between protecting the public interest and protecting the private affairs of ministers. The restrictions on business dealings of immediate family members were dropped. It did, however, specify that ministers must not hire their own immediate relatives (or other ministers' relatives) for government jobs.

During this period the government set up the 1984 Task Force on Conflict of Interest (Starr–Sharp Report) which reported on the need to tighten the rules. The report proposed the creation of two ethics officers — a counsellor and a commissioner. A *commissioner* would function as a police officer, responsible for seeking out and investigating potential conflicts of interest, whereas an *ethics counsellor* would inform ministers what the law and ethical code demanded of them so that they could obey it (Canada, 1984a). No immediate action was taken on this report but it was to have considerable significance later.

Ambiguity and lack of enforcement provisions in the new guidelines led to a major conflict of interest case when a cabinet minister, Sinclair Stevens, was faced with a series of allegations in 1986–87. Stevens had placed his assets in a blind trust — that is, he did not sell his assets but put them in the hands of someone else so that he would not be involved in the buying and selling process which might be influenced by his knowledge or actions as a minister. However, the trust was considerably less than 'blind' because of Stevens' connections with several involved individuals, including his wife (who remained an officer of York Centre Companies) and his secretary. It was revealed that Stevens' wife had obtained a $2.6 million loan from a consultant to a company that had received grants from Stevens' government department. Investigating the case, the Parker Commission concluded that Stevens had violated the guidelines 14 times. Further, that he 'knew about and was involved with the York Centre companies and thus with trust assets, because his wife and special assistant told him about the trust assets, and because his wife participated in joint management of the assets with him' (Canada, 1987, p. 329).

Concerned that Canadians were losing confidence in the integrity of politicians and politics in general and also that his government had an extremely poor image in this regard, Mulroney decided that guidelines were no longer sufficient. He introduced conflict of interest legislation in early 1988. Bill C114 attempted to force enough disclosure to keep the government leaders honest, yet not infringe on their private lives so much that highly qualified individuals would be deterred from practising politics. However, this Bill died on the Order Paper when the 1988 general election was called. Further attempts to legislate about conflict of interest also failed. In the last days of the Mulroney government, another, more stringent Bill, Bill C43, was introduced but it too expired when the 34th parliament was dissolved.

Although incidents of conflict of interest, patronage and unethical gains from public office have been fairly frequent in Canada, the laws and rules regulating such behaviour have usually been reactive. In other words, after a scandal erupted, politicians and others typically examined what to do about the behaviour that caused it. Otherwise the issue was ignored. In 1970, for example, on behalf of Allan MacEachen, President of the Privy Council, the author went to see Michael Pitfield, at that time the Clerk of the Privy Council and adviser to Prime Minister Trudeau, with a proposal to introduce comprehensive conflict of interest legislation. Pitfield's response was: 'Do you have any cases? Come back when you do, and we can do something'. The guiding rule was that politicians should be trusted, and only when their actions went badly should there be any action.

Crises and scandals have therefore often been catalysts to reforms in political systems because they have highlighted weaknesses in laws and rules. As a consequence the resultant reforms have been *ad hoc*, piecemeal and not very satisfactory. Simply getting a reform proposal on the agenda does not mean that it will be the one required. Scandals lead the media to a frenzy of recriminations and public criticism of individuals in the search for scapegoats. Vital energy is spent — energy that could be directed to the systemic causes of the problem and to systematic and coherent reforms. Moreover, reacting to crises often means that action is taken too quickly, without the benefit of sober thought or the reflection of experts. Reforms should not just punish the guilty. Guilt finding is not as important as finding ways to limit wrongful behaviour in the first place. The challenge is to reduce the incentives for unethical behaviour.

Contemporary Regime: Laws and Rules and Institutions

Throughout all of the above scandals and efforts to correct them, senior government officials were restricted by various rules about illegal and unethical conduct. Then and today the Criminal Code, the Parliament Act, Standing Orders of the House of Commons and Rules of the Senate continue to apply to any minister or ordinary member or senator involved in fraud, influence peddling or breach of trust. For example, the Criminal Code makes certain practices such as bribery illegal. The Parliament of Canada Act forbids MPs from holding government contracts; and the Standing Orders of the House of Commons and Senate rules prevent certain behaviour and require certain activities — such as the requirement to disclose a financial interest when speaking or voting in parliament. But much of the unethical conduct has not been illegal or even against parliamentary rules. Most of the conflict of interest, patronage and gains have been about broad unethical behaviour in grey or cloudy fields where changing notions of the public interest and ethics have come into play.

The written rules for ministers differ from jurisdiction to jurisdiction, with some of the provinces having more stringent rules than Ottawa. For example, Ontario appointed an Integrity Commissioner in 1988 and has an Integrity Act. British Columbia appointed a Conflict of Interest Commissioner in 1990. The federal government, in contrast, has never accepted the view that rules about ministerial ethics should be legislated or even that codes of conduct should apply to ordinary MPs (Greene and Shugarman, 1997).

When he came to office in 1993, Liberal Prime Minister Jean Chrétien made it clear that he wanted to set up an 'integrity regime' and make himself responsible for his ministers' actions. Arguing that this was what the Constitution required, he opted against passing laws or even regulations concerning ethics in his government. The new prime minister argued that integrity in government was not simply a matter of rules and regulations, it was also a matter of personal standards and conduct (House of Commons Debates, 16 June 1994). He hired former minister Mitchell Sharp as EA for one dollar a year to advise on the integrity of government. In June 1994 the prime minister unveiled a conflict of interest code for senior officials and lobbying rules. The code was a significant improvement on earlier prime ministerial efforts.

The code of conduct (Canada 1994b) states that 'public office holders shall act with honesty and uphold the highest ethical standards so that public confidence and trust in the integrity, objectivity and impartiality of government are conserved and enhanced' (s. 3(1)). It goes on to list the principles and compliance measures to prevent 'real, potential or apparent conflicts of interest' (s. 3(5)). The code covers all members of cabinet, parliamentary secretaries, members of the ministers' staff and over 1200 senior officials in the federal public service. The wives and dependants of ministers are also covered. They too must disclose their activities, but they are not required to follow the rules of the code with regard to disclosure (s. 9(1)). Ministers are prohibited from engaging in a profession, actively managing or operating a business or serving as a corporate director. Moreover, they cannot hold office in a union or professional association or act as a paid consultant.

Appointees' assets are also listed and monitored. Exempt assets such as homes, vacation properties, bank accounts and fixed income investments as well as mutual funds are not further controlled. 'Declarable' assets must be made public, but the office holder may continue to handle them. They include ownership of family or local businesses, farms under commercial operation and rental properties.

'Controllable' assets are those such as publicly traded securities, including shares in a stock market, which could be affected directly or indirectly by government action. Office holders are required to divest themselves of all these types of controlled instruments. (This is in contrast to Australia, for example, where ministers are required to conform to such rules only if the assets are within the minister's responsibility or portfolio.) Office holders may use one of three strategies. They may sell the assets, put them in a 'blind trust' or in certain cases create a 'blind management' agreement where, for example, a minister owns a private company which might do business with the government. In the latter case the office holder is prevented from making any decision on the management of his/her assets.

Although Sharp (who basically wrote the Sharp–Starr Report) was now on the prime minister's staff, only one position was created, not two as earlier envisioned. On 16 June 1994 Howard Wilson was appointed as Prime Minister Chrétien's EC.

Although there is no Ethics Commissioner, Wilson is frequently referred to by this title in the media and his staff believe that he performs the functions of a commissioner. In simple terms, the duty of the EC is to uphold the code of conduct for public office holders. The code also requires those covered to provide a report to the EC tabulating his/her asset, liabilities and outside activities. The EC reviews the list and tells the public official appointees what to do to be in compliance with the code. Wilson also has responsibility for enforcing a law, the Lobbyists Registration Act. However, although it is not legislated for, his most important responsibility is to probe the ethical conduct of cabinet ministers *whenever requested to do so by the prime minister*. His role does not include dealing with suspected breaches of the Criminal Code.

When the Liberals came to power Chrétien asked Sharp to interview prospective cabinet ministers in order to identify anything in their records that might embarrass the new government. Sharp interviewed each prospective cabinet minister in a 45-minute heart-to-heart session, asking them, among other things, whether they and their spouses could live with conflict of interest guidelines, and whether they had skeletons in their closet, tax arrears or personal problems. The survey kept two individuals out of cabinet, and caused a few others to request a change of portfolio in order to avoid potential conflicts.

Although the prime minister's actual letter to ministers[2] has never been disclosed, all it says on this topic is that senior officials are to follow the code and that the EC will be in touch with them about it. Despite the reasonable doubts and accusations of secrecy, there are no hidden rules in the prime minister's letter. In the code, public officials are instructed to disclose their assets and outside activities confidentially to the EC, who is responsible for both conflict of interest and lobbying rules.

Aside from the public code, the prime minister, with the advice of Wilson and Sharp, also declared that ministers may never communicate with government tribunals except under very specific circumstances. As publicly stated by the EC, 'ministers shall not intervene, or appear to intervene, on behalf of any person or entity, with federal quasi-judicial tribunals on any matter before them that requires a decision in their quasi-judicial capacity, unless otherwise authorized by law' (Wilson, 1999a, pp. 8–9). Ordinary MPs are not restricted in their dealings with administrative tribunals, but the guidelines hold ministers to a higher standard of accountability. At issue is finding the right balance between ensuring ministers do not use their clout to influence unduly quasi-judicial tribunals and giving them the appropriate amount of freedom to help their constituents.

Post-employment rules also exist for office holders. For two years ministers are restricted from taking a position or signing a contract with any organization with which they had direct or significant dealings while in government. (The rule is one year for other office holders.) Nor can they lobby their former departments during this 'cooling-off' period.

Significant Ethics Investigations since 1994 by the Ethics Counsellor

There have been quite a number of public allegations against Liberal cabinet ministers that the prime minister asked Wilson to investigate. On almost every occasion Wilson has publicly cleared the government of any wrongdoing. In 1994 Michel Dupuy, Heritage Minister, wrote to the Canadian Radio-Television Corporation (CRTC) and asked them to consider a constituent's application for a radio licence in Montreal. Despite the fact that the rule about ministers contacting quasi-judicial bodies was somewhat vague, Dupuy did break the prime minister's code. The prime minister defended Dupuy, but later dropped him from cabinet. Wilson told the Canadian Broadcasting Company he had never been asked to investigate the circumstances of Dupuy's letter to the CRTC, despite the fact that the agency reported to Dupuy. Wilson confirmed that he knew nothing about the letter until nearly a month after Dupuy had confessed to Chrétien that he had written it, and he was asked by a staffer for the prime minister to give his opinion only after the media got wind of the affair. Wilson said he regarded the failure to consult him earlier as 'water under the bridge', and, like Chrétien, he declined to discuss what his opinion was. 'I did give advice and that's between the two of us' (*Toronto Star*, 3 November 1994). Deputy prime minister Sheila Copps added that she had spoken to Chrétien and he advised her 'that if there are questions about the ethics of the government, the ultimate arbiter of those questions is not a bureaucrat, it is the prime minister' (*Vancouver Sun*, 10 June 1995). The guidelines for a minister writing to tribunals were then tightened.

In 1995 the Opposition urged the government to instruct the EC to examine an alleged improper relationship between Liberal Senator Pierre DeBane and *Canada Post* President George Clermont. The prime minister retorted that it was not up to the government to impose ethical standards on MPs and senators, it was up to parliament. Wilson never investigated and the government took no action (*Vancouver Sun*, 17 March 1995).

In 1996 Defence Minister David Collenette was accused of interfering with a quasi-judicial body after he wrote to the Immigration Board on behalf of a constituent. Collenette clearly had violated the rules and had to leave. 'He should have known what a quasi-judicial office was, as we went over it enough times' an aide told me. Wilson said that Collenette had broken the cabinet rules. The minister resigned but later returned to cabinet in another portfolio. Collenette is one of the prime minister's closest political friends and one of those responsible for bringing down former prime minister John Turner. Also in 1996 former Immigration Minister Sergio Marchi was questioned for writing a letter to the Immigration Board in relation to a board decision concerning a killer who successfully appealed his deportation order. Wilson declared that the letter was not an attempt to intervene and did not violate any cabinet guidelines. In the same year Youth Minister Ethel Blondin-Andrew was found to have used government credit cards to pay for her Hawaii vacation and a fur coat. She claimed that she paid the government back. Wilson concluded that there was no wrongdoing.

There were a number of incidents in 1998. Finance Minister Paul Martin was accused of a conflict of interest over changes to the Income Tax Act that benefited shipping companies. Opposition parties alleged that the changes could benefit Martin's company, Canada Steamship Lines Ltd. The EC concluded that Martin was unaware of the changes since a junior minister had handled the issue, and therefore cleared

Martin of any conflict. Former Transport Minister Doug Young was accused of a conflict when, after being defeated in the last election, he obtained a share in a toll highway company that received federal funding when he was Transport Minister. Again, Wilson found that there was no conflict. Solicitor-General Andy Scott's conversation about the Asian Pacific Economic Conference inquiry was overheard on an airplane and subsequently reported in the media. Sharp admitted in one news article that he discussed the Solicitor-General's conduct with the prime minister, but 'remained out of the loop'. When a journalist asked Wilson whether he expected the prime minster to ask him to investigate Scott, Wilson replied, 'no, I don't' (*Ottawa Citizen*, 17 October 1998).

The latest case concerns Jane Stewart, Minister for Human Resources. Stewart had to take responsibility for the 'job-creation scandal' in which grants and contribution programs such as the Canada Jobs Fund were shown to have been mismanaged in excess of $1 billion in annual spending. The department approved the majority of applications even though crucial information was missing, and then failed to follow up most of them. This launched a series of allegations about political interference and the department requested an audit. Stewart has not been accused of benefiting personally by anyone other than Deborah Grey (Deputy Leader of the former Reform Party). But if a minister provides benefits to his/her constituents is that ethical misconduct or simply an outcome of democratic practices? Just what is ethical misconduct in such a case? Wilson maintains that this does not come under the guidelines.

The above, of course, are only the ministerial cases on public record. Part of Wilson's mandate is to provide advice to the prime minister on the ethical conduct of his ministers when asked. There is no formal report, and because his findings qualify as advice to a minister they remain hidden from public scrutiny. Wilson will not say how many other times he has been asked to investigate a cabinet minister.

Criticisms of the Ethics Regime and Position of Counsellor

Four main criticisms of the current system emerge from the judgements in the above cases.

1. *The* ad hoc *nature of the rules* The rules are unique to each prime minister so that the next prime minister can change them at will. The rules are not regularized in the form of regulations or laws approved by parliament.
2. *Minimal consultation with Opposition leaders* The Liberal campaign platform (known as the Red Book) stated that Opposition leaders would participate in developing the ethical guidelines governing cabinet ministers. This was reaffirmed during the preliminary stages of creating this position; deputy prime minister Copps was quoted as saying that 'the government wants to consult *Bloc Quebecois* leader Lucien Bouchard and Reform Leader Preston Manning

before appointing a federal ethics counsellor' (*Ottawa Citizen*, 9 March 1994). However, the prime minister never consulted Opposition leaders on the office, only on the appointment itself. Furthermore, Prime Minister Chrétien stated that there would be a House of Commons debate before new guidelines were finalized, but this never occurred.

3. *No independent investigative powers* Wilson is responsible for investigating conflict-of-interest allegations against anyone the prime minister asks him to investigate in the prime minister's own government. The EC then reports his findings directly to the prime minister. There is nothing to compel the EC to investigate conflict of interest allegations raised in the media or by the Commons. Wilson is not an ethics commissioner as that position was described in the Sharp–Starr Task Force report: he does not actively seek out and investigate possible conflicts of interest, but merely advises those who ask him what the law is. There is no opportunity to investigate the prime minister. Or, put another way, there is no institution he can report to if the prime minister is in violation of the law or the guidelines.

4. *Lack of accountability and openness* The Liberals promised that the '... ethics counsellor would report directly to parliament' (Liberal Party of Canada, 1993). However, Wilson is not accountable to parliament. He reports, personally and privately, to the prime minister. Wilson sees nothing wrong with making private reports to the prime minister rather than to parliament and he attributes the criticism over whom he reports to as a misunderstanding of Canada's constitutional system. He says that he functions most effectively if he reports to the prime minister. 'The question of accountability resides ultimately with [him] ... anything that cuts away from accountability of the prime minister to parliament is, in my view, something that has to be very carefully examined' (*Ottawa Citizen*, 17 October 1998).

Sharp is nervous with the idea that an unelected official would have the authority to decide what is right and wrong in areas where issues often are not so black and white. He thinks an official operating as a free agent could lead to the kind of overzealous investigation seen in the USA with independent counsel Starr. This argument is refuted by the fact that the Auditor-General reports directly to parliament, as do the respective commissioners of privacy, information, official languages, and the watchdog of the Canadian Security Intelligence Service. These officials are the public's independent guardians against government waste and abuse of power. As such, they must be free, and be seen to be free of manipulation by the ruling party, which is precisely why they report directly to parliament.

The question raised by critics of the EC is why shouldn't the EC report to parliament as well? If the office reports to parliament, it is argued, it will gain a degree of independence that traditional cabinet appointees lack. In the present arrangement, if Wilson finds a corrupt cabinet minister, for example, it seems unlikely that he would take any action that would embarrass the government. What happens if the prime minister himself is in conflict of interest? It is left up to the prime minister to decide if there is anything improper going on in the government and whether or not any indiscretions that have occurred are made public.

Evaluations and Consequences

The effectiveness of the two new institutions (the EC and EA) on honesty in public life is difficult to assess as the officials carry out their activities in secret. Sharp's interviews with potential ministers produced notable successes when two potential ministers (Gagliano and Dhaliwal) withdrew their names for a cabinet appointment in 1994 after they were apprised of the conditions in the prime minister's guidelines. Both MPs were, however, able to put their private affairs in order so that they could join the cabinet at a later date. No potential ministers were prevented from joining the cabinet in the second Chrétien administration.

As EC, Wilson has proven to be an effective and wise administrator of the code as it is written. Wilson regards the fact that not a single government minister has had to resign over a conflict involving his/her personal interests with satisfaction, not as possible evidence that his office might be ineffective. Wilson has not publicly provided any names of ministers over potential or actual conflicts, and the EA, Sharp, says categorically, 'there have been no public accusations of misconduct in the seven years I have been in office'.[3] However, after agreeing with the prime minister's public statements to the effect that he is responsible for his ministers' conduct and that parliament is responsible for MPs' behaviour, Sharp seemed to change his position on the need for a code if another party were in government. 'We don't need a code. Why do people want one? It is only for curiosity. You wouldn't find anything with us. Mulroney's group was in violation of the law, but we don't do that sort of thing'.

Do these new offices and guidelines mean that the government and their ministers are now really acting more ethically? If you ask the government and EC's office, they would definitely say yes; however, the Opposition parties would undoubtedly say no. The Liberal government and the EC put more stress on what has been called 'integrity' while the Opposition and some reformers emphasize compliance and enforcement. Even this distinction indicates how evaluation in this field of ethics is tenuous and conclusions are often vacuous. We can attempt to study best practices but, alas, we have no measurement convention about ethics.

Intellectuals will always try to determine some external measure of success in this regard, and yet we may be measuring the unmeasurable. When we don't know the total amount of unethical conduct how can we measure the effectiveness of rules? Once we change the rules we soon find a need to change them again as more unethical behaviour is uncovered. For this reason the question arises as to whether rules or character training are better approaches to such issues. Recently, both the British Medical Association (BMA) and the British airline industry have been groping with this problem. The airline industry has already begun a system for reporting 'near misses' and the BMA is considering essentially the same thing.

The assumption of such efforts at organizational change is that risk can never be eliminated, but institutions can seek ways to assess patterns of poor practice and find ways to avoid common faults. In other words, lessons about errors can be learned. A no-fault acknowledgement of error might move some institutions from a secret, blame-centred culture to a more open, learning culture. But in politics is it possible to have no-fault acknowledgement of errors? If the facts about unethical behaviour are not reported to the public or other MPs does this not represent a wasted opportunity — like not knowing about near misses between aeroplanes or in hospitals? Or is it the essence of the democratic process that all error is attributable?

Sustaining Reform

In attempting to come up with proper morality and ethics for ministers, MPs and other public office holders, commentators tend to accept the idea that the subject of ethics can be handled by experts or professors. However, ethics is really about negotiated compromises that result from a dialogue between politicians, experts and the public — that is, stakeholders in the democratic process. In other words, the final rules and their institutional arrangements result from negotiations rather than from deductions from a set of high principles. The roles that the various stakeholders play affect their notions of what the proper rules should be. Rules are not so much the product of ethical genius but rather emerge from a context of relationships at any particular historical moment. They do not emerge from some objective, neutral form of academic inquiry as in 'it is evident that MPs should not lie' or ministers 'should never be in a conflict of interest'.

A self-critical spirit should infuse reformers — do they never get into conflicts of interest themselves, do they never fudge the truth when dealing with administrators, clients, students or parents? Do they never compromise with principles? Of course they do, and so do individuals in all private and public sector employment.

However, it is still reasonable to assume that the image of the individual minister and member would be enhanced if parliament were to adopt a strict code in the area of conflict of interest. Any private financial interests a minister or member can retain should be carefully supervised by a parliamentary committee and by the courts. We need reforms that are sustainable and that means institutionalized. It is necessary to make them difficult to reverse. In order to obtain such reforms there will be a need for proponents inside and outside the system to help augment support for new institutions among politicians, public servants, journalists and the public.

There is a significant need for balance between reform and democratic responsiveness. Arguments about scandals, prurient voyeurism and political opportunism should not be used to negate reasonable arguments for practical reforms. There is an increasing recognition of the need for written rules — but also for ethics education and practical management of the rules. Rules cannot be expected to solve all problems. While regulations make management more efficient, voluntary compliance will still be at the heart of the issue.

Notes

1. The author gratefully acknowledges the financial assistance of the Fletcher Jones Foundation on this and other projects. Professor Maureen Mancuso's research and advice on this topic were particularly helpful.
2. When a minister is appointed, the prime minister sends him/her a letter which includes a statement of the guidelines and often a list of things the prime minister wants accomplished in the portfolio.
3. Personal interview with author.

Chapter 10

Integrity and Ministerial Office: The Queensland Integrity Commissioner

Noel Preston

In contrast to Canada's federal and provincial legislatures, Australian federal and state governments have been reluctant to embrace, or even to discuss, the idea of a specialized, independent ethics adviser within executive government responsible for providing counsel to ministers on conflict of interest matters and other ethical concerns. Across the years and across Australian jurisdictions various practices, such as consulting senior political colleagues, have been adopted to resolve dilemmas troubling ethically conscientious ministers. More recently, and with debatable results, Prime Minister Howard has delegated to the head of the Department of Prime Minister and Cabinet the supervision of cabinet rules on ministerial conduct.

Those opposed to enhancing further the ethics infrastructure in government sometimes argue that the number of integrity measures instituted in the past decade or so, such as anti-corruption bodies and public registers of pecuniary interests, is already prolific enough (Hayden, 1998), and that, after all, the ultimate accountability of governments is to the ballot box. Moreover, some assert that the over-regulation of political life ignores the morally ambiguous nature of political practice and sets unrealistic standards (see Uhr, Chapter 15). Maintaining the irrelevance or futility of locating an official ethics adviser in government, opponents might cynically quote Machiavelli: 'For a man who wants to make a profession of good in all regards must come to ruin among so many who are not so good' (Machiavelli, 1985, Chapter xv, p. 61). Alternatively, they might put the plausible view that people who need the services of an ethics adviser to define the difference between right and wrong should not be in charge of government anyway.

Arguably, these objections mask the more fundamental reasons for the reluctance of governments to adopt proposals for an official ethics adviser within government. Those reasons are located in politicians' instincts that ministers should be accountable to the fewest possible number of officials and regulations. By and large, the reality is that governments are more inclined to use their numbers to tough out ethical crises than to facilitate ethics reforms. I maintain that the arguments for resisting such ethics measures are dubious inasmuch as they misrepresent the capacity of an ethics infrastructure in government, centred on an ethics adviser, to support cabinet ministers and motivate ethical behaviour while enhancing better public administration (Burgmann, 1998; Kernot, 1998; Preston, 1998; Thompson, 1995; Wilson, 1998, 1999b; Uhr, 1998c).

Providing evidence to support the case for institutionalized ethics advice within Australian governments, unlike in Canada, is virtually non-existent.[1] However, one Australian jurisdiction has recently taken steps that may eventually provide data for testing the view that ethics advice should be institutionalized within government. This chapter describes and analyses this particular, first Australian example: the establishment of an ethics adviser (entitled Integrity Commissioner) within the government of Queensland led by Premier Peter Beattie. This move is an exception to the Australian trend of reluctance to go down such a road, though, not surprisingly, there are indicators in its development of the resistance, delay and doubt typical of moves to establish public sector ethics regimes.

Legislating for an Integrity Commissioner

In June 1998 the Australian Labor Party in Queensland led by Peter Beattie included a section in its election policy platform entitled 'Good Government'. This was intended to differentiate it in terms of ethics and accountability from the incumbent conservative administration under Premier Rob Borbidge, which was perceived as still vulnerable to the tags of cronyism and unethical practice left over from the government of Joh Bjelke-Petersen, premier of Queensland from 1969 to 1988. Bjelke-Petersen had left office under the pressure of a Commission of Inquiry into Possible Illegal Activities and Associated Police Misconduct (Fitzgerald Inquiry) chaired by Tony Fitzgerald QC, (Fitzgerald, 1989). Among other things the inquiry revealed significant corruption in the state's political institutions. Among the several 'Good Government' initiatives promised by Beattie was a policy proposal, without detail, for a Queensland Integrity Commissioner. This was, in part, a response to research conducted by several academics into the implementation of Queensland's Public Sector Ethics Act 1994. This research was presented to both sides of Queensland politics. It argued for a range of initiatives to give more substance to the ethics regime under the legislation.

Following the Fitzgerald Inquiry report (1989), the Queensland public sector was transformed by a number of administrative and ethical reforms. These included the adoption of the Public Sector Ethics Act. This Act contains a set of five fundamental ethical obligations for the public sector and requires the development of codes of conduct consistent with these obligations by all Queensland public sector agencies. Members of parliament (including members of cabinet) were not covered by these codes. The National Party government led by Premier Mike Ahern had earlier introduced a Ministerial Code of Ethics. The Register of Members' Interests, first established by resolution of the House on 19 April 1989, also covers ministers. A subsequent proposal from the Members' Ethics and Privileges Parliamentary Committee that there be a more detailed register for ministers kept with the premier was rejected by both sides of Queensland politics — a demonstration that reluctance to institutionalizing ethics measures in government is often bipartisan.

A couple of months after taking office in 1998, Premier Beattie sought advice in relation to whether his pecuniary arrangements indicated any potential conflicts of interest. Later, Peter Beattie publicly announced he had taken this action and, as a result, had sold a certain parcel of shares. In May 1999 the premier introduced the detailed proposal for the Integrity Commissioner in a Bill to amend the Public Sector Ethics Act 1994. Parliament resumed debate on the matter in November of that year, passing the legislation the same day. Two months later, the Department of Premier and Cabinet invited applications for the part-time position. On 21 August 2000, more than two years after the Beattie government assumed office, the appointment of the Integrity Commissioner was announced. This followed a second year in office when the government had found itself embroiled in a number of dubious ethical situations. This included the so-called Net Bet Affair which resulted in the treasurer, David Hamill, standing aside while his action in approving an Internet Gaming Licence to a company involving certain Labor Party identities was examined by the Auditor-General and the Queensland Criminal Justice Commission (Queensland Audit Office, 1999). The delay in implementation of the Integrity Commissioner proposal was partly due to the determination of some in the cabinet to carefully proscribe the bounds of the role.

The purpose behind the creation of the Queensland Integrity Commissioner as stated in the legislation is to help ministers and others to avoid conflicts of interest and in so doing to encourage confidence in public institutions (Div. 1, s. 25). The functions of the office described in the Public Sector Ethics Amendment Act 1999 are threefold:

1. To give advice to designated persons about conflict of interest issues;
2. To give advice to the premier, when the premier asks, on issues concerning ethics and integrity, including standard setting for issues concerning ethics and integrity;
3. To contribute to public understanding on these matters by contributing to public discussion of policy and practice relevant to the Integrity Commissioner's functions (Div. 4, s. 28).

This range of functions clearly moves the purpose of the office beyond mere advice giving on particular cases of conflicts of interest, although the extent to which the commissioner can act proactively is dependent on the relationship with, and attitude of, the premier of the day. The commissioner's capacity to take initiatives to promote an ethics and integrity agenda within government will also be constrained by the resources provided. The appointment is under the Public Sector Ethics Amendment Act, not the Public Service Act 1996, and is part-time (40 per cent) for up to five years, though initially only for three years. A staff of two persons is proposed, though a revamped Ethics and Integrity branch in the Department of Premier and Cabinet also supports the commissioner. The qualities required by the Act for appointment as commissioner are 'knowledge, experience, personal qualities and standing within the community suitable to the office' (Div. 7, s. 37.2). The person currently appointed is a recently retired state Supreme Court judge.

In his second reading speech of the Bill, the premier linked this initiative to the range of 'pioneering reforms' established by Queensland Labor governments since the Fitzgerald Inquiry. He emphasized that this was the first such appointment in Australia. His justification for a specialized ethics adviser focusing on conflicts of interest was made in the following terms:

> It can be overwhelming to work through these situations alone. My government believes that a source of voluntary, confidential and expert advice on ethical dilemmas can be a real benefit in resolving potential conflicts before they happen (Queensland, Parliamentary Debates, 26 May 1999, p. 1941).

In concluding his speech the premier said he expected the commissioner would provide 'independent and tough-minded advice'. The advertisement for the position claimed that the Integrity Commissioner 'will assist in improving standards of integrity and probity in Government and public administration, and thereby make an important contribution to raising community confidence in public institutions' (*Courier-Mail*, 22 January 2000).

As a functionary within, rather than alongside, government and directly responsible to the premier, the Queensland position is undoubtedly influenced by, rather than modelled on, the Canadian federal government's Ethics Counsellor (see Jackson, Chapter 9). Its powers are much more restricted than the Canadian model. Indeed the premier did not make an explicit reference to the Canadian institution in his second reading parliamentary speech, though Opposition Leader Rob Borbidge did. The Opposition, while acknowledging the Integrity Commissioner initiative was a 'positive one', did not support the Bill when the premier rejected most of its own amendments.

The range of officials, or 'designated persons', able to seek advice from the commissioner on conflicts of interest is considerable (Div. 3, s. 27.1). Effectively, they fall into four groupings: first, the premier, all ministers, parliamentary secretaries and those employed in their offices; second, all government members (as well as any independents appointed by the government to parliamentary committees); third, public sector chief executive officers and certain senior executive officers or equivalents; and fourth, statutory office holders. The constituency potentially covers about 5 000 persons. It is not simply the ministry but also those most politically significant in the ranks of executive government. The ethical conduct of others in the bureaucracy is subject to the administration of the Public Sector Ethics Act 1994.

Designated persons are not compelled to seek advice on possible conflicts of interest. The advice is confidential (rather like that of a lawyer's to a client). Neither are they compelled to follow the advice that must be sought in writing. An inducement to those wondering whether or not to seek advice is the immunity and protection provided

(Div. 6, s. 35.1). Any person taking action in compliance with the commissioner's advice is not liable in a civil action or an administrative procedure for that action, just as the commissioner himself is protected (Div. 6, s. 36). In apparent violation of the principle of transparency, the conflict of interest advice is exempt from freedom of information provisions.[2]

The secrecy provisions extend further. They prevent the commissioner from disclosing the request for advice as well as the advice itself. Only the person in receipt of the advice can disclose it. However, under certain circumstances the premier may be given a copy of the advice, as too may ministers and chief executives in the case of officials under their authority. The legislation stipulates that other senior officers may only seek advice with the permission of their chief executives. For instance, if the Integrity Commissioner believes an 'actual and significant' conflict of interest exists for a designated person and they have failed to resolve the conflict within seven days of receiving the advice, the commissioner must advise the premier, providing 'natural justice' is observed. That is, the person must be told of the commissioner's view and that this is a matter to put before the premier if the conflict is not resolved in seven days.

The Nature of the Initiative: Problems and Prospects

Though it has not been explicitly explained by the government, the use of the title 'Integrity Commissioner', rather than, say, 'Conflict of Interest Commissioner' or 'Ethics Counsellor' (both terms are used in North America), is worthy of note. Arguably, it implies a role wider than the advisory role on conflicts of interest that dominates the legislation setting up the office. The other functions provided for in the legislation, for example advice to the premier and the promotion of public understanding on ethics in government matters, are clearly important components of an integrity agenda.

Another way of understanding this choice of term is by distinguishing between, on the one hand, a negative, legalistic, 'compliance'- oriented public sector ethics system, and, on the other hand, a positive, 'integrity' system which is supportive, educative, preventive and promotes the ethical. Obviously the Integrity Commissioner is interested in compliance, but primarily the role emphasizes the positive integrity approach. As the premier reminded the parliament when introducing the legislation:

> The Integrity Commissioner will not, in general, be a watchdog for conflicts of interests. The functions of the Integrity Commissioner do not empower the Commissioner to conduct any independent investigation, decision making or enforcement, as this is currently the role of the Criminal Justice Commission and will remain so (Queensland, Parliamentary Debates, 26 May 1999, p. 1942).

It is in its 'integrity' orientation that the Queensland office is similar to the Canadian federal government's model. Commenting on the relationship between compliance and integrity in government ethics measures, Mr Howie Wilson, the Canadian Ethics

Counsellor, has observed:

> Our goal is to promote an attitude of integrity *and* compliance, not beat that cooperation out of people ... Over the past five years, we have seen that if you set a high, principled standard that seeks to prevent even the possibility for conflict, office holders do rise to it. People come forward with questions because they know they will get advice that should keep them out of trouble ... We have avoided the negative fallout of systems that obsess on compliance with rigid rules that never seem to encompass all possible problems. [These are] systems that assume that all public office holders are either crooks or are too dumb to know what is proper, no matter how senior they are, or how much money they make ... We have created a system that enables us to address the appearance as well as the reality of a conflict (Wilson, 1999b).

Yet, unlike its Queensland cousin, the Canadian process compels ministers to seek advice regarding their pecuniary interests and potential conflicts of interest. As well, it requires compliance with clear regulations about post-ministerial employment. The additional functions in the Queensland role, of general advice to the premier and the promotion of public understanding of ethics in government, potentially strengthen the Queensland model, but in terms of its capacity to encourage ethical compliance it is more like a basic sedan than a Rolls Royce.

A key element common to both the Canadian and Queensland positions is that neither report to parliament but rather to the prime minister or premier. It is argued that this is appropriate, for the functions differ in significant ways from other offices within their respective government integrity systems such as the Ombudsman, anti-corruption commissioners or the Auditor-General, each of which report directly to parliament. Their functions are different: an Auditor-General is entrusted to audit accounts to ensure that government is using its resources effectively and within the law, likewise the Queensland Criminal Justice Commission is concerned with official misconduct or actions which are allegedly illegal.

As an ethics adviser *within* government, the Integrity Commissioner is dealing with less precise matters, such as the appearance of conflict and matters that go beyond what the law requires. Were the Integrity Commissioner to become too public a player in the political process, he/she would be seen as an 'ethics police officer'. This perception would undermine the confidence of the designated persons in the office. For these reasons it is contended that a reporting obligation to the premier alone is appropriate. The annual report to the premier provided for in the legislation must not refer to particular cases but to how the integrity and advice-giving system is working overall (Div. 7 s. 43.2). There is, of course, no reason why this annual report should not be tabled in parliament or be publicly accessible — unless it is based on a government's self-interested need to prevent the Integrity Commissioner from being able to appeal to forums outside government.

Viewed optimistically, the office of the Integrity Commissioner provides an enhanced opportunity for the integration and monitoring of how various ethics measures across the Queensland government are working, especially with respect to ministers. Furthermore, it provides the opportunity to place these matters on the premier's desk. Currently, ministerial conduct is guided by a *Ministerial Handbook* which covers matters such as entitlements and gifts administered through the Ministerial Services Branch, a body which is neither equipped nor mandated to give authoritative advice on the most difficult of ethical issues. As previously mentioned, as members of parliament ministers are subject to requirements that they lodge their pecuniary interests in the Members' Register. Like all parliamentarians, ministers have access to advice on ethics and privilege matters from the parliamentary committee. Ministers will also be subject to a code of ethical standards, currently under review in the Queensland parliament. That parliamentary code is potentially an important tool for the Integrity Commissioner with respect to ministers and government backbenchers, though the Members' Ethics and Parliamentary Privileges Committee (MEPPC) is likely to be jealous of its jurisdiction in relation to the Integrity Commissioner (MEPPC, 2000).

Some problems with the proposal will only emerge over time. One that can be anticipated is the issue of 'conflicting advice'. For instance, in the case of ministers and other members of parliament, the MEPPC is empowered to give advice on ethical matters. What happens then if the Integrity Commissioner gives different advice on a matter? Of course, no one is compelled to take the Commissioner's advice, though if they do not they may forfeit the statutory protections.

The Queensland Minister's Code of Ethics (published in the *Ministerial Handbook* and a completely different document from the proposed parliamentary code) has received little attention in public disputes over ministerial conduct. Its exhortation to ministers to observe 'high standards in the execution of their public duties' is followed by 10 more specific injunctions, which range from a restatement of cabinet conventions to pecuniary interest responsibilities of disclosure and divestment where appropriate. It also cautions ministers to 'avoid falling under an obligation to those in the hospitality or travel industry'. Arguably the ministerial code is deficient in several respects; for instance, it is silent about post-employment obligations or potential conflicts with party-political roles facing ministers. The ministerial code is clearly fundamental to the Integrity commissioner's role, and its deficiencies are arguably important matters for the commissioner to address. It remains to be seen whether a review of the code is one of the tasks of the commissioner's first year in office.

In terms of its capacity to motivate ministerial ethics there are significant problems with the Integrity Commissioner proposal. One problem is that a literal interpretation of the legislation leaves the commissioner with a merely reactive role, potentially waiting in the office for the phone to ring. The voluntary nature of the relationship between the commissioner and ministers (as well as other 'designated persons') means that particular ministers and their colleagues may avoid any engagement with the commissioner. Obviously the urges of the premier and strategies adopted by the Integrity Commissioner to win the confidence of designated persons will become important in fostering motivation to seek assistance. Much will depend then on the individual in the office as to whether, in a part-time capacity, time and energy will be found to promote the agenda potentially associated with the role. At the end of the day, though, the Integrity Commissioner will always be constrained by the fact that, although the office is designed to enhance accountability, it is gravely limited in its capacity to demonstrate publicly its record in achieving that good.

The secrecy and protection provisions surrounding the advice are presented as a means to encourage people to make use of the commissioner. The downside of those provisions (as is also the case in Canada) is that they may undermine public confidence in the role because the Integrity Commissioner will have no capacity to comment on any particular case or to assure the public that he/she is intervening in a particular case. These provisions make the following scenario perfectly feasible: under the privilege of parliament a minister may untruthfully announce that he/she has received certain advice from the commissioner when he/she has not even approached the commissioner, yet the commissioner is unable to contradict publicly the minister's claim. What is more, the premier may refuse to act on a particular matter under the terms of the Act, and the commissioner again has no capacity to raise this directly in the public domain. Unlikely as each of these scenarios may be, the possibility of them occurring (and some other chapters in this book testify to that possibility becoming a reality), when combined with the voluntary and reactive nature of the commissioner's position, might undermine public confidence in this office.

Further, the commissioner's advice itself, if disclosed by the recipient, is likely to be controversial and embroil the commissioner in a political brawl. The antidote to this problematic situation can only be public belief that the holder of the office is of such integrity that he/she would resign in such circumstances. But is this so weak a position as to be implausible? Given such worst-case scenarios, is this office a prisoner of government?

Already the Opposition has predictably decried the Integrity Commissioner proposal as mere window-dressing. Yet a danger for government is that it will raise public expectations regarding solving ethical problems in government which cannot be met. A problem this initiative confronts is to demonstrate to the cynics that it is an initiative of integrity, not a partisan political weapon. To some, a major difficulty with this model is that it excludes Opposition members (potential ministerial office holders) from the process. These were themes in the Opposition Leader's address to parliament in November 1999: a reminder of how easily ethics issues are politicized (Preston, 1998, pp. 149–51). The incumbent of this office faces an ongoing challenge to convince all sides of Queensland politics that this office is suitably independent and effective. Opposition Leader Borbidge described this challenge colourfully in parliament:

> How are we to view the proposed Integrity Commissioner? Is he or she to be employed to keep the stables clean? Is their job to keep the stable door locked? Is it a job that is there on a stand-by basis so that if the horse bolts, the stable door can be slammed shut straight after the breakout instead of when an event becomes public knowledge? Is it more of a veterinarian's job;

one that will provide a handy in house gelding facility? Is it intended that this surgery should be performed as a preventive measure before the fact or as an on site sanction available to deal with transgressors who have actually bolted through the door and been returned only after a public hue and cry? (Queensland, Parliamentary Debates, 11 November 1999, p. 4982).

Conclusion

Because the Queensland Integrity Commissioner has been appointed very recently, this discussion has been limited to a description and critique of the institutional design of this model of ethics advice to ministers and senior members of government. An analysis of how this model actually operates must await the passage of time. However, it is interesting to speculate how such a position may have influenced the management of recent ethics crises in government. Arguably it has the potential to forestall problems like those that confronted the first-term Howard government when a few of its ministers faced embarrassment over conflict of interest allegations in 1996, or the Beattie government in relation to the so-called Net Bet affair referred to above.

At the core of the Net Bet affair was a question of the minister's judgement with respect to approaches by Labor Party identities including parliamentarians who were in a conflict of interest as shareholders in the successful Internet gaming company. In this case, the ethics adviser, in the Queensland model, could only make a difference if the relevant ministers first recognized the conflict of interest issue and took the initiative of seeking advice. Other ethical issues have arisen recently in Queensland where the presence of an Integrity Commissioner would probably have no effect. These are occasions (as when one member of the cabinet involved himself in an alleged fight with another Labor figure) when it is unlikely that the premier would listen to the commissioner to the exclusion of other political considerations. Another major ethical matter, which bedevilled the Beattie government in late 2000, involved a public inquiry about party members and officials rorting or manipulating internal party pre-selection ballots by falsifying electoral enrolments. In the midst of this inquiry, the premier was reported as telling journalists that he had not sought advice from the Integrity Commissioner on these questions because they belonged to the jurisdiction of the Criminal Justice Commission (*Courier-Mail*, 19 December 2000). This, notwithstanding the fact that, according to the Public Sector Ethics Amendment Act, the premier may seek advice from the Integrity Commissioner on 'issues involving ethics and integrity'.

Nonetheless, there is scope for ongoing ethical reform arising from the Integrity Commissioner's functions, including the promotion of public understanding of ethics in government, regardless of how seldom ministers knock on the commissioner's door. Despite its problems, the Queensland approach has possibilities and strengthens the government integrity management system overall. The existence of this office will at least emphasize enhanced ethical expectations to ministers. On the really tough issues of political ethics, when motivating ministerial morality comes into question, the

Integrity Commissioner's capacity will be no stronger than the premier's integrity. The workability of this model as a catalyst in motivating ministerial morality hinges on that relationship.

Notes

1   Though the New South Wales parliament has a part-time ethics counsellor for all members of parliament. In addition, legislation was introduced into the Australian Senate in 2000 by the Opposition and minority Australian Democrats for an adviser for MPs regarding entitlements and other ethics matters.
2   There is a view that the advice to designated persons may be released if the reviewing officer deems it to be 'in the public interest', which probably implies 'with the agreement of the designated person'. It is possible that there may have to be some testing of this question before the courts.

Chapter 11

Conduct Unbecoming: Independent Commissions and Ministerial Adversaries

Jenny Fleming[1]

The tradition of parliamentary sovereignty assumes that parliaments will monitor their own behaviour and punish miscreants according to their own conventions. The notion that an external body can judge the morality, rather than the legality, of ministerial or parliamentary behaviour is rejected precisely because it reduces that supremacy, which is such a crucial part of the Westminster system. But is such an absolute position tenable? There are experiments where external bodies have been given the responsibility to judge ministers. Their success may be a matter of dispute, but their experiences suggest that there are lessons to be taken for broader application.

This chapter is concerned with two institutions that are somewhat unique in Westminster systems of government: the Criminal Justice Commission in Queensland and the Independent Commission against Corruption in New South Wales (NSW).[2] External oversight bodies were established in the late 1980s in response to a perception that high-level corruption existed in the states' political institutions. Traditional investigatory bodies such as specialized police units were considered inappropriate and ineffective to combat such behaviour. The responsibilities of these bodies include the misconduct by public officials and elected members of parliament. Bi-partisan parliamentary committees monitor these institutions and they are regarded as 'independent' bodies[3] with discretionary power, autonomy and status. The existence of these bodies has created a political dilemma for governments. How do they publicly acknowledge and accept the oversight from a body they have created and maintain appropriate parliamentary supervision over a body that in turn monitors them? This chapter suggests that these bodies can have a significant impact, even though there are several strategies that governments can employ to undermine these politically sensitive organizations.

In examining whether bodies external to parliament can make ministers accountable, or even ethical, this chapter suggests that these organizations can have a positive influence, providing they retain strong community support, a factor that limits the extent to which the executive can constrain them. Yet, as this chapter demonstrates, the organization's discretion and autonomy is still vulnerable to political intervention. As a mechanism for motivating ministers to more ethical behaviour an independent oversight agency has to balance independence with parliamentary sensitivity.

Criminal Justice Commission

Origins

In 1987 the Queensland government established an inquiry into 'possible illegal activities and associated police misconduct', was chaired by Tony Fitzgerald QC. Over a period of two years the inquiry revealed extensive corruption in Queensland's political institutions and serious misconduct in the state's police force (Fitzgerald, 1989, pp. 2–10). Among other proposals, Fitzgerald recommended the establishment of an independent body, the Criminal Justice Commission (CJC), 'permanently charged with the monitoring, reviewing, co-ordinating, and initiating reform of the administration of criminal justice' (Fitzgerald, 1989, p. 308). The CJC's responsibility was primarily focused on police misconduct, but because the inquiry's evidence led to four ministers being found guilty of misusing ministerial expenses,[4] the CJC's mandate extended to members of the state's Legislative Assembly, the Parliamentary Service, the Executive Council and local government members and officials. For this reason, Fitzgerald emphasized the need for the 'exclusion or reduction of party political considerations and processes from the decision-making process' with respect to the CJC:

> ... executive authority and connection with the CJC must be limited to what is necessary to finance it, provide administrative and resource needs, and that necessary for public financial and other accounting purposes. For those purposes, and not otherwise, a Minister should be responsible for the CJC[5] (Fitzgerald, 1989, p. 309).

Fitzgerald's recommendation was lost in what became the very politicized environment in which the CJC operated.

The relationship between the inaugural Chair of the CJC, Sir Max Bingham, appointed by a government in its death throes, and the newly elected Labor government was constantly strained. The structural difficulties for independent oversight bodies lie primarily in what is often perceived as an unconstitutional interference with the traditional Westminster system of government, where ministers are held to be solely accountable to parliament for their departments. The problems were inherent in the structure Fitzgerald recommended. As Lewis points out, tensions arise when an external agency reports directly to parliament, bypassing the 'authority and influence of the executive' (1999, p. 152). In Queensland, the real problems began in 1991 when the CJC exercised its power to investigate the ethical behaviour of ministers and parliamentarians. While governments acknowledged the right of the CJC to propose policy and publish research findings, they became aggrieved when the commission publicly assessed their own behaviour.

Travel Entitlement Investigation

The CJC's investigation and subsequent report (CJC, 1991) into the alleged misuse of parliamentary travel entitlements took over 12 months to complete. Some of the delay was due to the Auditor-General's insistence that the CJC produce an authority from the Supreme Court prior to his releasing documentation. Under the Criminal Justice Act, the Auditor-General was not bound by the Financial Administration and Audit Act and according to the commission his 'well-intentioned' caution was costly and time consuming (CJC, 1991, pp. 10–11). Many parliamentarians believed that the commission had 'exceeded its authority by launching the investigation'. Bingham received many 'distinctly menacing' telephone calls advising him of the vulnerability of the commission. He was told, 'the future of the commission was at risk — and its prospects would not be helped if the inquiry were to continue' (Walker, 1995, p. 173). Thirty-seven members of parliament refused to relinquish travel records and other documentation to the CJC voluntarily, and as a result the CJC had to exercise its legislative powers to obtain the information it required (CJC, 1991, pp. 51–3). This reluctance was understandable. The CJC had written to the leaders of each political party in May 1991, advising them of the process by which the commission would proceed with its investigation. Despite the 'commission's best intentions one or more of the party leaders or his staff chose to disclose this correspondence to the media'. As a result of this disclosure, 'some members were disinclined to co-operate with the commission for fear that any information provided by them would be leaked to the media' (CJC, 1991, p. 52). As the Chief Investigator, Forbes Smith, pointed out, ' ... if the public knew that a specific member had helped us with our inquiries or indeed attended a meeting at the CJC, a number of unfortunate, if mistaken conclusions could have been drawn. For politicians, it's all about perception' (Smith, 2000). The CJC was aware of the politically sensitive nature of the inquiry. 'There were only two of us on the investigation to limit the possibility of information becoming public property. We knew the whole issue was dynamite politically but there was no reluctance on our part to conduct such an investigation. That was part of the job' (Smith, 2000).

Not only was there a disinclination to proffer information, there was also some resistance to attending hearings. Out of 13 members called to an investigative hearing, one had to be officially summoned by the commission (CJC, 1991, p. 54). Under the Criminal Justice Act, a witness may object to answering questions on the grounds that it may incriminate him/her. If such an objection occurs, the information furnished is 'not admissible in evidence against the person or witness in civil or criminal proceedings in a court'. Out of the 15 individuals questioned, seven chose to take advantage of this protection (CJC, 1991, p. 55). The apprehension reflected an earlier investigation arising out of the Fitzgerald Inquiry where five ministers had been charged and three imprisoned (Wanna, 1991, pp. 217–18). The new government wanted no repetition.

Given the volume of travel claims, the CJC restricted its investigation to daily travelling allowances. But the lack of records and documentation was a problem:

> In essence there was nothing to investigate because no records had been required or kept and that was the nature of the investigation. In the absence of any definitive guidelines we were rendered at some points incapable of

effective investigation. Almost no one volunteered the information and very little information was written down for us to check (Smith, 2000).

Legal experts advised the CJC that the lack of guidelines and paperwork relating to travel entitlements would mitigate against successful criminal proceedings. As a result, anonymous case studies were used in the report rather than names (CJC, 1991, pp. vii–viii). But names were soon put to cases. After a number of existing and former ministers were forced to resign from their respective positions on the front bench, relations between the CJC and all politicians became problematic (Walker, 1995, pp. 173–80). Politicians from both sides of the parliament decried the 'unprofessional, subjective, sloppy, judgmental, and pathetic travel entitlements' report (cited in Lewis, 1999, p. 155). The deteriorating relationship between the government and the CJC illustrated the difficulties for an external oversight body investigating its master.

Under intense media focus, the investigation itself was tough – 'proceed[ing] despite allegations of interference with, and of attempted intimidation of, the Commission' (CJC, 1991, p. ii). A political power game was played out in the press as the government sought to assert its authority and remind the CJC of its vulnerability. The commission forwarded its final report to the Parliamentary Criminal Justice Committee (PCJC), the seven member all-party committee of the Queensland Legislative Assembly, for review. The CJC was not prepared to discuss its recommendations with the government and 'was very glad to see the end of the inquiry' (Smith, 2000).

The adverse findings of the report, coming so soon after the revelations of the Fitzgerald Inquiry, undermined the government's disparaging comments about the CJC's handling of the investigation. If there was any intention to act on what the CJC had perceived as the government's intimidating threats, the findings of the investigation, the high media profile of the CJC and its apparently strong community support ensured that any 'government action was kept in check by the weight of public opinion' (Lewis, 1999, p. 155).

The Mundingburra By-Election — The Government Response

In 1996 a by-election was held in Mundingburra in North Queensland which would decide whether or not the government retained office. The Queensland Police Union (QPU), taking advantage of contemporary law and order debates, campaigned in the electorate for more police, using extensive advertising to promote its cause. The by-election delivered government to the National–Liberal Party coalition. Soon afterwards it was revealed that the QPU had signed a Memorandum of Understanding (MOU) with the soon to be appointed police minister and the incoming premier. Among other things, the agreement sought to limit the power of the CJC in its dealings with the state's police service. Under strong media pressure the now Police Minister forwarded the MOU to the CJC for its perusal. Following legal advice, the CJC engaged a retired Supreme Court judge from another Australian state, Ken Carruthers QC, to conduct an inquiry into the signing of the MOU.

Throughout the Carruthers Inquiry (CJC, 1996)[6] the government attacked the CJC, particularly as Carruthers began to speculate publicly on the inappropriate activities of Premier Rob Borbidge and the Police Minister, Russell Cooper. The government also reduced the CJC's operating funds by $2.7 million. This amounted to 10 per cent of the commission's budget. Given the lack of discretionary funds already available to the CJC, the cut resulted in a number of staff being laid off (CJC, 1996-97, p. 3). The government's action was a reminder of the commission's political vulnerability. For the government the unethical conduct of one of its members was not the only issue at stake. The loss of government was a real possibility. But there were other strategies it could employ.

While Carruthers worked on his report a member of the National Party made allegations in parliament about one of the CJC's senior officials, Mark Le Grand.[7] On the basis of these allegations the government announced an inquiry into the CJC, an inquiry that would include an investigation of the Carruthers Inquiry. Carruthers resigned in protest and the CJC was obliged to rely on two barristers to collate his evidence to provide a report. As the MOU had not given anyone concerned any tangible benefits, they absolved the premier, the Police Minister and the police union executive of any illegality (CJC, 1996).

The government's attack on the CJC continued. The inquiry into the CJC became known as the Connolly–Ryan Inquiry after its investigators. The choice of Peter Connolly was surprising. The former Liberal member of the Legislative Assembly and Queensland Supreme Court judge had acted as adviser to the Police Minister on the MOU some months earlier. Connolly's overtly political comments in the press and his inappropriate behaviour during the hearings prompted the CJC to commence Supreme Court action to stop the inquiry on the grounds of bias (Smith, 2000). The court found in favour of the CJC and the inquiry was terminated in August 1997.

Clearly the government had reservations about the CJC and its independent status. While the community seemed supportive of the organization and the media strongly advocated the role it should play, members of parliament disagreed. Allegations were made, not only about individuals but about the general way in which the CJC operated. Choosing what to investigate was one such concern. There was some evidence, for example, that legal opinion had recommended against the CJC undertaking the MOU inquiry and yet the CJC had proceeded (Dickie,[8] 1999a). The government deemed it an auspicious time to provide some legislative restraint to the organization it had created from the Fitzgerald blueprint.

The Criminal Justice Amendment Act

In September 1997 a Bill to amend the Criminal Justice Act was introduced into parliament. The Bill strengthened the PCJC's role, increased ministerial control over the organization's budget and introduced a permanent commission of inquiry in the shape of a PCJC Commissioner. It was the CJC's perceived loss of independence that raised the most protest (Queensland, Parliamentary Debates, 1997; Homel, 1997; Clair, 1997).

Under the Act the PCJC moved from its monitoring and reviewing role to assume a more significant directive and decision-making role. It was given new powers to issue mandatory guidelines and policy directions. The PCJC could now order the CJC to initiate and pursue specific investigations into any conduct or activities of CJC commissioners or staff. The all-party Scrutiny of Legislation Committee, the Labor Opposition, the CJC's Commissioner, Frank Clair, and the Queensland Law Commission expressed concern about giving the PCJC an 'executive role ... in circumstances where it itself is not accountable to the parliament ... through the processes of ministerial responsibility' (Queensland, Parliamentary Debates, 1997, pp. 3885–6, 4012). The Law Society put it more bluntly and observed:

> ... to give the power of direction to the parliamentary committee would enable politicians to use the CJC to target persons or groups in the community (Queensland, Parliamentary Debates, 1997, p. 4013).

The PCJC's revised role included the handling of all complaints against the CJC, and a power of veto on legal practitioners conducting hearings on behalf of the organization. It had the prerogative to inspect and copy all operational material (including that gathered using listening devices) for information purposes, and the power to insist that the CJC turn over confidential information when requested.

The new legislation directed that the CJC obtain the Police Minister's approval to any changes relating to wages, allowances, conditions of employment, promotion and salaries. The minister could now legitimately request details of proposed and actual expenditure of the commission. Clearly under the proposed legislation the minister was in a position where he/she could exercise considerable control over the CJC's investigatory duties. As Frank Clair pointed out:

> ... this legislation has the potential to destroy the effective operation of the CJC. It will be impossible to recruit persons of integrity and ability to serve under such conditions. Impossible to ensure that the hard decisions are made in future without fear, favour or an eye to avoiding unfair investigation (Clair, 1997).

For an organization that was designed to be independent of political intervention, the proposals were undeniably intrusive.

Office of Parliamentary Criminal Justice Commissioner

The legislation established the office of a parliamentary commissioner (PC) as a standing Commission of Inquiry. Its wide ranging powers included the power to audit records and activities of the CJC and the investigation of complaints against the CJC referred to it by the PCJC. Its investigations, however, could only be triggered by a request of a bi-partisan majority of members of the PCJC.[9] The PC would have full access to information, including the records of the discredited Connolly–Ryan Inquiry. Under the legislation, information held by the CJC could be directed back to the PCJC by the PC for re-evaluation. Given the history of the Connolly–Ryan Inquiry and the Supreme Court's judgement of bias, this seemed inappropriate.

Another concern of the CJC was the loss of legal rights of CJC commissioners and staff generally. As the CJC pointed out in its submission to the Attorney General, the legislation left the CJC with little entitlement for justice review or most of the other legal rights that would protect it from excessive zeal on the part of the PC (Homel, 1997).

The PC could decide whether the CJC was exercising its powers appropriately or even whether matters already under investigation were 'appropriate to be investigated by the CJC'. The PC could also, on the advice of the PCJC, target the CJC for what could be a purely political investigation. As one CJC commissioner observed, 'the investigation of government politicians will be very difficult' (Homel, 1997).

This was arguably the government's intent. The government itself did little to persuade observers otherwise; the Minister for Transport questioned the independence of Carruthers during parliamentary debate and suggested that the Carruthers Inquiry 'was a vendetta against the coalition'. The Opposition welcomed the minister's interjection because 'that is precisely the view which has prompted the government to bring in the legislation ... the CJC [would] pay a very high price for [its] audacity in investigating Premier Borbidge and Police Minister Cooper' (Queensland, Parliamentary Debates, 1997, pp. 3880–2). Whatever the reasoning, the legislation clearly restricted the CJC's activities, sought to diminish its credibility as an independent organization and severely impeded its ability to investigate politicians. In Labor's words, the CJC had been 'neutered' (Queensland, Parliamentary Debates, 1997, p. 3919).

Despite this less than conducive environment, the CJC, through vigorous investigation and the assistance of an inquisitive press, has been responsible for removing a number of ministers from frontbench positions. Despite attempts by Queensland governments to undermine and control the CJC, the importance of an independent organization committed to promoting ethical standards in the public sector ensures its survival. Whether or not the CJC-conducted surveys that reveal high levels of community support (CJC, 2000) have any merit (Dickie, 1999b), it is probably accurate to observe that the public are more likely to 'trust' the CJC than they are to trust politicians. This support has promoted its political importance to an extent that governments are limited in what they can do to constrain its activities. The Independent Commission Against Corruption in NSW has had a less publicly hostile relationship with its government and yet there are signs that this organization too is becoming increasingly vulnerable to government pressure to conform to a more politically manageable status.

Independent Commission Against Corruption

Origins

The Independent Commission Against Corruption (ICAC) was established in 1988 after years of political controversy about high-level corruption in NSW politics (Sturgess, 1994, p.107) and was invested with extensive powers (Furness, 1994, pp. 198–202). Over time these powers have been the focus of criticism from interest groups, politicians and other interested parties (Sturgess, 1994, p. 114).

The ICAC's independence is crucially important to the organization. The absence of any statutory provision that subjects it to the control or direction of a minister assures this independence. Like the CJC, the ICAC is accountable to the state's parliament through a bi-partisan Parliamentary Joint Committee (PJC). The PJC is responsible for monitoring and reviewing its activities and reports, reporting to the parliament and acting as an intermediary when questions are asked of the ICAC. The PJC cannot reconsider operational decisions made by the commission or examine operational matters. This is the role of the Operations Review Committee (ORC), which advises the ICAC Commissioner whether the ICAC should pursue an investigation and must be consulted before an investigation can be discontinued. The ORC includes representatives from the community and key government agencies and usually meets once a month (Furness, 1994, pp. 205–6).

In its first two years the ICAC received over 2 500 complaints and initiated over 30 formal investigations (1991a). Only a minority of these investigations directly focused on the role of a minister. However, they afforded the ICAC opportunities to comment on the ethical standards of the parliament. The first, the investigation into the Silverwater Filling Operation in February 1990 (ICAC, 1990a), concerned an already imprisoned Minister for Corrective Services. The ICAC took the opportunity to raise the issue of ministerial interference in public administration and included in its report a description of the ideal relationship between a minister and a public official. Given that the minister in question was already imprisoned, the ICAC's findings did not embarrass the government and little attention was paid to the report's observations.

In October 1990 the ICAC published its report into the Walsh Bay Redevelopment Project. It was alleged that the responsible minister interfered in the tendering process for a large development project. No corrupt conduct was found (ICAC, 1990b). A third report, the North Coast Land Development investigation, cited a number of MLAs including the deputy premier, the Lands Minister and a number of parliamentarians from both sides of the House. Its strong recommendations about the law on political donations and political lobbying practices (ICAC, 1990c) were largely ignored by the government. It preferred to criticize publicly the ICAC's power to hold public hearings that could embarrass the government (Sturgess, 1994, p. 117). Indeed this concern with public humiliation drives the government's discomfiture about the ICAC and similar organizations. So while politicians' ethical status remains low (McAllister, 2000) and organizations such as the ICAC and the CJC retain credibility within the community, governments are constrained by their own creation, and as Warhurst has pointed out are effectively 'hoisted on their own petard' (1980, p. 151).

Following an investigation into bribery allegations against a member of parliament in 1991, the ICAC once again offered advice on the ethical standards of politicians. The Neal Report concluded with an examination of the position of parliamentarians in Australia generally and in NSW especially and recommended a code of conduct be developed. It also commented on the relationship between members and professional lobbyists and recommended the establishment of a Register of Lobbyists (ICAC, 1991b). The recommendations were forwarded to the PJC for further consideration. It would be another seven years before they were acted upon. The NSW parliament seemed resolute that it was not the role of the ICAC to divine the ethical standards governing politicians. The Metherell case would confirm their thinking.

The Metherell Affair

In April 1992 the ICAC was requested by the Legislative Council and the Legislative Assembly of NSW to inquire into the circumstances surrounding Dr Terry Metherell's resignation from parliament and subsequent appointment to a senior public service position. Following hearings throughout May, its report contained findings of corrupt conduct (Commissioner Temby based his allegation of 'corrupt conduct' on his understanding of S8 and S9 of the ICAC Act that defines corruption) against the then premier, Nick Greiner, and the then Minister for the Environment. The report suggested that their conduct could warrant dismissal from their ministerial posts. In the face of considerable public hostility, the premier protested in parliament:

> I refuse to be judged according to a standard which has only emerged after the event and which I am assumed to have understood and agreed to. By all means let's change the rules. But let's do so prospectively and on a known and agreed basis (cited in Sturgess, 1994, p. 123).

Following an appeal to the Supreme Court both the premier and the minister resigned (ICAC, 1992a; Chaples and Page, 1995, pp. 62–7). In August 1992, the Court of Appeal found that the ICAC had erred in its application of S9 (that is, in relation to corrupt conduct). It argued that in the absence of any legally recognizable standards for assessing a minister's conduct, a minister's behaviour could not be judged under S9. The ICAC prepared another report in order to 'correct the record' (Chaples and Page, 1995, pp. 66–7; ICAC 1992a, b). Commissioner Temby had some criticisms of his own, particularly about conventions that placed ministers 'in a special category':

> [They] can be removed from office by parliamentary action, and generally no other means of removal is available. So to such people, there are no

> disciplinary offences. Accordingly, in terms of S9 of the ICAC Act, the practical reality of the Court decision is that if their conduct is not such as could constitute or involve a criminal offence, they are not at risk of finding a corrupt conduct. This interpretation means behaviour such as bias, favouritism, nepotism and jobs for the boys may be 'corrupt' if done by a public servant but not if done by the holder of a high office (ICAC, 1992b, p. 10).

Despite Greiner's admonitions to 'change the rules', it would be two years before the parliament amended the ICAC legislation to include a sanction against ministers who substantially breached an applicable code of conduct. It would be another seven years before an applicable code of conduct was officially tabled in parliament.

Travel Entitlements Investigation

Following revelations in the Commonwealth parliament in 1996 of abuses by MPs of travel and other allowances, the ICAC considered an investigation of the same issues in NSW. The ICAC was advised by the Auditor-General that the parliamentary records were virtually 'unauditable' in relation to travel and that considerable resources would be necessary if the ICAC was to undertake an investigation. With declining budgets, the ICAC deferred the issue. In 1997, however, in possession of information relating to alleged abuses of travel allowances by NSW MPs, the ICAC seconded audit officers from the Auditor-General's department and began its inquiry.

The investigation spanned the period 1990 to 1997. It reported corrupt conduct on the part of Brian Langton, the Minister for Fair Trading and Minister for Emergency Services, in which he was engaged before becoming a minister. The ICAC recommended that consideration be given to prosecution and dismissal. As in Queensland seven years previously, the ICAC's investigation into high-profile members of the state parliament was not an easy task with administrative and cultural problems identified by the organization as a hindrance to investigators.

One of the difficulties was the bicameral nature of the NSW parliament[10] that ensured separate administrations for the Assembly and the Council. As the ICAC noted, the structure did not allow for the independent management of pecuniary systems without 'undue influence from Members or others who serve the interest of such Members' (ICAC, 1998a). In its second report to parliament, the ICAC recommended the merging of the two administrations, with one officer to manage it. This solution would make redundant the roles of the Clerk of the Parliament and the Clerk of the Assembly, the most senior public servants in the administration of the parliament (ICAC, 1998b). The ICAC's recommendation was not received well by government officials. Other administrative problems identified by the ICAC concerned a lack of resources, ambiguous expenditure and process guidelines, no effective internal reporting systems, no fraud prevention strategies and, as in Queensland, a prevailing view that 'things were done as they had always been done' (ICAC, 1998b; Stathis, 2000).

From the outset parliamentarians objected to the ICAC's intrusion on their sovereignty. The idea that as a sovereign body the parliament deserved to be 'naturally' trusted seemed to be widespread — a culture perpetuated by 'existing structures, systems and some personnel'. There was also a view that the investigation was 'exacerbating the declining public respect for parliamentarians' (Stathis, 2000). In a second report to parliament, the ICAC noted that in the absence of a code of conduct,[11] training or education programs about an MP's role and responsibilities, the traditional way of doing things was always going to take precedence.

With the ICAC's second report and its 63 recommendations, the investigation became less than cordial. A few members of parliament became the focus of media headlines. Parliamentarians were concerned that the detailed level of information in the media identified particular members and depicted them poorly in the eyes of the community (PJC, 1999a, pp. 85–6). They were angry at what they perceived as a lack of consultation.

Subsequently the ICAC adopted a more conciliatory stance, 'crucial for achieving sustainable reform in the long term' (Stathis, 2000). Its third report acknowledged the criticism while attempting to explain its rationale (ICAC, 1999, pp. 2–4). The report noted the parliament's response to the ICAC's recommendations in the previous report. Only nine of them had been actively implemented with others deferred for budgetary consultation or committee consideration. Twenty recommendations were partially implemented and three recommendations were rejected outright. The ICAC suggested that significant progress had been made in relation to its recommendations and that the investigation had proceeded satisfactorily (ICAC, 1999, pp. 6-40). Yet even while the ICAC remained optimistic about future reform, the government via its parliamentary committee was considering legislative changes that would bring the independent organization into a much closer relationship with the government.

Changes

The new PJC constituted in March 1999 resumed the review of the ICAC begun in 1997. During its first meeting with Commissioner Barry O' Keefe, the PJC revealed parliament's concerns about the ICAC's investigation into travel entitlements, its dealings with parliamentary officers and its recommendations. Many of the recommendations were criticized as impractical. The focus in the meeting on the recommendations was very specific and the discussion about the inadequate consultation processes was vigorous. References in the report to parliamentarians' use of holiday destinations was vilified as a purposeful strategy to gain 'a cheap headline and at the same time [to demean] the position of parliamentarians' (PJC, 1999a, pp. 85–6).

Other sources of heated debate included the ICAC's method of determining which matters should be the subject of an inquiry, what factors were taken into account, how the ICAC dealt with vexatious complaints and the advantages of private hearings (PJC, 1999a, pp. 85–6). The committee was particularly interested in the ORC and the lack of attention it received in the ICAC's annual report (PJC, 1999a, pp. 103–5). A further meeting in November returned to the subject of parliamentary travel. The commissioner was reminded of the importance of consultation and the problems of sensationalizing and bringing inappropriate detail to the community (PJC, 1999b, pp. 152–4). The bi-partisan committee was unanimous in its disapproval of the way the ICAC had conducted its review of parliamentary travel entitlements.

The committee's review of the ICAC revealed what was perceived as a 'significant gap' in the consideration of complaints against the commission and its officers. In June 2000 the committee tabled its report on accountability and determined that there was a need for an independent means of proactively monitoring the ICAC. Having looked closely at other Australian models and that of the ICAC in Hong Kong it determined that the most suitable model for the ICAC would be that of the Inspector (PJC, 2000).

The inspector model is less legalistic and formal than the Queensland one but essentially works on the same principle – that is, it will render the ICAC more open to parliamentary scrutiny and will serve as a prior warning system to a government that has been constantly frustrated in its attempts to monitor the progress and substance of investigations. Unlike the parliamentary commissioner in Queensland, the proposed inspector would be able to conduct investigations into the ICAC on his/her own initiative, at the behest of a minister, in response to a complaint or through a referral from another agency (PJC, 2000, p. 8). In short, these recommendations empower the inspector 'to do anything that is necessary to be done for the exercise of his or her functions (PJC, 2000, pp. 63–7).

At the time of writing, the PJC's recommendations relating to an Inspector are still just proposals. Yet there is clearly an agenda on both sides of politics to rein in the independence of the oversight body and render its activities more accessible to government and parliament via a third party. As pointed out in the PJC's report, it would be inappropriate to extend the PJC's powers because of the threat to the ICAC's independence. Hence the need for a third institution. It is difficult to see how this institution would 'safeguard the independence of the ICAC' or 'contribute significantly to the enhanced nature of the ICAC's performance and procedures' (PJC, 2000, p. 5).

How Well Do They Work?

How effective are these institutions then in motivating ministers to better behaviour? To what extent can they be classified as independent? Both the CJC and the ICAC were established in an environment of public disenchantment with political institutions. Both organizations have sustained a high level of public legitimacy despite attempts by all sides of parliament to undermine their credibility in times of political crisis.

The CJC's relationship with its political masters in Queensland has always been characterized by friction and suspicion. Much of the early conflict was a combination of inevitable tensions, given the expectations of a new government, and a conflict of roles and personalities between the commission, its chairperson, the government and the PCJC. The obligation of the CJC to draw attention to politically sensitive questions of ethics and the appropriate behaviour of parliamentarians intensified the conflict. The travel entitlement investigation in 1991 cost the new government three ministers and considerable adverse publicity. In 1996 the CJC's investigation into the Mundingburra by-election once again generated adverse and unwelcome publicity in the media.

It is not surprising then that both governments tried to undermine the activities of the CJC publicly and to expose the organization's activities to a more stringent reporting system. No particular political party was primarily responsible. All parties are apprehensive of an organization that has the propensity to humiliate them politically and destabilize their time in office. Thus, the bi-partisan nature of the PCJC has not been a successful means of rendering the CJC independent of the government. Parliamentarians all agree they would rather not be investigated or monitored by an external body whose ethical parameters may not be the same as their own.

Possibly the CJC's very existence and its public support have ensured a measure of compliance within political circles in Queensland. So on one level the existence of such an organization has had a deterrent effect. The government's 1997 legislation has had its own impact. When allegations about electoral rorting in the state emerged, the CJC was initially reticent to begin any investigation, citing a lack of jurisdiction as a reason for its hesitancy. Brisbane's *Courier-Mail* scornfully pointed out that the 'CJC was created to keep politicians honest. If the allegation is that politicians are engaged in electoral rorting, it is hard to see how the CJC cannot act'. The newspaper also reminded readers about the CJC's 'weak-kneed' investigation of the Housing Minister, Robert Schwarten's, public fistfight earlier in the year. There, the *Courier-Mail* asserted, the 'CJC had showed all the independent courage of a fieldmouse'. The 'investigation of serious allegations against a politician was at best cursory, and at worst a whitewash. It's high time the CJC started doing its job' (*Courier-Mail*, 16 August 2000).

For an organization that depends on its masters for its budget and for the very parameters within which it works, it is not difficult to see why the CJC was reluctant to investigate another political timebomb. The issue of jurisdiction is still pertinent. Under the Act the CJC may only conduct an inquiry into a member of the Legislative Assembly if the conduct under investigation could constitute a criminal offence. Legal interpretation of this clause seems indecisive. Following *Courier-Mail* criticism, the CJC appointed P. D. McMurdo QC to conduct preliminary inquiries (CJC, 2000a). Part of his brief was to decide whether such allegations come within the definition of official misconduct. Following McMurdo's recommendation to proceed with an open inquiry and public pressure for the organization to proceed, the CJC began its investigations into electoral rorting practices. At the time of writing the Shepherdson Inquiry has completed its investigation into the electoral rorting affair and is preparing its report for parliament. To date, as a consequence of the inquiry, the deputy premier and Lands Minister and two high-profile Labor backbenchers have resigned. One of the CJC's staunchest critics, former premier and now leader of the Opposition, Rob Borbidge, has withdrawn his criticism of the organization and its independence:

> I'm quite happy to admit that I am pleased the CJC has restored my public confidence in them ... I have no proposals or plans to change the structure of the CJC ... for the first time in a long time [the CJC has] demonstrated a complete lack of political bias (*Courier-Mail*, 1 December).

Thus speak Oppositions. Governments tend to think differently.

In NSW the ICAC no longer has the jurisdiction to oversee the conduct of the state's police officers[12] and therefore has more time and resources to conduct its investigations into public affairs. Originally more publicly committed to promoting public sector ethics, the ICAC has arguably enjoyed greater compliance because of its more detailed brief. However, politicians have shown a reluctance to subject themselves to the ICAC's ethical standards and judgements and the aftermath of the Metherell affair has been a sobering reminder to the ICAC of the limitations of its role.

In recent years the ICAC's budget has been declining and a new commissioner is now faced with a PJC committed to a stronger monitoring role of the ICAC in the shape of an inspector. This model has been agreed to by the PJC, a committee comprising politicians from all sides of parliament. The bi-partisan nature of this committee is intended to suggest that the government is unable to persuade or influence the operations of the committee and, indirectly, the ICAC. The proposed inspector would form a bridge between this committee and the minister and arguably leave the committee open to 'gentle persuasion' by the minister. The inspector model has the potential to restrict and limit the ICAC's activities. Just as the CJC enjoys community support, so does the ICAC. Whether or not this will allow the ICAC to pursue its ethical agenda in the context of parliamentarians remains to be seen.

Conclusion

Both histories show similar patterns. The institutions are designed in the midst of political crisis and a rush of enthusiasm for honest politics. As their investigators move to monitor and review the activities of politicians and ministers, enthusiasm wanes and hostility emerges. The defence of parliamentary sovereignty is raised and a variety of strategies are used to restrain this action. Yet these have never included proposals to abolish either the ICAC or the CJC. They are too much a part of the political infrastructure and while the organizations may not be as popular as their 'surveys' suggest, there is clearly an expectation from the public that they should be allowed to do their job and do it vigilantly.

This is probably the main conclusion to be drawn from the discussion in this chapter. External bodies with adequate powers can provide an investigatory environment that makes ministers nervous and arguably more cautious. When these external bodies investigate they may find cases of inappropriate behaviour. When they do, they can expect politicians to retaliate and to seek to reduce their influence. Politicians, though, cannot eradicate community support for these organizations. In the wake of the Metherell case, the organizations may be cautious about basing their reports on ethical value judgements. However they are not prohibited from making recommendations in relation to ethical reform nor are they precluded from making public statements about appropriate standards. Indeed the public expects it of them. As long as they retain public support and adequate resolve, external oversight bodies can have an influence — flawed perhaps, but more effective than the old system of parliamentary self-censorship.

Notes

1 Thanks to Forbes Smith (CJC) and Peter Stathis (ICAC) for their cooperation and assistance throughout.
2 The Anti-Corruption Commission in Western Australia is another example of such an organization.
3 That is, not specifically accountable to government.
4 The ministers were subsequently jailed. For more detail of the political context see Fitzgerald (1989, pp. 123–37).
5 The CJC is currently administered by the Department of Justice and Attorney-General.
6 The following account of the Mundingburra issue is, unless specified otherwise, taken from Colleen Lewis's book, *Complaints against Police, The Politics of Reform* (1999).
7 The allegation concerned the leak of details to the federal government of a CJC/police investigation into alleged relationships between former federal minister, Graham Richardson and Gold Coast prostitutes.
8 Phil Dickie is an independent journalist and former special adviser to the CJC.
9 The original Bill suggested that the majority decision would only need to come from government members of the PCJC. The Opposition successfully amended the clause at Committee.
10 Queensland has a unicameral system.
11 The NSW parliament brought down its code of conduct on 12 May 1999, eight years after ICAC had suggested it and six years after the Supreme Court had cited its absence as a reason why ministers could not be cited for corrupt conduct.
12 This function now belongs to the Police Integrity Commission, legislatively established in 1996.

Chapter 12

The Role of the Auditor-General in Scrutinizing Ministerial Ethics

John Wanna and Alexander Gash

In Australia, the office of the Commonwealth Auditor-General was established by legislation in 1901 as a *single* statutory office holder responsible for providing independent opinion on the financial statements of the government. Such arrangements followed evolving Westminster practice (in the UK, Canada, New Zealand and the Australian colonies) of separating responsibility for auditing and reporting on the accuracy of the public account from the head of the government's budget agency (e.g. the Chancellor, Treasurer or President of Treasury Board who would have reported annually on the state of the books). Some Australian jurisdictions had adopted multiple auditors-general and divided aspects of the audit function across two or more officials who were usually charged with other statutory or administrative duties. However, at the Commonwealth level it was felt more appropriate that a single, independent office holder be given responsibility for scrutinizing the public accounts, auditing the books and stocks of public entities and reporting on the end of year financial statements.[1] The establishment of a dedicated statutory officer in Australia underlined the importance of money, revenues and expenses in a young federal nation where the regional colonies had surrendered some of their financial powers to a central government. The fact that multiple public auditors could be appointed, however, is an important precedent to which we later return.

The Commonwealth government attempted to separate the Auditor-General (A-G) from the executive in a number of important ways. For example, the A-G's salary was stipulated in legislation and itemized separately in annual appropriations; the A-G was given wide inquisitorial powers to summon officials, inspect records and search premises; the A-G was provided with secure tenure and protection from dismissal; and, in the annual report presented to parliament, the A-G was unconstrained as to the matters on which he/she could report (other than that a report on the Treasurer's end of year financial statements had to be presented). But in other important ways the A-G was dependent on the executive. The office holder remains an executive appointment. The position has never been advertised and, although appointed by the Governor-General, remains at the discretion of the prime minister, Treasurer and later the Finance Minister.[2] The annual budget of the Audit Office has until very recently been policed by the government budget agency (Treasury and Finance); in effect, the Audit Office has had to extract resources from the same government it is auditing. And, while the A-G enjoys wide powers of inspection, in practice the A-G and audit staff have experienced instances where requested information has been denied or delayed. For the A-G to be effective in dispensing his/her statutory duties requires good working relationships and the cooperation of agencies and ministers. The A-G is inevitably walking a very fine line.

The argument put forward in this chapter is that for much of the twentieth century successive Auditors-General, and the Audit Office,[3] have not generally investigated or reported on ministerial ethics or ministerial behaviour. In the last decade, however, there are signs the A-G's mandate has been extended, both through interpretation and statutory provision, to include *aspects of ministerial behaviour*. But the bounds of the A-G's investigatory powers in this area remain unclear. Principally, topics for investigation would be confined to the financial or procedural aspects of administration and in particular the capacity to undertake performance audits that in some way involve the minister. Such powers are at present dependent on a broad and convoluted set of statutory powers that under certain circumstances can include ministers. But these powers are also couched in conventions and protocols. While the A-G can initiate or extend an investigation to include some aspects of ministerial behaviour, the more likely occurrence is for matters to be referred to the A-G by the relevant minister (or the prime minister or Finance Minister), with the ministers then agreeing to cooperate with the audit investigation.

It could be argued that during the 1990s the A-G became a reluctant volunteer or even conscript involved in scrutinizing the administrative-ethical behaviour of ministers. Such developments occurred not so much because of the personal motivation of the A-G. Rather, they occurred as a result of performance audit investigations or requests from ministers for the A-G to investigate their behaviour. Circumstances, not auditor motivation, brought ministerial behaviour more into focus.

While this may be viewed in a positive light (i.e. as a means of enhancing scrutiny of the executive, bringing wayward ministers to heel, providing Oppositions with independent judgements with which to score political points), we argue that there are substantial risks in relying on the A-G to perform this function. There are political dangers associated with an extension of the role of the A-G into areas where auditors may or will be required to investigate the ethical behaviour of ministers. Increasing the involvement of the A-G in such matters is likely to compromise the office and expose the A-G to various forms of political attack or denigration. Also affected may be the A-G's core activities in auditing public sector agencies and maintaining effective working relations with departments. We question whether the A-G is the appropriate office holder or has the capacity to scrutinize effectively the privileged domain of ministers. A better alternative may be to establish a separate auditor with the powers to investigate parliamentary and ministerial allowances and entitlements.

Ministers and the Body Politic: Beyond Effective Reach?

Officially, ministers are appointed by the head of state generally to administer a department or area of administration. But they are elected representatives enjoying both parliamentary and executive privileges. Cabinet proceedings remain confidential and cabinet records are only selectively released publicly after 30 years (although the A-G can gain confidential access to cabinet documents providing they relate to an audit and reasons are provided).[4] Ministerial decisions were traditionally regarded as privileged, although the procedural and substantive nature of those decisions has increasingly come under review through administrative law and the courts. Ministers have traditionally enjoyed protection under public interest immunity (previously known as Crown privilege) in their deliberations and for most of their decisions. Such privileges have also been accepted as extending to their behaviour and practices. The minister's private office and immediate staff were similarly considered sacrosanct — not part of the general area of administration — and more recently governed by the Members of Parliament (Staff) Act 1984.[5]

For the most part the decisions and behaviour of ministers can be debated in parliament but are beyond (or at least appear to be beyond) the purview of other officials and accountability officers. The notion of 'ministerial provenance' has existed to define an area that is off limits to other investigators, although the actual boundaries of this domain remain unclear and often untested. But, if ministers are beyond effective reach it may not be because they are formally excluded but because they are conventionally regarded as outside the parameters of statutory investigators.

Role of the Auditor-General in Scrutinizing Ethics in the Public Sector Generally

The Audit Act 1901 limited the scope of the audit function but provided a wide range of powers for the A-G within those limits. As Funnell (1994, p. 344) has argued: 'The original intent of the *Audit Act* was to limit the state auditor to the auditing of Consolidated Revenue Fund, the Loan Fund and the Trust Fund'. The auditor was meant to give an opinion on the Treasurer's end of year financial statements. As such, 'much of the Act dealt with detailed financial procedures, such as the operation of bank accounts and the proper procedures for the payment and collection of monies' (Funnell, 1994, p. 299). In other words, the A-G's mandate and authority was limited to transactions involving the three main public funds operated by the Commonwealth, but otherwise he/she had wide powers of investigation, surveillance and cross-examination under oath. There is also little specific detail in the original Act as to how the A-G should discharge his/her responsibilities and undertake actual audits. For example, issues of whether the A-G and Audit Office staff should visit the site (the 'travelling audit'), conduct a comprehensive audit or a sample audit, chase small amounts of money or investigate systems of assurance, or even initiate an investigation are left to the discretion of the A-G.

Initially, one of the A-G's main roles was to report and eliminate instances of fraud, financial malpractice and corruption. So, although the role of the A-G was presented as one of independent verification and assurance, the darker side of the job originally was to perform the bloodhound role and seek out miscreants and corrupt practices involving the use of public money. But over the years the emphasis on catching the culprit in personal cases of fraud has tended to decline. In part this is due to the growth in size of the Australian Public Service (making the identification of individuals increasingly difficult) and in part because of greater administrative regulations and, later, more sophisticated computer systems which served to minimize opportunities for fraud. The Audit Office instead prefers to review internal audit control systems, financial and management information systems in order to eliminate possibilities of non-compliance or malfeasance. Individual fraud cases are still referred to the relevant authorities to initiate criminal proceedings, but the overwhelming orientation of the Audit Office is the move away from the 'gotcha mentality' in public auditing to an ethos of improving internal systems of assurance to prevent suspect behaviour — a philosophy that would presumably guide any investigation into cases of ministerial abuse.

Role the Auditor-General Plays in Scrutinizing Ministerial Behaviour

Until recently, Auditors-General have not played a major role in scrutinizing the behaviour of ministers. Moreover, Auditors-General have rarely attempted to clarify their powers in relation to the auditing of ministers. So what held the auditors back? Several factors are often seen as constraining the A-G from engaging in ministerial investigations of a more substantive nature.

Australia, along with many other Westminster-derived systems, traditionally operated with a mixture of statutes and conventions. It could be argued the Audit Act 1901 was one of the main factors inhibiting Auditors-General from investigating ministers, but neither the original Act nor its subsequent amendments specifically prohibited the A-G from investigating ministers (or other parliamentarians). Section 14 of the original Act states that the A-G is 'authorized and required to examine upon oath declaration of affirmation ... all persons whom he shall think fit to examine respecting the receipt or expenditure of money or any stores respectively affecting the provisions of this act'. A subsequent section (s. 14(b), inserted in 1948 and amended again in 1969) stated that the A-G shall have 'full and free access to all accounts, books, documents and papers in the possession of (a) any authority established or appointed under any law of the Commonwealth; (b) any officer or employee under the control of any such authority; and (c) any other person'. Such clauses applied to those areas of public administration that auditors *could* audit, though they did not appear to exempt ministers.

One area of the public sector explicitly excluded from the Audit Act in 1961 was the parliamentary refreshment rooms. Section 2A(3) stated: 'The provisions of this Act do not apply to or in relation to affairs and transactions (including the receipt or expenditure of money) in relation to the Parliamentary Refreshment Rooms except affairs of transactions involving expenditure of moneys for the purpose of which the Consolidated Revenue Fund has been appropriated.' Nevertheless, this specific amendment does not provide a general statutory exemption of ministerial entitlements under the Act.

Under the new Auditor-General Act 1997, the A-G has a wide mandate to audit Commonwealth agencies, authorities, companies and subsidiaries. The Act specifies the main functions of the A-G as twofold: auditing financial statements and conducting performance audits. Moreover, the A-G can audit any Commonwealth entity 'at any time' and can also ask the responsible minister, the Finance Minister or the Joint Committee of Public Accounts and Audit to request a particular audit of an entity. While the main provisions of the Act relate principally to legal entities (agencies, authorities and companies), other sections refer to 'any person or body', which has been interpreted to include ministers. Hence, it is clear that the A-G's core responsibilities are to audit the various listed public sector entities and activities. But it is also apparent that ministers and parliamentarians (as persons) are *not* excluded from the scope of the Act and, depending on the circumstances, their activities (including information they may have) are now clearly within the A-G's powers of investigation. So, although not specifically mentioned by the Act, ministers and ministerial activities can now become the target of investigation.

More persuasively, the powers of the A-G are limited by parliamentary privilege and the immunities enjoyed by members of each House of Parliament. The A-G may not use his/her powers so as to breach or infringe parliamentary privilege, but this statutory protection (under the Parliamentary Privileges Act 1987) may not cover *all* circumstances involving ministers, nor may an A-G's request for information from a minister necessarily be in breach of privilege. Ministerial offices, however, since the proclamation of the Members of Parliament (Staff) Act 1984, are exempt from falling under the A-G's mandate for the purposes of performance auditing. This provision is repeated in the Auditor-General's Act 1997, which states that a general capacity to undertake performance audits of agencies 'is taken not to include any persons who are employed or engaged under the Members of Parliament (Staff) Act 1984 and who are allocated to the Agency' (s. 15).

In addition, it appears that certain conventional understandings of Crown privilege or 'public interest immunity' have meant that many political participants and observers generally considered ministers beyond the purview of the A-G's mandate. Such conventional understandings of the 'area of ministerial provenance' may have discouraged Auditors-General from attempting to investigate ministerial behaviour, perhaps because they regarded ministers as outside their mandate. Indeed, some Auditors-General have gone on record as saying that they considered the ministerial and 'political' area to be outside their scope, and something they kept 'well out of' (Craik, 1980, p. 2).

Certainly, from the written documentation, Auditors-General have not reported much on matters involving ministerial behaviour or ethics since Federation. Excluding the decade of the 1990s, one could be forgiven for believing that successive Auditors-

General have shown little inclination to initiate or pursue an investigation into ministerial practice and ethics off their own bat.[6] Moreover, when traditional forms of auditing of agencies, programmes or administrative practices have in the course of investigation touched on ministerial involvement the A-G has generally either excluded such considerations from the final recommendations or not commented on ministerial behaviour *per se*.

But such conventions have been challenged in recent years with the intention of opening up a somewhat more significant role for the A-G in auditing the ethical behaviour of Commonwealth ministers, especially in relation to their expense claims and uses of public funds for official purposes. John Taylor (A-G from 1988 to 1995) did attempt to introduce a US-style system of ministerial ethics but was frustrated by the total lack of support in Canberra. He recalled that, 'I took this little thing around with me (a US General Accounting Office ethical code) whenever I could talk to anybody about ministerial ethics and the framework in which it could operate. I couldn't go into a minister's office, I had no power to go into a minister's office and inspect papers ... I don't think I had a hope of implementing anything significant in relation to a ministerial ethics framework' (Taylor, 2000).

The new Act does clarify some aspects of ministerial provenance. In relation to financial or assurance audits the ministerial office is not specifically excluded. Furthermore, Div. 3 s. 20 of the legislation specifically gives the A-G the power to undertake audits 'by arrangement with any person or body'. Already legal advice and a particular precedent (the Health Minister Michael Wooldridge) indicates this can include ministers (if they secure ministerial agreement). Section 20(1) of the Act states that:

> The Auditor-General may enter into an agreement with any person or body:
> (a) to audit financial statements of the person or body; or
> (b) to conduct a performance audit of the person or body, or
> (c) to provide services to the person or body that are of a kind commonly performed by auditors.

The only limitation to this power is that the A-G must not perform functions under s. 20(1) 'for a purpose that is outside the Commonwealth's legislative power'. This limitation was included to prevent the Commonwealth A-G straying into state or interjurisdictional affairs and to prevent the A-G operating as a private business. The limitation, however, does not exclude ministers or their offices. The new Act also extends the definition of minister of state to include the Speaker of the House and President of the Senate as ministers.

Audit of Ministers by Ministerial Invitation

There is no statutory or formal mechanism preventing ministers from requesting the A-G to investigate matters in which they have had a hand. However, while ministerial requests for audit investigations into agencies or programmes are reasonably frequent (and occur regularly for some organizations), it is hard to find any evidence where the A-G was requested by ministers to investigate *themselves* until 1997. Since 1997 there have been just two requests from ministers to investigate ministerial behaviour.

There are two ways by which ministers can request (but not direct) the A-G to investigate their behaviour. First, the prime minister and/or Finance Minister have the power to request the A-G to investigate matters in another portfolio that may involve another serving minister. Second, ministers are at liberty to write to the A-G requesting an investigation into matters where they personally may be involved or implicated. In both cases, such action may be taken for a variety of reasons. A prime minister or minister may wish to be seen to be transparent and publicly accountable, or they may hope to have the A-G exonerate their behaviour or that of their personal and/or departmental staff. The minister may be embarrassed by a scandal and consider an independent audit report the least damaging way out. To date, there have been two requests: the first from Prime Minister John Howard in 1997 and the second from Health Minister Michael Wooldridge in 1999.

On 24 September 1997 Prime Minister John Howard requested the A-G to conduct an investigation into matters relating to ministerial travel allowance claims. The prime minister's request was made amid accusations of impropriety raised about the travel claims lodged by the then Minister for Transport and Regional Development, John Sharp. The A-G was somewhat reluctant to undertake the audit, not because it involved a minister but because he considered an efficiency audit under the Audit Act 1901 would or could not reveal anything likely to be of benefit. But judging the matter to be sufficiently in the public interest, he responded to the prime minister's request by advising that the inquiry would involve the examination of 'any actions carried out by, or on behalf of, a minister which had any bearing on the operations of the relevant departments' (Australian National Audit Office (ANAO), 1997, p. xiv). He also reminded the government, however, that his 'statutory functions did not extend to examining the operations of a minister or a minister's office other than as they related to the conduct of the audit' (ANAO, 1997, p. xiv). While most of the A-G's findings centred around the lack of appropriate administrative systems in processing ministerial travel claims, the Audit Office was critical of the personal role the minister had played. The A-G went as far as to say that in a number of instances Sharp 'incorrectly' certified that he was entitled to a travel allowance — a damning finding which stopped short of accusing the minister of fraud. Sharp was found not to have taken due care in making travel claims. The A-G also warned all ministers that before lodging claims 'ministers should ensure that they are correct' (ANAO, 1997, p. xviii).

At that time, systems of payment of ministerial entitlements and reimbursement of expenses (separate from departmental expenses) were handled by ministers themselves through a self-authorizing procedure, assisted by their personal staff. Often a small unit was attached to the Prime Minister's department to process the claims and report totals. Historically, these amounts were relatively small but could still be audited. Over time the amounts involved increased while the system of checking and monitoring remained lax. Following the scandal of the 1997 'Travel Rorts' affair (see Tiernan, Chapter 8), responsibility for ministerial entitlements and expenses was transferred to a unit in the Department of Finance and Administration (DoFA) that established new, relatively strict guidelines and reporting practices. The processing of ministerial claims for expenses is now audited by the ANAO.[7] In other words, the amounts claimed in ministerial expenses and receipts produced are now audited by the A-G, as are the internal processes of administration adopted by DoFA to process these claims. But the reasons for the expenses or the substance of the claims is not itself audited — the A-G has agreed to trust the word of the minister providing the correct disclosure procedure has been adopted.[8]

The second case involved a request made in October 1999 by the Minister for Health, Michael Wooldridge. The minister requested the A-G investigate a matter in which the minister was personally involved and which in effect asked the A-G to investigate aspects of the minister's behaviour. The matter related to the budget round of the previous year (May 1998) when the Commonwealth government announced arrangements to fund improved access to magnetic resonance imaging (MRI) services under the Medicare benefits scheme — after intense negotiation with representatives from the Royal College of Radiologists. By February 1999 questions were raised in the Senate and subsequently in the House of Representatives over a number of accusations and suggestions of 'inappropriate behaviour by various parties involved in the negotiation process' (ANAO, 2000, p. 11). The accusations centred on the excessive placement of orders for MRI machines before budget night by persons who had access to confidential information about the scheme to be announced in the budget — thus providing certain individuals with a financial advantage. On 18 October 1999 the minister requested the A-G conduct an audit into the 'probity of the processes surrounding the negotiation of the Agreement between the Government and the diagnostic imaging profession' (ANAO, 2000, p. 12). In particular, the request invited the A-G to investigate why a sudden influx of MRI orders had occurred just prior to the scheme being officially announced.

The unique aspect of this inquiry is that for the first time in history the A-G had required a minister to give evidence under oath — an agreed procedure with the minister. Following legal advice, the Audit Office had used s. 20(1) of the Auditor-General Act 1997 to enter into an agreement with the minister to acquire full and free access to the relevant documents and information and to engage in the necessary discussions with the minister and his staff. The investigation extended beyond the routine grounds of a s. 18 audit and invoked previously unused access and information-gathering powers. However, the main focus of the A-G's investigation remained on probity and process issues. In collecting evidence, the audit revealed differing accounts of events given by people under oath — which then raised questions about what the A-G should do when confronted with such different recollections of the events.

From one perspective, the MRI audit may have set a precedent whereby ministers may be personally interrogated by an auditor in the process of an audit investigation. However, the Audit Office does not consider the Wooldridge case a precedent, preferring to regard it as a last resort and not normal practice. In many ways, the MRI audit has increased expectations of the Audit Office so that when a comparable case occurs sometime in the future the office may well be asked whether it is going to use its s. 20(1) powers and, if not, why not.

Audit by ministerial invitation also begs the question how far can the A-G initiate an investigation without the minister's invitation. There may be many instances where matters under audit may involve the minister and where some questions of propriety or process are raised. Conventionally, were a minister to indicate that he/she did not wish to cooperate with the audit investigation the A-G would eschew that particular matter or redirect the line of investigation to focus the audit solely on administrative/ procedural matters. While the new Act enables the A-G to obtain information widely by directing 'a person' in writing to provide 'any information the Auditor-General requires' and if necessary to 'attend and give evidence before the Auditor-General or an authorised official' and 'produce to the Auditor-General any documents in the custody or under the control of the person' (s. 32(1)), these powers relate only to an A-G function. This section is not sufficiently encompassing to include ministers and their staff in their own right.

A scenario could conceivably unfold in which an A-G were to approach a minister to provide 'information or answers to questions' and for those to 'be verified or given on oath or affirmation'. Conceivably, the A-G could approach a minister and seek to put him/her under oath (which would bring them under the provisions of s. 32 of the Auditor-General Act 1997). Hence, the audit-related information-gathering powers of the A-G imply that the auditor can certainly approach ministers for information provided it relates to audit mandate functions. The A-G is empowered to write to ministers demanding information, and can seek to extract information orally from them under oath or affirmation.

Of course, ministers may elect to refuse to provide an oath or affirmation (claiming parliamentary privilege or ministerial provenance and challenging the specific provision that applies to ministers). But in circumstances where the A-G had formally directed they do so, a refusal to answer under oath could be either illegal or politically damaging to the minister concerned and erode his/her standing or credibility. The need to manage perceptions may force ministers increasingly to 'come clean' by providing the A-G with information and answers to questions under oath.

Performance Audits as a Means to Explore Ethical Behaviour by Ministers

The Royal Commission into Australian Government Administration (1976) recommended that the A-G's mandate be extended to encompass the ability to report on the efficiency and economy of government agencies. Subsequent legislative changes extended the powers of the A-G in 1979. Since that time the Audit Office has gradually moved away from solely concentrating on traditional concerns of probity and financial compliance to include also an ethos of accountability through performance and economic efficiency. Certainly, the main target of efficiency audits was routine administration in departments and agencies, but this extension of the A-G's powers may have increased (perhaps unintentionally) the possibility of the A-G investigating the ethical practices or integrity of ministers (e.g. the trajectory of the 'Sports Rorts' affair efficiency audit tabled in 1993).

The 1993 'Sports Rorts' affair became an infamous case in which an efficiency audit found irregularities in the administrative procedures of Ros Kelly, the then Minister for Arts, Sport, the Environment and Territories. A political row exploded between the then Keating Labor government and the Coalition over grant allocations from the *Community Cultural, Recreational and Sporting Facilities Program*. The unproven but ultimately damaging allegation was that she had 'interfered with the due process of public administration and exercised her ministerial influence' for political party purposes (Uhr, 1998b, p. 153). As a result of an efficiency audit report tabled in 1993, the Opposition parties claimed that marginal government seats had received a disproportionate percentage of funding (ANAO, 1993, p. 11). The audit report, however, was more cautious in its findings. Other than making a brief statistical comparison to the percentage of Labor and Liberal seats that received funding, the auditor shied away from accusations of unethical conduct by concluding that the statistical analysis did not 'demonstrate one way or the other that projects were approved on party political grounds' (ANAO, 1993, p. 12).

Further claims of inappropriate conduct centred on the minister's lack of cooperation with the audit inquiry, the extent and use of departmental documentation in her ministerial office and incidents where the minister had ignored departmental advice. The A-G's report did not accuse the minister of impropriety. Rather, recommendations concentrated on the department's administration of the programme and improving the criteria upon which community cultural, recreation and sporting grants were allocated. The minister concerned eventually agreed to present evidence to a House of Representatives committee investigating the administrative procedures. She was ultimately damaged not as much by the audit report as by her own decisions to tough it out. Her admissions brought further embarrassment to her when she personally admitted allocating grants on a whiteboard in the minister's office. Under mounting political pressure she then elected to resign from office.

The Auditor-General Act 1997 now lists the main functions and powers of the A-G to conduct performance audits, special audits by arrangement and 'extra audits'. The general scope of these audits is directed toward Commonwealth organizations, but three important points arise from this statutory power. First, the A-G can initiate these types of audits independently without waiting for a request and without needing to obtain a court order to force people to comply with directions to provide information. Second, the A-G is required after undertaking these types of audits to 'bring to the attention of the responsible minister any important matter that comes to the attention of the Auditor-General'. The definition of 'important matter' being 'any matter that, in the Auditor-General's opinion, is important enough to justify it being brought to the attention of the responsible minister'. And, third, the A-G can undertake performance audits *by arrangement* with individuals or bodies (which has been interpreted as extending the potential scope of such audits subject to agreement). So, if in the process of conducting an audit the ANAO discovers some apparent anomalies, questionable procedures or unethical behaviour by the minister, the A-G is empowered to draw that matter to the attention of the responsible minister and approach the minister with the intention of arranging an agreement to audit the person. Moreover, the A-G is also able to draw such matters to the attention of the prime minister and/or Finance Minister and present a special report to parliament.

Conclusions

The degree to which the A-G can perform an effective accountability function in relation to ministerial behaviour is ambiguous. Much relies on agreements, interpretations of powers, understandings of conventions and the circumstances involved in particular cases. The new Act has significantly enhanced the role and power of the A-G in scrutinizing administrative and financial behaviours across the public sector, including in certain circumstances ministers themselves. However, if the A-G is to become more heavily involved in the scrutinizing of ministers, there is a significant risk that this will lead to the unfortunate politicization of the office of the Auditor-General, perhaps exposing the incumbent to invidious political situations or the risk of appearing as a pawn in a partisan conflict. Extending the A-G's investigations explicitly into the ministerial domain may indeed undermine the Audit Office's capacities to undertake the core responsibilities with which it is charged (the assurance and performance auditing of the public sector at large).

There are some fundamental problems in relying on the A-G to investigate incidences of ministerial breaches of accountability. There has been a reluctance in the past to explore this domain and uncertainty about the extent of the A-G's powers or mandate. Moreover, auditors may only operate within the audit function, and many issues of ministerial behaviour or ethics may fall outside such bounds (e.g. judicial or statutory appointments, discrimination, improper personal relations). In addition, if the A-G becomes more active in this respect, it may sour working relations with executive government and parliament, therefore inhibiting the A-G's effectiveness in scrutinizing public expenditure. This would most certainly be a 'high price to pay' for what is in effect an assurance function relating to a relatively minor aspect of public expenditure.

A better solution may be to place fewer expectations on the A-G by the establishment of a dedicated ministerial and parliamentary auditor.[9] This would not necessarily remove the A-G from the picture, but complement his/her endeavours with a specialist and equally independent office holder enjoying equivalent powers of investigation but narrower responsibilities. The role of a ministerial and parliamentary auditor, responsible to the parliament, could focus on financial matters and practices (allowances, entitlements, travel claims, etc.) but could entail a wider ethical mission.

The officer could also be used to investigate complaints almost as a specialist ombudsman, provide advice or counselling, and codify and monitor ethical standards for parliament as a whole. This position need only require a part-time officer and a small staff whose sole concern is the auditing of ministers, parliamentarians and their support staff. By appointing a parliamentary auditor, the parliament would allow the A-G to concentrate on improving financial accountability and issues of value for money in the broader public sector. And, the existence of a parliamentary auditor would arguably have a stronger deterrent effect on parliamentary and ministerial behaviour — and at least require adequate documentation to be maintained and procedures followed.

Notes

1 At Federation, the Head of State, High Court judges, the Crown Solicitor, the Auditor-General and the Public Service Commissioner were regarded as key public officials who should be provided with independent (constitutional-statutory) powers and other protections of their positions given they were (or could be) expected to form independent opinions. Later other statutory office holders and commissioners with independent powers were gradually added (e.g. the privacy commissioner, ombudsman).
2 The original Audit Act did not stipulate an appointment process or criteria for appointment for the A-G. The 1997 Act still requires the proposed appointee to be nominated by the executive but now also requires the responsible minister to seek the agreement of the Joint Committee of Public Accounts and Audit on the proposal.
3 The Audit Office has appeared under many different titles since its establishment in 1902. Initially the office was referred to as the Auditor-General's Department, occasionally the Federal Audit Office or Commonwealth Audit Office. In 1984 it became known as the Australian Audit Office, and in 1991 the Australian National Audit Office. This latter name is enshrined in the new Auditor-General Act 1997 and the office is established as a statutory authority in its own right for the first time.
4 The new Act requires that the A-G not disclose information in reports that 'would involve the disclosure of deliberations or decisions of the Cabinet or a Committee of the Cabinet' (s. 37(2b)). The wording of this clause suggests that the A-G may well come across information relating to the deliberations of federal cabinet (presumably only from ministers or the cabinet secretary) but that such confidential information should not be incorporated in the final report to parliament and/or the relevant minister. A further section allows the Attorney-General to issue the A-G with a certificate stating that in the opinion of the legal officer the disclosure of certain information 'would be contrary to the public interest for any of the reasons' set out in the Act (national security, cabinet confidentiality, prejudice of Commonwealth–state relations, unfairly prejudice commercial interests, or 'any other reason that could form the basis of a claim' to the courts) and that the information not be disclosed. However, should the Attorney-General prohibit disclosure, the A-G is required to state in the report that certain information has been omitted and provide the reasons given by the Attorney-General. The A-G is also able to issue a non-public report on the matters and present copies to the prime minister, the Finance Minister and the minister(s) responsible, if any.

5   The Members of Parliament (Staff) Act 1984 (in conjunction with the Financial Management and Accountability Act) provides that ministerial staff are exempt from performance audit by the A-G. Ministerial staff are employed by office holders (ministers) on behalf of the Commonwealth, and their remuneration is paid by separate appropriation provided to the department to which they are attached.
6   A former A-G, John Taylor, recalled that he had wanted to investigate the circumstances surrounding Paul Keating's investment in a piggery business — but although he may have wished to investigate, he did not proceed because he felt that 'I was in enough trouble already'. Other audit staff have different recollections, believing Taylor had never sought to proceed with such an investigation.
7   A memorandum of understanding (1998) and a protocol on ANAO access to cabinet documents (2000) have been negotiated between the DoFA and the ANAO relating to the auditors' access to information and records of the department. This protocol mainly concerns cabinet and confidential government decisions/papers and the streamlining of access or cooperation — but neither extends to ministerial offices or ministerial office correspondence.
8   In a subsequent audit in 1999 tabled in parliament on 3 February 2000 into the Cultural and Heritage Projects Program and the way in which it was administrated, the Audit Office reported that when ministers were asked to provide reasons for their decisions concerning successful grant applications it was two months before they responded. The ANAO noted: '... the Ministers have documented their reasons for approving successful applications, details of their reasons have not been made available for public release. It is difficult to engender confidence in a system of open and transparent decision-making, as part of a sound framework of public accountability, if access to documentation, explaining the reasons for approving particular projects, is not reasonably forthcoming' (ANAO, 1999–2000, p. 42).
9   One possible proposal of this type is the Auditor of Parliamentary Allowances and Entitlements Bill 2000 — a Bill for an Act to establish the office of Auditor of Parliamentary Allowances and Entitlements, and for related purposes. At the time of writing, the Bill is currently before the Senate Standing Committee on Finance and Public Administration Legislation.

Chapter 13

Ministerial Ethics and the Media

Stephen Tanner

Since the mid-1980s the Australian media spotlight has been regularly turned on to the behaviour of ministerial office holders. Via newspapers, television and radio, Australians have become accustomed to ministers, premiers and even prime ministers defending their own or colleagues' behaviour. In some cases the individuals were able to weather the political storm, in others they were forced to succumb to political pressures and resign their ministries, and in a small number of cases involving illegal, as opposed to unethical, conduct they were jailed. In all cases, the media played an important role in either exposing the behaviour or in covering the subsequent political and legal events that followed.

This chapter will argue that the media can play an important role in motivating ministers to act ethically. This capacity results from their 'fourth estate' or watchdog function by which they are able to monitor public office on behalf of voters. By pursuing such a role, the media is able to generate debate about appropriate ministerial standards. It will be contended that by focusing political and public attention on particular incidents the media can sometimes secure admissions of wrongdoing, occasionally even ministerial resignations. However, the chapter will use two case studies to demonstrate that the media's success can be limited and will depend upon a range of factors, including:

1. their ability to access information about the particular allegations;
2. their relationship with the individual who has been accused of an ethical breach;
3. how media 'savvy' that person is; and
4. the political consequences that attach to a particular incident.

Understanding the Media's Interest in Ethical Misdeeds

Central to liberal democratic theory is the view that members of parliament remain accountable to their electors and that they should not abuse their positions for personal or partisan advantage. Related to that is the belief that the media play an important watchdog role, informing electors of ethical breaches. The media work as a conduit, providing a two-way flow of information between voters and their elected representatives (Meyrowitz, 1993; White, 1989, p. 29). Not only do they inform electors of the apparent breach, and attempts by the politician to justify or explain his/her behaviour, but they can also provide MPs with the public's response through letters to the editor columns. Under this model the media's role is an important one — in addition to being informational they also help to ensure that the trust upon which liberal democracies depend for their legitimacy is maintained.

To appreciate the media's interest in ministerial ethics it is necessary to understand the relationship between politicians and journalists. This relationship has been widely documented over the years (Western, 1987; Greiner, 1993; Moore, 1993; Bennett, 1988; Sigal, 1973; Sabato, 1991). Often described as 'symbiotic' or 'parasitic' (Western, 1987), it is a relationship based on mutual need. For their part, journalists and media organizations need access to the information ministers have at their disposal. Equally, politicians depend on the media to publicize their achievements, their concerns and their criticisms of each other. Without the news media, publicity would be prohibitively difficult and expensive to obtain. As well, without access to politicians, the media's newsgathering and dissemination role (and especially its watchdog functions) would be fraught with difficulties, particularly given the time and legal constraints under which journalists operate (Tanner, 1999a, p. 80). Some of these problems were particularly noticeable in the two case studies selected for this chapter.

The Background

The Metherell Affair

The background to the Metherell affair has been widely documented (Tanner 1998, 1999a, 1999b, 1999c; Gleeson *et al.*, 1992; Independent Committee Against Corruption (ICAC), 1992a, b). Briefly, the crisis developed when New South Wales (NSW) Premier Nick Greiner agreed that a former ministerial colleague-turned-Independent MP, Terry Metherell, be appointed to a $110 000-a-year position in the NSW Environment Protection Authority (EPA), allegedly to create a parliamentary vacancy the government expected to win. While not that different from a host of other 'jobs for the boys' appointments that had characterized Australian politics for decades, in this case it generated a strong outcry. The outcry could be attributed to a number of factors. First and foremost was a perception that when campaigning for office Greiner had eschewed jobs for the boys. Journalists and Greiner's political opponents believed the premier had breached this promise when appointing Metherell. Second, they believed that he had supported the appointment to shore up the government's hold on office, not because of any particular qualifications Metherell might bring to the position. And while he could fall back on a moral justification for the appointment, namely that Metherell was elected as a Liberal, and thus he was simply restoring the balance of the house, he still had to contend with the argument that he was acting in a self-serving manner and thus had breached the trust placed in him by the people of NSW.

The appointment was ultimately investigated by the ICAC, which found that Greiner and his Environment Minister, Tim Moore, had acted corruptly (see Fleming, Chapter 11). While they were subsequently cleared by the NSW Supreme Court, their political fates had already been decided by the non-aligned independents who held the balance of power in the NSW lower house.[1] The Independents demanded — and secured — their resignations as premier and minister respectively, arguing that if they did not resign, they would support a proposed Opposition no-confidence motion which would have led to a change of government. In demanding their resignations, the Independents said the decision to appoint Metherell was a clear breach of the higher standards Greiner had promised the people of NSW when campaigning in 1988.

Kennett — Share Trading on the Side

In 1997 Victorian Premier Jeff Kennett had been accused by Stephen Mayne, a former press secretary to the then Treasurer, Alan Stockdale, of using his position to buy shares in floats that had previously closed. The two purchases — 50 000 shares in Guangdong Corporation and 20 000 shares in Arthur Yates and Co, a horticulture company — had been bought in the name of the premier's wife, Felicity. Mayne made his allegations on the Australian Broadcasting Corporation (ABC) programme *'Four Corners'*, claiming that the premier had arranged the purchases even though there had been public announcements that both floats had closed. The intimation was that Kennett had used his position as premier to purchase shares that were not available to members of the broader community, and thus he had used his public office for personal gain. However, Kennett was in a different position from Greiner when responding to the allegations. First, he had not been elected on a promise to clean up public sector standards. Second, whereas Greiner was forced to resign because he did not control the balance of power in the parliament, Kennett was under no such pressure. He commanded a clear majority in both Houses and thus was able to take a different approach when dealing with his political foes and journalists. This was confirmed when Kennett weathered his political storm, but Greiner and Moore became victims of theirs.

Managing the Issues

The two issues provide important contrasts in approaches to media management by political leaders forced to deal with ethical problems. Metherell's resignation from parliament and appointment to the EPA were announced at a press conference, on a Saturday morning, after parliament had risen for its Easter recess and when senior political journalists were expected to be on leave. Greiner and Moore had expected some outcry, but believed the issue would die after a few days. Instead, the issue spiralled out of control, with four major newspapers publishing 940 articles on this issue over its four and a half month lifespan (Tanner, 1999a). One reason why this issue developed was the government's decision not to provide journalists with information about the appointment process. Tim Moore refused to talk to journalists once the press conference had concluded, and Greiner played down his role. He also tried to convince journalists that the proper processes were followed and that Metherell was qualified for the position. However, given the numbers in the parliament, the journalists had a range of other sources they could turn to in order to develop the story (including the Opposition, Independent members of parliament and Greiner's colleagues who were irate at not being told about the appointment). One of these sources, Independent member Clover Moore (no relation to Tim), proved a major ally for the media.

Whereas Greiner and Tim Moore refused to bow to journalists' requests for detail about the appointment process, they could not deny Clover Moore's request for the information, given the power she wielded in the parliament. When she received the information Moore passed it on to the media. This information not only reinforced journalists' views that Metherell had received preferential treatment, but further inflamed the political situation, meaning that the government would struggle to control the issue, particularly once Greiner succumbed to calls for an inquiry.

While the political situation in NSW meant that Greiner would struggle to tough out his situation, in Victoria Kennett was able to adopt a much stronger stance. Immediately the story was aired he went on the attack, criticizing the media and accusing Mayne of disloyalty (*The Sydney Morning Herald (SMH)*, 25 September, p. 9). Both Kennett and his press secretary claimed that the allegations aired on the programme were not new, having first been aired and dismissed in 1993. They painted it as a non-story — much the same as Greiner and Moore had attempted to do. But in this case, Kennett successfully thwarted the media's attempts to develop the story. In doing so he was aided by the fact that:

1. He wasn't holding government documents that might have undermined his case;
2. He did not have to deal with independents;
3. The incident was not seen as an attempt to shore up his hold on office; and
4. He was much tougher in his relationship with the media. Nonetheless, he was accused of using his public office for private gain.

Kennett was also aided by the fact that key sources refused to talk to the media or, if they did, said nothing to undermine the premier's argument. Two of these sources, the managing director and chairman of Guangdong Corporation, and the stockbroker who provided the Yates shares, refused to answer journalists' questions and denied that he had been granted preferential treatment (*The Age*, 9 September, p. 4). The premier was aided, perhaps unintentionally, by a story in *The Age* featuring a statement from a stockbroker not associated with either float who said that the preferential distribution of shares was not unusual and that the Guangdong and Yates prospectuses both included a clause that permitted such allocations. This meant that journalists were forced to rely on the original source of the allegations, Stephen Mayne, and the predictable political response from the Opposition. Their only hope of the issue developing an extended political life was if other former advisers or disaffected public servants were prepared to come forward with more information against the premier. But these were not forthcoming.

Reactions to the Metherell Appointment

While the initial reactions of journalists to the Metherell appointment were mixed, within a few days there appeared to be a unanimous view among newsroom staff that the appointment was wrong and should be condemned. The tenor of the media's attitude to the appointment is reflected in the first editorials. The *SMH*, for example, described it as 'an outrageous political appointment' that some people would see as a 'grubby attempt to hold on to power'. It also referred to the 'shabbiness' of the appointment, describing it as 'an ill-conceived deal' and 'an extraordinary deal' (14 April 1992, p. 10). The *Daily Telegraph Mirror (DTM)* described it as 'outrageous' and a 'cosy little deal' (14 April 1992, p. 10). *The Australian* was equally critical, describing it as 'ham fisted', 'inept', 'abysmal politics' and 'hypocritical' (14 April 1992, p. 10). These initial reactions set the tone for subsequent editorials. In fact the attitudes of editorial writers were reflected in the descriptors they employed to portray the appointment and the involvement of the key players therein. The newspapers quickly adopted the pejorative 'affair' and 'deal' to describe the appointment and its aftermath. They did not, however, use the suffix 'gate' as has been the tendency among the US media organizations when describing scandals.

Two key themes emerged in the media's coverage of the appointment:

1. it was a political appointment and a poorly orchestrated one at that; and
2. it involved a breach of promise that would undermine Greiner's carefully nurtured reputation for political probity.

In relation to the second theme, the attitude of journalists was encapsulated in the *DTM's* first editorial. It said:

> Lest we forget, Greiner arrived in 1988 with a clear pledge to clean up the political game in NSW, to knock rorts on the head and ban jobs for the girls and boys. Roughly, four years later he is capping a record of providing an employment agency for Liberals by giving Metherell a senior posting in the Environment Protection Authority (14 April 1992, p. 10).

These views were also reflected in the general news stories. The attitude of journalists was captured by Matthew Moore when he said that the premier's involvement was: 'proof that at the end of the day Greiner is just like the rest of them — he'd sell his grandmother if he thought it might keep him in power' (*SMH*, 13 April 1992, p. 2). Taking a similar approach, Jeni Cooper described the appointment as 'cynical politics at its worst' (*The Australian*, 14 April 1992, p. 1). Moore said that journalists felt aggrieved because they had believed Greiner was 'somehow different, but that at the end of the day he wasn't' (*SMH*, 13 April 1992, p. 2).

Early media coverage painted a picture of a government under siege. Journalists wrote about the demands being placed on the government by the independents and Opposition, of the premier's own internal problems with his coalition colleagues, and of whisperings about his hold on the leadership. Significantly, they also highlighted the fact that in appointing Metherell to the EPA the premier had not conferred with his ministerial colleagues (other than Moore). Nor had he discussed the appointment with his senior advisers. Journalists saw this as evidence of his political inadequacies.

Media images of a government reeling from a problem of its own making were further highlighted during the inquiry phase. It was inevitable that the media would focus on the inquiry. First, it was easy journalism. That is, the journalists would be treated to a daily diet of high-profile political figures appearing before a quasi-judicial body. With all witnesses hiring high-powered legal teams, it was equally inevitable that the exchanges between lawyer and politician would become heated. Second, there was a sense of irony in the fact that Greiner was appearing before an anti-corruption commission that he had established as one of his first priorities after winning government to clean up public sector standards in NSW. It was a classic example of an MP being tripped up by his own stated standards.

While media organizations devoted enormous space to coverage of the pre inquiry and inquiry phases, perhaps the most important coverage of this issue from an ethics perspective was of the post inquiry period when the ICAC had handed down its report. At that time there was considerable debate in the opinion columns and editorials as to whether the ICAC's decision was appropriate or not. During that period, there was some support for Greiner's claim that he was only technically corrupt, particularly among editorial writers (*SMH*, 25 June 1992, p. 22; *The Australian*, 20–21 June 1992, p. 18). They said there was a need to distinguish between the narrow definition of 'corrupt conduct' as contained in the ICAC's governing legislation and the more popular views. In fact three of the four newspapers argued that the premier was not corrupt as the term is popularly understood. For example, the *SMH* argued: 'The premier is not corrupt, and his actions in the Metherell affair do not amount to corruption as most people would understand it' (*SMH*, 20 June 1992, p. 22). Editorial writers even pointed out that his conduct was no different from that of his predecessors (*SMH*, 30 June 1992, p. 12; *The Australian*, 20–21 June 1992, p. 18), with *The Australian Financial Review (AFR)* describing such appointments as the 'meat and drink of real politik' (*AFR*, 22 June 1992, p. 18).

Despite this show of sympathy, the newspapers argued that Greiner would be forced to resign. They said he would have to do this to ensure that the government stayed in office. The attitude of editorial writers, and of some journalists who covered the inquiry, was captured by the *AFR*, which described Greiner as fitting the 'classic definition of the tragic hero'. It also described him as 'a man of basic decency who, under pressure from a score of directions, is fatally tempted to cross the line of acceptable behaviour and ends up betraying himself and his cause' (*AFR*, 25 June 1992, p. 16). The *SMH* said that even if Greiner was able to hold on to office, the 'corrupt' tag would stay with him and prevent him from maintaining his reform program (*SMH*, 20 June 1992, p. 22).

Interestingly, media interest in the Metherell affair appeared to ease following Greiner's forced resignation as premier, even though his appeal to the NSW Supreme Court was still to be heard. This highlights the media's recognition of the practical political outcomes of such issues. Media interest may have been maintained had the non-aligned independents allowed Greiner and Moore their day in court. However, with a new government in place the issue had lost its potency, other than in terms of the possible consequences for the ICAC and the potential lessons to be learned by future generations of MPs.

Treating the Media with Contempt — Kennett

Despite the short lifespan of the shares issue (barely a week), Jeff Kennett still had to weather a series of negative stories. Perhaps the strongest criticism of the premier was published in an *Age* editorial. It accused him of being 'evasive' when questioned about the allegations (25 September 1997, p. 16). *The Age* argued that if Kennett had received the Yates shares after the float had closed then his conduct was 'inappropriate'. The editorial argued:

> Whether the Premier's requests in fact received special consideration is not the primary issue; what matters is whether his actions can be construed as taking advantage of his office.

The Australian said the premier 'had a case to answer', arguing that his previous explanations to parliament about the share transactions had been contradicted by Mayne's account (27–28 September 1997, p. 18). The *SMH* said the premier's refusal to discuss the allegations with the media: 'simply feeds the suspicion that [he] is running away from questions he does not want to answer' (24 September 1997, p. 14). The two Fairfax papers in particular were critical of Kennett from the outset, highlighting the fact that he had hosted a function at Parliament House to coincide with the launch of the Guangdong float. The *SMH* said this pointed to the unorthodox ways in which business was done between the government and the private sector in Victoria. The *SMH* said that a photo opportunity on the steps of Parliament House featuring the premier and directors of Guangdong Corp 'could have provided a handy leg-up to the share price — and thus to the Kennett family's private interests'

(27 September 1997, p. 38). The *SMH* and *The Age* both ran stories detailing how the share allocations in the Guangdong float set aside for two Victorian state government agencies had been 'mysteriously cut back'. While the intimation was that this had been to accommodate the premier, the papers also quoted a spokesperson from the Australian Securities Commission (ASC) who said that the premier's shares were believed to have come out of the directors' personal holdings and therefore there had been no impropriety (*SMH*, 27 September 1997, p. 38). To reinforce further the argument that there might well be a conflict of interest involved, the *SMH* said Mayne had claimed that stockbrokers and banks made $250 million out of the Victorian government's privatization program. It also gave another example, alleging that Kennett had used his contacts to put together a rescue package for a company in which his wife and sons held 80 000 shares. The bail-out was said to have involved media tycoon Kerry Stokes (27 September 1997, p. 38b). *The Age* and *The Australian* published a story in which it was alleged that Kennett had used his contacts in the media to have an earlier story on the Yates share deal pulled shortly before it was due to go to air (*The Age*, 23 September 1997, p. 2; *The Australian*, 23 September 1997, p. 1). There was also an intimation in some stories of an inappropriate link between Kennett and Bruce Mathieson, the owner of a large number of gaming machines in Victoria and also the chairman of Sino Securities, the company managing the Guangdong float.

These stories certainly give the impression that Kennett may have acted inappropriately and was using his position for personal gain. Given that, it is significant that media organizations did not tag the Kennett share story with 'scandal', 'corruption' or 'crisis' tags. It was referred to as the Kennett shares 'deal', but nothing more emotive. Nor were there calls for him to stand down (apart from predictable statements from the Opposition leader), or any serious discussion about the story affecting his hold on government or the leadership. This probably reflects the belief on the part of journalists that the story posed no threat to his leadership or to the government.

Despite this, there were a number of themes to emerge from the media's coverage of the issue. The first had to do with his relationship with the media. Sections of the media argued that in refusing to answer journalists' questions, Kennett was denying them the right to perform a traditional watchdog role (*The Australian*, 24 September 1997, p. 2). A number of journalists and letter writers argued that Kennett had used his power to stifle informed comment and dissent. One way he had achieved this, it was argued, was by intimidating critics. This was confirmed by Mayne, who responded to media criticism of him for waiting four years before going public with his allegations. He said there were a number of reasons for the delay. The first was that at the time of the share deals he did not have all the information. More important, however, was fear of the 'inevitable public backlash against him'. He said: 'Kennett's media culture is so aggressive. I thought that taking this step would put too much pressure on me and my job'. Mayne did not make the allegations until he was leaving Victoria for a job in NSW. Writing in *The Australian*, Nicholas Way said Kennett's tactic of shooting the messenger 'was a tactic that had worked and worked well for the premier: studiously ignore any substance to allegations of impropriety and lambast the organ carrying the message'.

While Kennett denied any impropriety, the media reminded readers that he did not have a good record on such issues. For example, *The Australian* said that the previous year he had rejected Opposition calls for all ministers to place shares in a blind trust so as to avoid any conflicts of interest. *The Australian* even quoted one un-named former Kennett minister who said that voters had not punished the premier electorally for his behaviour because he had 'conditioned them to expect lower ethical standards of politicians' (27–28 September 1997, p. 23). This was different from the situation in NSW under Greiner. It may help to explain the different reactions of journalists in Victoria and NSW to their respective stories. Rather than show contrition for his actions, as Greiner and Moore had belatedly done in an attempt to appease the independents and voters, Kennett thumbed his nose at his detractors, telling them that the 'Four Corners' story had inspired him to re-enter the stock market. He also attacked the media, claiming that his family had suffered in a material sense because of his 21 years in politics. He said:

> At the end of the day, you [journalists] would have us work seven days a week, 24 hours a day for one and sixpence and you don't care a damn what happens to our families or to our financial position (*The Australian*, 26 September 1997, p. 3).

Whereas the media's coverage of the Metherell affair was a case study into the appropriateness of the appointment, coverage of the Kennett share story focused primarily on Kennett's personality and his relationship with the media. For example, *The Age* published a cartoon showing a signpost, one arrow pointing to Victoria, and another, in the opposite direction, to democracy, free speech and open government (24 September 1997, p. 4) The focus on Kennett's personality was particularly noticeable in news stories and editorials. For example, writing in *The Age*, Kendall Hill said the premier had showed 'no visible signs of distress' (27 September, p. 3). *The Australian* also editorialized on this issue, arguing: 'But no-one will be surprised if he manages to tough it out'. It said: 'The obstinacy and brazenness he displays under attack are the other side of the Kennett can-do coin.' Shane Green, writing in *The Age*, said that the allegations were not enough to make or break the premier on the eve of his fifth anniversary in office (27 September 1997, p. 25). Green argued that, in the absence of a permanent anti-corruption body like the NSW ICAC or the Queensland-based Criminal Justice Commission, there was 'nowhere for the matter to go'. One of *The Australian's* journalists also noted that Kennett's federal colleagues recognized his ability to weather such attacks almost unscathed. He said it was: 'a mark of his political skill that he has been able to transform what might be perceived as a fatal flaw in other leaders into part of his winning package of positive entrepreneurial larrikinism' (27–28 September 1997, p. 23). Journalists pointed to the fact that rather than prompting calls for his resignation, Kennett had taken the initiative and suggested that he might take early retirement, although he had refused to nominate a departure date, the intimation being that his departure would be of greater cost to the people of Victoria than any personal benefit accrued from the shares (*The Australian*, 27–28 September 1997, p. 2).

Significantly, *The Australian* defended Kennett's behaviour towards the media, suggesting that *The Age* and the ABC had treated him as a 'buffoon' since the time of his election as Opposition leader 10 years earlier. It could also be argued that the newspapers were mischievous in some aspects of their coverage of this issue. For example, some stories reminded readers of earlier conflicts of interest involving the premier or his family. These included allegations over favouritism meted out to the premier's former advertising agency and his wife's free use of a $100 000 BMW motor car.

The Feedback Loop — Letters to the Editor

Earlier it was suggested that the media provided a two-way flow of information between ministers and voters. While media coverage of these two issues indicates clearly that journalists were critical of both Greiner and Kennett, it is often difficult to ascertain whether the views of journalists are representative of those in the wider community. One important indicator of community attitudes — for journalists and politicians alike — is the letters to the editor column. In the case of the Metherell affair it has been suggested that journalists responded to, rather than led, community sentiment (ICAC, 1992a). The letters to the editor column showed mixed attitudes towards the appointment (Tanner, 1999c). While the overwhelming proportion was critical of Greiner, there were others that supported him. Perhaps importantly, there was a significant number of letters that criticized the media's coverage of the story.

While there were only a small number of letters to the editor on the Kennett share deal, the views contained therein were also mixed. Kennett received some support from two senior public figures — one a former premier, the other the head of a business lobby group — who wrote letters to *The Age* complaining that they had been invited under false pretences to participate in the programme in which the allegations were aired. They said they were told the purpose of the programme was to discuss Kennett's first five years as premier. They were angered when their positive comments about the premier were not included in the programme. Generally, however, letters tended to be critical of Kennett and reflected the criticisms of the premier contained in news and opinion pieces.

Conclusion

The task confronting the media when covering political scandals, particularly those involving breaches of codes of conduct, is a difficult one. Nonetheless, as this chapter shows, the media can play an important role by generating debate about appropriate ministerial standards and by focusing attention on the behaviour in question. While in the case of the Metherell affair the media can hardly claim credit for the resignations of Greiner and Moore, journalists nonetheless played an important role in looking at the minutiae, including the appropriateness of defined standards. In this case the media were able to remind the premier, Moore and members of the wider community of Greiner's promise when campaigning for office, namely that he would improve ethical standards among ministers. The media's coverage of the Metherell affair also provided an important warning to ministers and their leaders: if you campaign on a platform that includes the promise of improved standards, make sure that you and your colleagues can meet those standards. It contained a second warning: make sure that the new standards are unambiguous. One of the difficulties Greiner experienced in seeking to justify the Metherell appointment was in convincing people that he was not compromising the promised standards. As many of the stories and at least half the letters to the editor on this issue showed, journalists and readers were not necessarily convinced by his arguments. His actions were perceived as self-serving.

In many respects the Kennett story provides stronger evidence of the difficulties confronting media organizations when covering ethical issues. Whereas Greiner had defined the standards by which he was to be judged, and thereby provided the public and journalists with the necessary benchmarks, in the Kennett case there was no such hook for media organizations. Because Kennett had not promised new standards of conduct, journalists were obliged to apply the traditional standards. These standards tended to be vague and subjective and couched in terms that highlighted the need for public trust in ministerial office holders and the need for leaders to serve the voters, rather than use public office for personal gain. The absence of clearly defined standards thus made it easier for Kennett to defend himself and added to the problems confronting journalists.

This clear distinction aside, both case studies also reveal some of the logistical hurdles journalists confront when trying to cover stories such as these. In the case of the Metherell affair the media's task was hindered early on by the failure of journalists to obtain important information about the appointment process. Early coverage of the Metherell affair shows how governments can control the flow of information. Once that information was released to the independents, who then passed it on to journalists, the government began to lose control of the issue. In this, the media's coverage of the Metherell affair — and thus its effectiveness as a watchdog of ministerial standards — can be contrasted with the coverage of the Kennett share deal. With the Kennett story, the media's attempts to expose the premier's share dealings as a misuse of office for personal gain failed when the information flow dried up.

In the latter case, journalists also had to confront a media-savvy premier, one who held them in low regard. Kennett's skills provided a stark contrast to those of Greiner and Moore, even though their early approaches to media management were similar. While this meant that the media struggled to perform an effective watchdog role in relation to the Kennett shares affair, one important conclusion does emerge. In their coverage of both stories, it was clear that the media respected institution and office, it was the individual they found wanting. As such, it is possible to argue that even if the media are not always successful in gaining political scalps in instances where it believes ministerial standards have been breached, they can still fulfil an important role in helping to ensure that ministers act ethically and acknowledge their accountability to the electorate.

One other point of contrast between the two case studies further highlights the difficulties confronting the media when covering ethical issues, namely the political consequences that attach to a particular incident. In the case of the Metherell affair it was obvious from the outset that the issue had the potential to bring down the government. This provided the media with a clear incentive to follow the story through to its conclusion. The Kennett share story, on the other hand, at no time appeared to threaten the premier's hold on government. Indeed there was evidence that some media coverage of the story was mischievous and inspired more by a dislike of the premier by journalists and media organizations than a genuine belief that he had seriously transgressed expected ethical standards. Nonetheless, the media's coverage of this story does show how a watchdog media can effectively raise questions about the appropriateness of particular conduct and, in the process, encourage members of the wider community to consider that behaviour.

Finally, it can be argued that the media played an important role as a feedback loop between electors and their representatives by publishing the views of readers in letters to the editor columns. In both cases the letters to the editor columns provided an important forum for readers to contribute their views on the appropriateness or otherwise of the conduct in question. While Kennett, Greiner or Moore might have ignored the views expressed, there is some evidence to suggest — at least in the Metherell case — that journalists were monitoring the views. Because of this, other ministers might use these columns as a barometer of popular opinion.

While this chapter looked specifically at two Australian case studies, it is contended that the conclusions drawn can be applied more widely. The relationship between politicians and journalists in other Western liberal democracies is similar to that which exists in Australia. Likewise, journalists and media organizations in other countries adhere to a watchdog role, and take seriously their obligation to ensure that ministers adhere to designated standards. Despite the constraints mentioned, if they continue to adopt a watchdog function and report upon possible breaches, then they will help to ensure that at least some ministers remain ethical.

Note

1   When Greiner won office in 1988 it was with a clear majority. While he was expected to be comfortably returned to power in 1991, the electors delivered a shock result, handing the balance of power to four Independent MPs. Greiner, who still commanded the largest single block of seats in the parliament, was able to hold on to government, but only with the support of the Independents. This meant that he had to negotiate before being able to pass his legislative programme, an outcome he found frustrating.

PART V:
MOTIVATING MINISTERIAL BEHAVIOUR

Chapter 14

Prior Advice is Better than Subsequent Investigation

Charles Sampford

This chapter argues that ethics reforms are stimulated by scandals whose subsequent investigation is massively diverting in time and energy. The various remedies that are tried — legal rules, public ethical standards or institutional reforms — cannot furnish a solution by themselves. To be effective they must be combined into an effective 'ethics regime' or 'integrity system' (Sampford, 1992). However, one of the most common reasons for not creating strong clear statements of political ethical standards is that they might later be used as a weapon against those who promulgated them. The problem lies not in the idea of ethical codes *per se* but in promulgating 'bare codes' of ethics without institutional backup. In particular, the creation of a credible 'ethics counsellor' or 'integrity commissioner' to provide prior advice on potential breaches of ethical codes could be a very effective means both of raising standards and of avoiding the scandals that lead to subsequent investigations. This chapter discusses some of the (still imperfect) institutions attempting to provide such advice, and some of the potential problems of political accountability and responsibility that arise from them.

The Love of Scandal

Ethics reforms are almost invariably prompted by political scandals. Accusations of wrongdoing are damaging to the individual and his/her party and demand from both a great deal of crisis management on the back foot. The media concentrate on seeking out culprits, individually or severally. Given the public perception of politicians, it is ironic that scandal is considered so newsworthy. If principled behaviour really were so rare, its news value would increase correspondingly, along the 'man bites dog' analogy. However, the media generally find it easier to report on stereotypes acting stereotypically.

Much less attention is devoted to institutional means to prevent such problems recurring.[1] The media show little interest in eliminating future scandals (which are, after all, their bread and butter) and the Opposition want to take the scalps of their individual opponents. To acknowledge that the system is flawed might be seen as an extenuating factor and might blur the political message that the government is in the wrong and the solution to the whole problem is simply to put the Opposition in power.

Ethics Regimes and the Prevention of Scandal

Much less attention is devoted to the means for preventing such problems arising in the future. Although after-the-event scandals may grab the headlines, preventive measures that protect against abuse of political office are clearly more important.

I have long argued that enforceable codes as a form of legal regulation are, on their own, largely ineffective in raising standards of institutional behaviour (Sampford, 1992, 1994; Sampford and Wood, 1993). They are useful as a backstop, at setting the minimum acceptable threshold, but will not help to raise conduct above that minimum. They have to be read narrowly to preserve the rights of the 'accused'; and if all ministers need do is to comply with the bare minimum, the code becomes more like tax legislation than a set of principles guiding their political behaviour. Accordingly, improving the standards of conduct of key participants requires an integrated approach which combines:

- ethical standard setting;
- legal regulation; and
- institutional reform.

The key to achieving this integration is the public 'justification' of the institution whose standards we are trying to improve. Such institutions begin by articulating the values or public benefits which that institution is meant to safeguard or promote — the *raison d'être* of the institution, the reason why it should continue to exist and why it deserves public support in one form or another. These values not only offer the core of the ethical standards, but also the principles underlying the legal regulation (and its interpretation) and the standards for assessing the design and performance of the institution.

Such an approach recognizes that institutional behaviour falls into a normative continuum from the highest standards, down through good work, to sub-par work, misconduct and outright criminality. This integrated strategy aims to raise standards of behaviour by, simultaneously, articulating ethical principles about what it means to be a good member, minister or staffer as the case may be and providing legal rules which provide sanctions for behaviour that falls so far below that standard as to deserve condemnation (this argument is further developed in Sampford and Blencowe, 2001).

Compliance regimes aim to ensure that minimum standards are not broken. By contrast, an ethics regime does not concentrate on the legal backstop but, more ambitiously, 'plays from the front' by seeking to improve standards. Ethics regimes add this positive dimension of articulating the highest, aspirational standards (and thus emphasize 'positive' rather than 'negative' ethics — see Sampford and Wood, 1993). The legally enforceable elements (and institutions in the style of the NSW Independent Commission Against Corruption (ICAC) that investigate and enforce them) do resemble a simple compliance regime, since they do impose negative sanctions. But an ethics regime, in addition, seeks to raise behaviour well above that minimum — by exhortation, example and positive rewards (Sampford and Blencowe, 2001).[2]

A Perceived Problem

One frequent and substantial objection to implementing the kind of approach outlined above is the concern that introducing a code of conduct will expose the incumbent government to criticism from both the Opposition and media for failing to comply with its own guidelines. This has been a strong disincentive to many who were otherwise well-disposed toward improving ethical standards. In 1996, a colleague and I approached the National–Liberal Party government and the Australian Labor Party Opposition in relation to a code of ethics for parliamentarians and ministers and the creation of an independent office to give them ethical advice about the code's meaning and effect. Both government and Opposition raised the same concern — that once a code was introduced it would be open to anyone to interpret in their own favour, allowing interested parties to claim triumphantly that the government was in breach of its own rules (Sampford, 1997). This was precisely the accusation levelled at the Howard government (see Weller, Chapter 5), which felt that it had in effect been penalized for setting high standards.

However, the real problem was not that the standards had been set too high. As Weller emphasizes, Howard's principles were entirely in keeping with previous unpublished standards. The problem was that the publication had highlighted and articulated a set of public norms with no means of advising ministers on what they must do to comply, nor any means of authoritatively interpreting these norms to determine if ministerial behaviour fell below the sanctionable minimum. In the absence of any sources of prior advice and interpretation, ministers breached the rules without understanding them and made themselves vulnerable to subsequent political attack by press and Opposition.

This mistake would never have been made when drafting the kinds of normative rules that governments are most familiar with — legislation. There are numerous guides to interpretation of statutes, outlining their justification, purpose and detailed meaning. Lawyers give advice in advance, and judges rule authoritatively after claimed breaches are committed and challenged. However, because it seems to be generally assumed that ethical norms are completely different from legal norms, it is rarely asked who will advise, interpret and rule on ethical standards. Ethical norms are different, in that individual conscience and interpretation play a larger role, and the courts do not have the final say (although courts do regulate the decision-making processes of others whose final say may reflect adversely on the interests of those affected). But ethical norms are not so different from law that those subject to them do not need advice, or that avenues for determining, developing and changing their meanings are not needed.[3] Nor are they so different from legal norms that it becomes acceptable for the one body to make, interpret, rule and punish. If such institutional arrangements were applied to legal rules, they would not only breach the rule of law but also result in a loss of public confidence — and be largely ineffective.

So the mistake lies not in introducing and publicizing ethics reforms, but in introducing a 'bare code' of ethics that is not part of an 'ethics regime' and not supported by other institutions. Agencies that investigate breaches of legal norms are important. But one of the most important institutions is one that provides ethical advice to ministers before they take any actions that might be subsequently questioned and investigated.

Institutions Offering Prior Advice

United States

In the USA, this problem with the interpretation of ethical codes of conduct has to some extent been addressed by the Office of Government Ethics (OGE). Although the rules set out by the OGE may be criticized for being overly detailed and legalistic, one feature of the process adopted by the OGE is particularly deserving of note. The OGE does not confine itself to the usual sending out of reminders and questionnaires and the organization of ethics training seminars. The OGE process starts with a standard measure: the declarations of all financial interests must be publicly filed. Some 25 000 appointees must make such declarations — including the president, vice president, members of cabinet, heads of agencies, all employees paid above a set minimum, senior military officers, administrative law judges, and the ethics officer of each agency (OGE 2000). All of the above must file within 30 days of their appointment, thereafter annually and within 30 days of their leaving office. They must include any interests of their spouses and dependent children. Those officials whose appointments must be ratified by the Senate (including all those of cabinet-level rank — 'ministers' (in the terminology of this project) must have their disclosure statement filed, and cleared by the OGE, before they are formally nominated by the president.

For most appointees, their declarations are checked by their own agency and any issues are discussed. One important practice, however, is that the agency ethics officer goes through the document with the appointee. For cabinet-level appointments the procedures are even more comprehensive. The agency ethics officer goes through the financial disclosure form with the prospective nominee. The form then goes to the OGE, to the nominee's employing agency and to the White House, where any potential conflicts of interest are discussed. The OGE is prepared to sit down with cabinet nominees and take a second look if necessary. Any potential conflict of interest must be resolved before the nomination is made to the relevant Senate Committee, which will discuss any forms of assets that could cause problems.

Standard procedures are available for resolving most conflicts of interest — including divestiture, recusal from participation in relevant decisions or an OGE-approved form of blind trust (which is so blind that the appointee will not even know whether the assets that caused the potential conflict of interest remain in the portfolio). This procedure is particularly relevant to Australia, where there are strong indications that at least some of the ministers caught out by the Howard code did not deliberately intend to flout the conflict of interest rules in relation to private investments, but rather acted (or failed to act at all) inadvertently. It is certainly hard to see Finance Minister Jim Short's breach (holding on to a few bank shares) as a deliberate breach of the rules.

Of course, there are particular reasons for following such careful procedures in the USA, where Senate Committees vet cabinet nominees publicly, a process in which there is a strong desire to avoid controversy. However, Westminster parliamentary democracies like Australia and the UK have shown that post-appointment questioning in parliament can cause enormous embarrassment to questionable appointees. The quick turnaround of governments in some parliamentary systems means that Oppositions would be best to consider these issues when selecting members of their shadow cabinet. Indeed, they might find this a good political move to embarrass any government that was not going through processes that were as stringent for their current ministers. Certainly the process of having officials sit down with ministers, alerting them to their portfolio's particular requirements and going through potential problems would be a useful development. This may be the best way to help ministers learn about ethics — one-to-one education is generally perceived to be the most effective, especially if it is practical and task oriented.

Canada and Australia

More comprehensive in its content, but less comprehensive in the personnel it covers, is the advice provided by the Canadian Ethics Counsellor and the Queensland Integrity Commissioner (see Jackson, Chapter 9, and Preston, Chapter 10). These officers are available to advise the head of government (HOG) and, generally when approved by the HOG, other ministers and senior public servants. One of the most important features of both these positions is that, if a minister seeks prior advice and follows it, the counsellor or commissioner will subsequently defend the decision in public — either personally (in Canada) or by publishing the advice they gave (in Queensland).

Effective Ethical Advisory Institutions

The above discussion has identified some key elements for the provision of prior advice as part of an effective ethics regime. These are:

1. An established practice of combing through every minister's financial affairs to identify potential problems and avoid them. This helps to avoid major conflict of interest problems and provides effective prior clearance as well as sensitizing ministers to ethical issues;
2. The availability of ongoing prior advice on ethical issues; and
3. The power of such advice to nullify, or at least largely deflect, any later criticism of actions taken in accordance with that advice.

The availability of this public defence addresses the very real concern that interpretation of any code of conduct is so open ended and that those who create such codes make themselves hostage to any interpretation that journalists or Opposition legislators can put on it. If the counsellor/commissioner enjoys genuine bipartisan respect, fewer problems will arise. It will certainly deter some of the more blatantly partisan or dishonest interpretations of ethics codes and may make the more ideological uses of codes more difficult (see Kultgen, 1998). But it does not close off all further ethical debate — nor should it. It may mitigate the tendency for governments otherwise to leave all ethics decisions, especially about breaches, in the hands of the HOG.

However, under such a model the dynamics of debate change fundamentally. The issue is no longer whether the relevant minister acted in an unethical (or worse) way, even less whether the minister is a good or bad person. The minister has done the right thing by seeking advice and following it or, in the case of conflicts of interest, taking the advice offered. The remaining issues are likely to be more substantive and systematic:

1. What is the correct interpretation of the norm?
2. Does the norm need to be changed, added to, etc?
3. Should the process be refined?

Such issues should be handled by a bipartisan committee or review panel with community representation to consider issues arising and interpretations given over the previous year and make prospective recommendations for changes to norms or procedures.

Bipartisan Support

It is crucial that the counsellor/commissioner has bipartisan respect. The best way to achieve this is if the process actively involves all major political parties in the first place. An appointment that is made by one side alone is always subject to subsequent criticism if the counsellor's advice seems too lenient for the government. Indeed, it may be perceived that the only cases that are likely to come to light are those in which the counsellor has given the action a clear bill of health. But if the Opposition takes part in the appointment, it is committed to supporting both the process and the appointee.

A preferred model would involve a formal process of appointment by a committee with nominees of all major parliamentary parties and a requirement that at least one Opposition committee member concur with the appointment before it can be made. In a parliamentary system, the committee could be a committee of parliament; this may be preferred as part of a process where the parliament is seen to be in control of the ethics of ministers as well as of its backbench members. If the chosen committee were responsible for the ethics of members, this would have the advantage of providing a coherent overview of the ethical issues confronting both members and ministers.

The argument against appointment by a parliamentary committee is that the committee might fail to distinguish between the standards appropriate to ministers and the standards appropriate for ordinary members of parliament. Ordinary members exercise very general, legislative, power collectively and in open session. Ministers exercise — individually and in private — significant executive power with the capacity to benefit or harm individual citizens and large corporations. This would provide a strong justification for a separate committee for the appointment of a ministerial ethics adviser. A non-parliamentary committee could also include political outsiders — as did the committee that advised the Queensland premier on the selection of his Integrity Commissioner. However, I would still argue for at least one politician from either side of politics, each of whom would have power of veto.

Separation of Ethics Advice and Ethics Investigation Functions

While arguing for institutions providing prior ethical advice, I am much more wary of bodies carrying out ethical 'investigations'. Investigation into breaches of laws and disciplinary codes (seen as effectively another form of law in Sampford, 1992) and the imposition of sanctions on those whose behaviour falls below the tolerable minimum form part of a well-designed 'ethics regime' or 'integrity system'.

In the absence of such formal sanctions, debates about ethical standards should remain matters for public debate. Prior ethical advice provides a defence in that debate and turns the question away from the individual minister's personal behaviour to the clarification of the rules. Where ministers have not sought that advice, the debate will still be focused on ministerial behaviour — with the added question of why they had not sought ethical advice.

Others have taken a different view, preferring to establish a body that is adjudicatory as well as advisory. The Canadian Starr–Sharp Report proposed an Ethics Commissioner to subsequently investigate allegations as well as a separate position of Ethics Counsellor to give prior advice. As Jackson reports, this aspect of the Starr–Sharp Report was ignored and the two distinct roles were combined. The Canadian Ethics Counsellor has not only been used to give prior advice but has also been asked to investigate past behaviour of ministers after that behaviour has already become a political issue. The subsequent report then involves matters on which at least one side of politics has already taken a position. It would appear that it is this aspect of the Ethics Counsellor's role that has been most controversial (see Jackson, Chapter 9).

The close relationship necessary for the giving of advice compromises the requirement of impartiality required of subsequent investigation. I am not convinced that establishing an ethics commissioner armed with investigatory powers is desirable anyway, and the model suggested here does not include one. However, if subsequent investigation of ethical (as opposed to legal) issues does take place, the government's ethical adviser should not be the one to perform this task.

Failure to Take Advice

The ability of ministers to keep themselves in the clear by giving the facts to an ethics counsellor/integrity commissioner and seeking advice has two natural corollaries. First, the minister must state the facts accurately. If an important fact is missed out (deliberately or inadvertently), this may negate the minister's protection. Indeed, it will expose the minister to suspicions that ethical clearance was given only because of the omission of that fact. Any such omission also raises questions about the minister's bona fides in seeking the advice. Was this omission deliberate, to mislead the commissioner and get the advice the minister wanted all along? Such situations could lead to interminable debate about which 'facts' were relevant. The system could offer ministers some protection by allowing the commissioner to find that the omission was trivial and would have made no difference to the advice given. This might be seen as placing undue pressure on the commissioner. However, an independent commissioner has protection from such pressure and any report of such pressure would be enormously damaging to the government. The rational strategy for a minister genuinely seeking ethical clearance is to state, fully and accurately, all the facts that he/she thinks might be relevant. It is the only way to get good advice and it is the only way to secure the subsequent protection from an integrity commissioner. This is a principle that is well understood in seeking prior legal advice, as compared to engaging a criminal lawyer to defend you.

Second, the protection provided by the commissioner is so valuable, and the dangers of seeking and taking it are so great, that it leads to another potential objection. Does this hand too much power to the commissioner, effectively transferring power from elected officials to an appointed official and making ministers effectively responsible and accountable to the ethics adviser (even, or perhaps especially, if the commissioner is appointed with bipartisan support)? There are four answers to this objection:

1. It is not in the ethics commissioner's own interests to get involved in political issues because the commissioner's reputation and authority depends on being seen as aloof from them.
2. The ethics commissioner's reasoning will have to be in terms of the previously agreed ethical standards and will have to be in terms that are general and not policy specific.

3. Subsequent concerns about the commissioner's rulings can be dealt with within the review process discussed below.
4. The commissioner has no legal power to fine, suspend, unseat, jail or otherwise punish ministers, only to shame them (the sting from any such rebukes will be diminished if it is perceived in parliament or among the general public that the commissioner is biased or has let power go to his/her head).

One solution, adopted in both Canada and Queensland, is to limit the range of issues with which the counsellor/commissioner may be involved. In both cases, they deal only with conflict of interest issues. However, the problem with limiting the range of issues is that it leaves the government open to claims of unethical behaviour in all the areas excepted with no means of defending its members against Opposition and media allegations that they have breached its ethical code. The very argument that was erroneously raised against ethical codes applies with full force against these limitations. The very silence of the counsellor/commissioner might be politically damaging. Finally, if there was any argument over the meaning of the exceptions, the minister could be portrayed as foolishly avoiding advice in order to pursue unethical practices. The suggested solution is that the advice be available on all areas of behaviour covered by any ministerial codes (the distinction is not 'public' versus 'private' behaviour — though any well-constructed code will consider such issues and, in particular, the conflict between the public and private involved in 'conflict of interest').

This does not provide a perfect solution (there is none). Like most issues of principle, it is important to have a clearly understandable public rationale for the range of issues covered by the ethics commissioner and the range of issues that are not. Blurred boundaries will remain in difficult cases, but most issues will be either clearly in or clearly out. In any case, the wise minister will consult in areas of uncertainty. Therein lies his/her protection.

Why Have Separate Advisers at all? Why Not Leave It to the Head of Government?

Professor Weller (Chapter 5), argues primarily against an outsider acting as a judge, and is sceptical about having an independent adviser. Having an adviser might complicate an already complicated situation further and blurs the line of Westminster accountability. He points to the 'old', 'but still good', solution 'that prime ministers who preside over a long list of scandals will face electoral justice'.

This argument highlights the basic principle of parliamentary democracy — the periodic summative judgement passed on government by electors. Other feedback loops can interfere with that core accountability and responsibility. I am in total agreement with the principle and the general philosophy behind it. I have long argued for parliamentary over presidential forms of executive government and against entrenched constitutional rights (Sampford, 1986). However, I would still argue in favour of this particular 'complication'. It addresses a real obstacle in getting politicians to sign up to codes of ethics. Without it, ministers are demotivated from supporting public statements of ethical standards. Such a failure would not only involve a politically unsustainable reversal, but would also run contrary to one of the core ideas of what it is to be ethical — 'asking hard questions about your values, giving honest and public answers, and trying to live by them' (Sampford and Wood, 1993).

If ethical judgements are left in the hands of the HOG (prime minister or premier), the maintenance and advancement of ethical standards will be less effective for a number of reasons:

1. HOGs would be in the position of making, interpreting and enforcing the rules of ministerial ethics. That sits ill with the idea of the rule of law and the separation of powers, and reduces confidence in the impartiality of such rules and enforcement.
2. For these and other reasons, an HOG's clearance of a minister will never have the same degree of credibility as that provided by an independent adviser — especially one provided in advance.
3. Although HOGs have an interest in avoiding the 'electoral justice' meted out upon leaders who are seen as presiding over a long list of scandals, it is dangerous to place too much reliance on this. HOGs may seek other means of avoiding electoral harm. They may rely on spin-doctors and on personal attacks against those who give opinions contrary to their own. They may seek to dilute and confuse the meaning of existing norms, rendering them less and less effective. Indeed, if they come to believe that publicly stated standards inevitably leave them defenceless against attack by press and Opposition, using any interpretation that suits such attacks, behaving like this is entirely rational.
4. Although having apparently ethical ministers is generally in the long-term self-interest of HOGs, their short-term interest in political survival is stronger. The motivation to power that fuelled their rise to the top is likely to propel them to risk, even abandon, ethical principle rather than sacrifice power when faced with a choice. If we leave such decisions entirely in the hands of HOGs, we are making a choice against ethical principles in those actual and potential crises where ethics are most needed.
5. It is in the interests of our democracy to have strong public institutions with high levels of legitimacy and public support. It can be argued that it is generally in the interests of the democratic politicians who seek power within those institutions for those institutions to be strong. However, if faced with a choice, most politicians would prefer to hold on to power within weaker, less legitimate institutions than to lose power. Accordingly, if the choice is left in the HOG's hands, we can assume that most rational HOGs will be prepared to put those institutions at risk to preserve their control of them. A strong case could be made out that the

decline in the legitimacy of our institutions and the respect for the politicians who run them can be traced to a series of such decisions by successive HOGs. This is not to deny that, where such attempts collapse, there may be a strong public reaction and some politicians may deservedly make political capital in seeking to improve the integrity of public institutions. However, if they and their successors are left to decide which to sacrifice — the integrity and strength of democratic institutions or their own grip on power — it is standards that will lose out. The public's reaction may be to elect reformist new faces. On the other hand, it might also lead to public cynicism and a spiralling decline in confidence in our democratic institutions.
6. Once ethical standards are introduced into public life without any means for interpreting them, it may become too easy to frame every issue in terms of attacks on the ethics of individual politicians. Personal vilification may replace policy debate. The provision for independent advice acts as a defence against such specious and self-serving Opposition charges.

We can conclude that there are some decisions that cannot be safely left in the hands of politicians. The core idea of democracy is that the people delegate executive and/or legislative power to politicians whom the electors believe will best use that power to serve electors' interests. It is in the interests of governments to use that power in ways that will earn approval and convince a majority that it is the better choice. However, there is always a temptation to use governmental power to secure re-election by avoiding or distorting that choice. The crudest form of avoiding that choice involves a cancellation or postponement of elections. However, there are many other means of avoiding that choice — distorting electorates and electoral boundaries, manipulating electoral practices and electoral machinery, using governmental power to silence opposition or promote government policies. The temptation is so great that it might seem that only strong laws will suffice. Certainly there is a need for clear constitutional provisions, electoral laws with teeth and independent electoral commissions with clear procedures for calling elections and counting the votes. There is a need for clear legal rules on electoral advertising, election funding and government advertising.

Wherever there is power there is a temptation for abuse and it is important that the fundamental democratic principles underlying those legal rules be clearly and publicly articulated and attempts made to live by them. Politicians in a democracy are members of a very important public profession. Politicians seek to articulate policy choices and put them before the people. If they believe that their policies and the general philosophy underlying them are correct, they should be proud to do so and to believe that those public values and public policies deserve to be chosen on their merits by their fellow citizens. To seek to win by other means discredits those values and policies and dishonours their profession.

Preventing the abuse of power for the purpose of holding on to power requires the support of a strong ethics regime — including strong laws, ethical standards and independent institutions (courts and electoral commissions *and* ethics advisers whose prior advice is available to those who want to keep to principle and the absence of whose advice could be politically damaging).

Institutional Emphasis on Subsequent Investigation

This chapter has argued that prior advice to ministers is better than subsequent investigation of alleged wrongdoing. However, virtually all the major public expenditure and effort remains focused on 'after-the-fact' investigations and investigatory bodies such as the ICAC and the Criminal Justice Commission (CJC). These have an important place in any ethics regime or integrity system, that is, investigating breaches of legal standards set in advance.

However, where standards are unclear and/or not established in advance, real difficulties have emerged. For example, Fleming (see Chapter 11) reports the 'lack of guidelines and paperwork' in the Queensland 'travel rorts' case and the 'absence of legally recognizable standards' found by the Supreme Court in the Metherell affair. In such cases the investigatory body not only investigates alleged breaches of standards after the event but must also determine what those standards are and interpret them. Fleming refers to Greiner's complaints that new and higher standards were being applied to him retrospectively. It is easy to mock such complaints — 'what a terrible thing for politicians to be expected to do the right thing and behave ethically when they never did in the past'. But it is generally seen as unfair to sanction somebody for the breach of a rule which had not been articulated at the time the action was taken. It is also inefficient because rules that are not communicated cannot be followed. These are the classic arguments in favour of the rule of law and the general case against retrospective activity.

Fleming points out that 'politicians have shown a reluctance to subject themselves to the ICAC's ethical standards'. However, that expression reflects the fact that, in the absence of prior standards, the ICAC had to set these standards. Setting aside the not unattractive view that the ethical standards for politicians should be set by them and not the ICAC, the idea that investigators should make the rules whose breaches they are investigating is contrary to our normal conception of the separation of powers between those who make and enforce rules.

In Queensland it is easy to see why so much emphasis was put on the CJC. The apparent success of and public support for a one-off inquiry led many to expect a permanent investigatory body to achieve similar success and respect. However, one of the great strengths of the Fitzgerald Report (1989) was that it recommended a permanent body, the Electoral and Administrative Review Commission (EARC), to consider reforms to the constitutional, legal and administrative mechanisms of government. Unfortunately, it dealt with ethics last rather than first — bringing down wholesale reform before discussing the values that reform was intended to generate. It was also given a sunset clause so it was unable to continue its work. In the interim, the CJC was expected to deal with the task of improving behaviour — whether in matters involving travel expenses or issues that go to the constitution of the government such as vote-rorting scandals or securing covert police union support for a change of government. This forced the CJC to combine both roles, of investigatory body and ethical adviser/reformer, which inevitably meant that there would be far more conflict over the CJC and that its ability to fulfil either function would be compromised.

Efficiency and Cost Effectiveness

Subsequent investigations cost a great deal in terms of time and resources and create high stakes for those who are investigated — including findings of improper conduct and potential loss of office, power and influence. The latter means that such investigations will be resisted strongly, which in turn drives up the cost of conducting them. As noted above, fairness demands that sanctions can only be imposed for clear breaches of previously established rules. The costs of giving prior advice are far less and some of the issues on which ministers have been embarrassed, exposed and investigated could have been settled in minutes. There may be resistance to the advice if it means that the policy end must be abandoned. However, in most cases it will merely mean that different means may have to be adopted. These different means may impose extra political hurdles but, once alerted to the ethical difficulties and the potential political backlash involved from subsequent investigation, politicians will have an incentive to follow the ethically defensible course. The sensible politician will be thankful for having avoided the potential flak and will seek it eagerly.

This will make prior advice more effective. There is also a good chance that higher standards may be developed as a result. There is an analogy in the sphere of law. If an individual's actions are challenged in court, the defendant seeks a lawyer to defend his/her action and argue that he/she did not fall below the lowest acceptable standard. However, if advice is sought beforehand, the advice that will be given is how to avoid legal problems and the likelihood of investigation and legal sanction (Sampford and Blencowe, 1998). In avoiding legally questionable conduct, the behaviour of the individual concerned will be of a higher standard than that which is questioned and successfully defended in court. It is even higher than that which is *not* successfully defended. We can assume that similar standards-raising effects will flow from prior ethical advice.

Conclusion

There are many ways in which laws may achieve their goals of changing behaviour. Although much of the public perception and fascination with law concerns its punitive element, law achieves most of its effects by non-punitive means. Concentrating on the criminal law is no way to pursue effective institutional or social reform. Compliance occurs because citizens know about the law and if they are uncertain they seek legal advice. It should not be surprising if this is even more true of other, non-legal, norms about ministerial conduct.

In this chapter I have argued that one of the best ways to encourage ministers to comply with ethical codes is to offer them the facility of seeking prior advice — advice which they can act on in the confidence that even if the advice is subsequently criticized, they will bear no blame. This will motivate ministers to consider whether contemplated actions involve ethical issues and to seek that advice if there is any doubt that they may. This is a significant carrot.

Most carrots are made more tempting by coexisting with a painful stick. Those ministers who do not seek the advice are likely to find themselves in the midst of controversy and a subsequent investigation of their actions. This will reinforce advice seeking in the remaining ministers. I do not anticipate that this will turn politicians into by-words of ethical probity. However, in conjunction with other elements of the ethics regime/integrity system, it has the capacity to raise ministerial standards. There is a real chance that it will also encourage ministers to consider ethical issues when contemplating future action just as they consider the legality of their actions before they seek formal legal advice. In such cases, ethics would not be an afterthought but a part of the way that policy is formed and justified. One dare not hope that this will become the norm. However, if prior advice is available, one can hope that most ministers will have the common sense to seek advance ethical clearance and avoid potential problems. Those lacking such common sense will soon find themselves out of ministerial office.

Notes

1 This concentration on individual rather than institutional problems is not confined to the media but is found even among public sector ethicists — for example Bailey (1964).

2 This raises the question of whether discretionary standards that are part of ethics regimes provide space for behaviour to fall below the minimum. The discretionary space is an essential element of the regime — see Sampford (1992). However, the discretionary space is above the minimum because that is provided by law acting as backstop. The whole scheme here is that law provides the legally enforceable minimum and ethics provides the principles that guide the formulation and interpretation of the law (see Sampford and Wood, 1993). To suggest that we rely on legal norms alone rejects the idea of ethics and limits the weapons deployed to improve ministerial behaviour.

3 Twining has emphasized that many of the problems with legal rules are problems of rules in general — and vice versa (Twining and Miers, 1983). The problem highlighted here is the need for rules (and institutions) for identity, adjudication and change which Hart argued as so necessary for law and which are seen here as necessary for ethical norms (Hart, 1961).

Chapter 15

Moderating Ministerial Ethics: Putting Political Ethics in its Place

John Uhr[1]

Introduction

Many contributors to the debate over ethics and politics argue that contemporary politicians pay too little attention to ethics. It is common to argue that democratic governance would be better if only governments took ethics seriously. In this view, politics needs more ethics. I can sympathize but in this chapter I want to disagree. Too much ethics can be as bad as too little ethics. Here my interest is directed to moderating two extreme tendencies in the field of ethics and politics: the first associated with unrealistic reliance on chief ministers to regulate ministerial conduct; and the second associated with idealistic over-reactions against this executive-centred model, and the search for alternative models with the capacity to promote moral virtue among public officials.

As my subtitle suggests, my aim is to put ministerial ethics back in its place: institutionally as an object of parliamentary and not simply executive regulation; and substantively as a project designed to prevent public harm from ministerial misconduct rather than promote personal virtue among ministers and their closest advisers. A parliament willing to exercise institutional leadership could do much to set appropriate standards for ministerial conduct and devise mechanisms to investigate alleged misuse of ministerial office. The task is then for parliaments to use the power of publicity and related forms of institutional leverage to ensure that political executives play fair with public office.

I can clarify the political theory informing my analysis by using two illustrations. First, in relation to the institutional norms of responsible government, I refer to the 1940s classic debate between Friedrich and Finer over administrative responsibility in democratic governance, especially Finer's defence of legislative oversight over executive government (Friedrich, 1966; Finer, 1966). My position here is consistent with Finer's warning about the dangers of official zeal in government agencies, even or particularly when that zeal is motivated by public-spirited concern for cleansing politics of its impurities. Finer appreciated that modern democratic politics works through elective institutions, to which all executive agencies are publicly accountable.

Although political and bureaucratic discretion is an inevitable and largely welcome fact of modern government, community confidence in government depends more on the exercise of public accountability through elected political assemblies than on government-appointed ethics agencies.

This brings me to my second illustration of the political theory informing my analysis. In relation to liberal-democratic political philosophy, I refer to the argument made by Judith Shklar about the necessarily limited place of personal ethical virtue in the public life of modern government (Shklar, 1984, 1992). Shklar's case is now the classic counterbalance to that made by advocates of virtue ethics who are uncomfortable with liberalism's reliance on models of self-interested individualism. As the author of a book entitled *Ordinary Vices*, Shklar contends that liberal democracy draws its ethical inspiration from an ambitious vision of 'justice without virtue'. This summary formula succinctly conveys Shklar's orientation: the ethical basis of liberalism rests on a civic commitment to political justice, without demanding that citizens or officials commit themselves to higher virtues of moral excellence (Yack, 1999). My position is consistent with Shklar's implied public policy priority of tackling the common but unacceptable vice of injustice over the alternative of cultivating, through government agency, the admirable but rare virtues of moral excellence.

Two Worrying Tendencies

In the area of ministerial ethics, two worrying tendencies require moderation. One is the cynical self-interest of political executives retaining control over the regulation of ministerial ethics. The other is the over-reaction of idealistic reformers who turn to non-political ethics agencies to clean up public life. My preferred path of moderation falls in between these extremes and involves a greater role for parliament as the centrepiece of ministerial ethics.

The first tendency requiring moderation is the self-interest of political executives and particularly chief ministers who are determined to retain regulatory control over ministerial conduct. Their responsibilities as party leaders mean that their approach will almost always be defensive. It is expecting too much of chief executives to expect them to be law maker, judge and jury when it comes to ministerial ethics. Chief ministers have a vital role to play in setting the tone of an administration but that role should not be expanded to include exclusive monitoring of ministerial ethics. In contrast, I defend the rights of parliaments to set standards of ministerial conduct and devise mechanisms for securing compliance and investigating alleged breaches.

Parliament is relevant because, as political executives also argue, the task of setting appropriate standards of ministerial conduct is a political rather than simply a legal or ethical matter. Parliament as the elected legislature is the right institution to establish publicly acceptable standards for ministerial conduct. Parliament's claim to establish community standards derives from its representative role as the forum for community deliberation over law and policy. Parliament is capable of securing community agreement for appropriate standards of political conduct, and of establishing public mechanisms capable of maintaining public trust in ministerial compliance with approved standards.

The second tendency requiring moderation is the misplaced enthusiasm of reformers determined to clean up politics by imposing standards of selfless public service and exemplary personal virtue (Chapman and Galston, 1992). In my view, it is asking too much of elected politicians that they exemplify the highest standards of ethical virtue at the personal as well as the public level. It is also asking too much of ethics and integrity commissioners to expect that they can protect the public interest by promoting moral excellence among public officials. I defend an alternative approach that takes as its policy priority the minimization of vice in the misuse of public office, as distinct from the maximization of personal virtue among public officials. In an ideal world there would be less need for my harm-minimization strategy if public officials were selected and retained on the basis of their ethical excellence. But this ideal world would not be a liberal-democratic world that, while far from perfect, has much to recommend it as the prevailing intellectual model of contemporary democracy. Liberal-democratic norms of public spirit might lack ethical purity, but their models of official probity are strong enough to inspire the contemporary international support for liberalization and democratization.

Even if non-liberal regimes of democracy might be superior in theory, there is a considerable risk of letting the excellent get in the way of the good. A basic consideration in ethics is first to ensure that as little harm as possible is done, before beginning the more difficult task of promoting the good (Frankena, 1973, pp. 45–8). The challenge is to chart a politically prudent course between the cynicism of self-regulating ministers and the idealism of ethics advocates. This might sound like an argument against ethics but it is really against the misguided expectation that government agencies, such as ethics commissions, can generate the type of ethical qualities among political leaders that liberal regimes draw on for their perpetuation. The cultivation and generation of exemplary ethics in liberal regimes owes more to institutions of civil society — such as the family, schools and universities — than to governmental bodies. The task for ethics or integrity commissions is to crack down on misuse of office as distinct from cranking up moral excellence.

We can distinguish the desirable goal of political ethics from the dream of ethical politics. My theme is that political ethics can be achieved short of striving for moral excellence among public officials. I acknowledge that political ethics can be 'read down' to include the political stage-management of ethics, which is a cynical practice dangerously within reach of one of the two extremes that I am opposing. To leave the management of ministerial ethics solely to the ministry would court just such a danger. But ethical politics can be 'read up' to take the routine practice of politics out of reach of ordinary citizens. The danger here would be that extra-political bodies would be called into play to supervise politics, along the lines of a kind of moral equivalent to the court system, with ethics regulators and moral censors intervening to protect the community against officials' lapses of selfless public spirit. While it is true that tighter ethics regulation is increasingly called for, debates over ministerial ethics highlight the degree to which resolution turns on community agreement on what constitutes appropriate political conduct. This is where parliaments have a role to play as standards setters: the standards of official integrity and appropriate political conduct are most suitably made by parliamentary institutions, acting in between the body of ministerial actors and the recommended body of ethics advocates.

Theories of Ministerial Responsibility

The conventional approach to ministerial ethics separates the field into two broad classes of misconduct: official and personal. Official conduct relates to official decision making and conduct either by the minister or by other officials such as public servants working as delegates of the minister. Personal conduct relates generally to the private conduct of ministers on matters that have nothing to do with their official responsibilities. A central preoccupation of the existing commentary on ministerial ethics relates to real or potential conflicts of interest between ministers' public duties and their personal *interests*, even though the study of political morality reaches higher and wider themes of conflicting *responsibilities* (see, for example, Applbaum, 1999; Sutherland, 2000; Thompson, 1987).

The reason for the weight of commentary on this facet of ministerial ethics is that powerful public officials inevitably find themselves in real, or potential, or externally perceived, conflicts of interests that call out for a regulatory framework. Even where pursuit of private interests involves no real threat to public duty, as in the many examples of private sexual conduct that have damaged ministers' public reputations, there is still the risk that a minister's conduct might amount to misuse of office, for example by using their power to extract favours or get special treatment. More usually, instances of inappropriate private conduct simply sully a minister's reputation, thereby threatening the minister's public career. Private misconduct can excite charges of hypocrisy and this too can severely damage the credibility of ministers, whose reputation as a trustworthy character has been placed in doubt.

This conventional orientation to the regulation of ministerial conduct is well summarized in recent comparative reviews of ministerial responsibility in parliamentary systems (Woodhouse, 1994, pp. 265–81; Butler, 1997; Bovens, 1998, pp. 85–9; Thompson and Tillotsen, 1999; Weller, 1999). Generally the focus is on resignations as an indicator of the force of sanctions, as classically argued by Dicey in his elaboration of 'constitutional morality' (Dicey, 1959, Ch. 11; but cf. Woodhouse, 1994, pp. 27–8, 33–8, 282–5). The general conclusion is: 'Politics, not theories of accountability, determines the fate of ministers' (Thompson and Tillotsen, 1999, p. 49). Butler provides a good illustration of the conventional political analysis of ministerial ethics relating the two fields of official and private misconduct to the conventional sanction of resignation from office (Butler, 1997; cf. Butler, 1973, pp. 49–69; Weller and Jaensch, 1980). The framework of analysis deals with misconduct primarily in terms of conflicts of interest, with the hope of unearthing patterns of ministerial resignation that might reveal enduring political standards. Butler reserves a small section of his analysis for debates, dealing not with conflicts of interest but with defective policy management by ministers. Typically these are not given as much attention as the conflict cases since the policy failings only seldom involve ministerial resignation. Of these the most prominent are the 'Crichel Down'-type cases of administrative failings for which ministers (once upon a time) took full parliamentary responsibility (Tomkins, 1998, pp. 52–7).

One weakness of the conventional approach to ministerial ethics is that it marginalizes the cases of lapsed ministerial responsibility in relation to policy management, which constitute the bulk of the cases of parliamentary and public dispute over ministerial responsibility. These policy-failure cases illustrate the very heartland of ministerial ethics, where that is understood in terms of parliamentary disputes over appropriate standards of conduct expected of ministers in the exercise of their official responsibilities. These cases relate rarely to clashes of personal and official interests but deal mainly with standards of competence expected of ministers in their official dealings. They *might* involve issues of conflict of interest but that covers only a part, and not necessarily the major part, of the debated ethical conduct.

These cases deal with ministers' official competence (or their 'professional ethics' as you will) and specifically with ministerial conduct in managing their dealings with parliament. Explanation, justification and defence of ministerial performance is itself a core part of the ministerial job. The office is a parliamentary one before it is an executive one. Only elected officials can hold cabinet office. Elevation to the ministry means taking on additional parliamentary duties and accountability obligations, as well as the very many executive responsibilities. Ministers are ministers because they are, in the first place, members of parliament; their ethics of office is broadly a political one but more specifically a parliamentary one (Reid, 1980). Their conduct is judged according to their ability to manage their parliamentary responsibilities, including their justification of their right to sustained parliamentary confidence in high executive office.

Specifying Ministerial Roles and Responsibilities

The limits of ministerial self-regulation are evident in the current trend to adopt codes of conduct. These ministerial codes illustrate the basic characteristics of the responsible government model with its bias towards giving the political executive all the 'responsibility' that their command of their parliamentary majority deserves. The executive 'takes responsibility' based on the 'confidence' parliament places in it to exercise the duties of office. Having responsibility is a sign of the 'trust' that the parliament has placed in the executive to rule within the generous boundaries of formal requirements of parliamentary approval for annual budgets, which act as periodic reauthorizations of the executive's right to the responsibilities of office.

The 1997 UK ministerial code is one of the most recent and influential ministerial codes. It has a Foreword by Prime Minister Blair about the importance of 'restoring the bond of trust between the British people and their Government'. One finds nothing directly here about parliament but a lot about the chief political executive's own expectations of the ministerial team, which include an expectation that ministers will honour their accountability obligations to parliament (Neill, 2000, paras 4.3–4.9; cf. Tomkins, 1998, pp. 38–49). Ministers are advised that 'they can only remain in office for so long as they retain the prime minister's confidence'. Consistent with this, the current standards committee has recommended against the establishment of a new ethics commissioner to deal with ministerial ethics, in part because the political realities of ministerial performance really mean that it is for the prime minister alone to judge whether ministerial conduct is fitting or inappropriate (see, for example, Neill, 2000, paras 4.15–4.30, 4.59–4.64, 4.76–4.78).

This preference for leaving the regulation of ministerial conduct solely in the hands of the political executive is not a view I support. The 1997 ministerial code was prompted by the prior action of parliament in generating a rare resolution on ministerial accountability as promoted by a House of Commons select committee. This parliamentary resolution forms a core part of the Blair code, stipulating that ministers have obligations to provide 'accurate and truthful information' and to be 'as open as possible with parliament and the public'. But the placement of these parliamentary-sourced obligations in an executive code highlights a potential tension (or as the Committee on Standards in Public Life style it, the 'awkward amalgam' or 'twin-faced nature' of this dated doctrine: Neill, 2000, paras 4.11, 4.64, 4.76) in the priorities of conduct expected of ministers, who must effect a balance of the competing confidences of prime minister and of parliament.

The UK House of Commons Public Service Committee published two inquiries in the mid-1990s identifying the institutional weaknesses affecting the responsibility of individual ministers in systems of responsible government (Public Service Committee (PSC), 1995–96, 1996–97). These two inquiries are rare examples of parliamentary committees investigating general principles and theoretical standards of ministerial responsibility (Tomkins, 1998, pp. 57–63). The basic constitutional context is structured around collective ministerial responsibility, meaning that the ministry holds executive office by virtue of its ability as a body to maintain the confidence of the House of Commons; this form of collective responsibility is potentially at odds with the ethical obligations of individual ministerial responsibility (Woodhouse, 1994, pp. 3–11; Tomkins, 1998, pp. 38–41).

Ministerial Credibility *v* Public Trust

A common weakness of ministerial codes is that they allow ministers to arrange their affairs in ways that bolster their personal credibility without really shoring up public trust in government. This results in something of a trade-off between ministerial credibility and public trust. Ministers defend their conduct with pleas that they have been misunderstood and that their actions are more credible than their accusers make out. In looking more closely at the fine grain of ministerial codes, we generally find applications of the wider theory of responsible government which holds that members of the political executive deserve to be trusted with the powers of government until they explicitly lose parliamentary confidence. In practice, the main test of that loss is not an Opposition claim of breaches of trust but the chief minister's decision that the price of responding to such claims exceeds the benefits accruing to the ministry.

The Australian situation illustrates broader problems encountered in Westminster-derived systems of responsible government (Encel, 1974, pp. 107–23; Reid, 1980; Weller and Jaensch, 1980; Weller, 1999). The classic Australian policy statement on the limited nature of the Westminster norm of ministerial resignation is that made in 1965 by then Attorney-General Snedden, who argued strongly against 'vicarious liability' on the premise that the obligation to answer *to* parliament did not imply a duty to answer *for* all departmental failures (Encel, 1974, pp. 117, 123). Against this realistic background, the classic policy document at the source of recent Australian developments in ministerial standard setting is the 1979 report of the Bowen Inquiry on desirable regulatory protections against undue private interests in public decision-making (Bowen, 1979, Chs 4 and 8).

Prime Minister John Howard's *Guide to Key Elements of Ministerial Responsibility* contains a valuable if succinct account of where ministers stand in the constitutional arrangements of responsible government and of their obligations to parliament, which is the relevant forum for resolving political disputes over alleged misconduct by ministers (Howard, 1996a; cf. Uhr, 1998b, pp. 194–6; Uhr, 1998c).

The existence of this so-called ministerial code, and its associated cabinet-office system for the registration of interests, is one thing; its implementation is another. The defect in this improved system of declared ministerial standards is that the one official who polices the system is the very same prime minister who devised it. In effect, the guidelines mean whatever the prime minister wants them to mean. The prime minister is both legislator and judge. This situation has given rise to frequent disputes over the prime minister's discretionary use of the guidelines to exempt some ministers from Opposition calls for their resignation, while accepting the voluntary resignations of some other ministers facing similar calls. Since Howard's code came into effect in 1996, three ministers have resigned for alleged breaches of the conflict provisions of the code and three others for misleading parliament when defending themselves against allegations of misuse of office (Thompson and Tillotsen, 1999, pp. 52–4; Uhr, 1998c).

The Australian ministerial code is a good illustration of the practical operation of the norms of responsible government, with the norms of *collective* ministerial responsibility setting the tone for the practical operation of *individual* ministerial responsibility (Thompson and Tillotsen, 1999, p. 54; cf. Encel, 1974, pp. 133–40). The two major responsibilities of ministers are identified as: management of their portfolios; and management of 'their accountability obligations' to parliament (Howard, 1996a, s. 1). The test of correct conduct for ministers is avoiding activity that might 'undermine public confidence in them or the government' (Howard, 1996a, s. 5). This gives rise to two operational rules. The first is biased towards the interest of the political executive: ministers should 'ensure that their conduct is defensible', that is, susceptible to public justification or plausible as distinct from credible. The second is more compatible with greater parliamentary involvement: ministers must be 'honest in their public dealings' and particularly avoid any intentional misleading of parliament which, should it occur, must be corrected 'at earliest opportunity'. This second rule provides parliament with considerable leverage over ministers who are liable for procedural as well as substantive failings.

The Howard guidelines also stipulate the limits to private business that may be conducted by ministers on the general rule that there should be 'no conflict or apparent conflict between interests and duties' (Howard, 1996a, s. 5). The emphasis on avoiding the appearance of wrong doing can be traced back to the Bowen Inquiry where 'the test of appearance' was formulated in terms of avoiding interests that 'look to the reasonable person the sort of interest that may influence' (Bowen, 1979, para. 2.24). This recognition of the importance of appearances might suggest that the test is in the eyes of parliament.

Ethical Overreach

The second sphere of moderation I foreshadowed relates to the tendency among external expert commentary to inflate ministerial standards to unrealistic heights. Traditional warnings about the dangers of corruption have been replaced by exhortations to promote ethics. The UK standards committee has recently canvassed the options for the 'external adjudicator' model of an ethics commissioner (Neill, 2000, paras 4.31–4.80). In the UK environment, this would involve a separation of the two roles of the existing Parliamentary Commissioner for Standards and the proposed office dealing with ministerial ethics. This committee investigated the 'crucial confusion' associated with all such models which slip between being merely advisory to being fully investigatory. The political executive prefers to rely instead on the traditional competence of the courts when dealing with criminal misconduct. But the possibility of alternative strategies to inspire ethical conduct is already in place. The Committee on Standards in Public Life set out such a framework in its initial report based on the 'seven principles of public life', beginning with the demanding virtue of 'selflessness' (Nolan, 1995).

This influential formulation of the ethics of public office has had enormous impact, a recent example being on the Committee of Independent Experts advising the European Commission (CIE, 1999, para. 7.4). But the most significant impact of the standards committee was the 1995 code of conduct for members of the UK House of Commons, which includes the 'seven principles of public life' originally devised by the standards committee (see Preston *et al.*, 1998, pp. 165–7). Given the central place of accountability in this list, I am reluctant to criticize this attempt to formulate standards appropriate to elected public officials. The one element that deserves comment here is the 'selflessness' as the leading occurrence of the seven model qualities, thereby setting the tone for public expectations of political leaders.

The virtue of selflessness requires office holders to 'take decisions solely in terms of the public interest' (Nolan, 1995). If this call for impartiality is designed to reinforce the prohibition against using office 'to gain financial or other material benefits for themselves, their family, or their friends' (as is also included in the seven principles), there can be little resistance. But 'selflessness' can be interpreted as quite a strict standard, requiring of elected members of parliament that they chart their course by reference to the map of 'disinterested' community service. Although not directed specifically to holders of ministerial office, and although intended more as an aspiration than a standard for strict compliance, this call for selfless elected politicians illustrates the contemporary inflation of expectations about the need for personal virtue in public life.

An Australian illustration of this pro-ethics orientation is the Queensland Public Sector Ethics Act 1994, which states that all public officials should strive to 'advance the common good of the community the official serves' and also comply with the obligation to promote the public interest, when that comes into conflict with 'the official's personal interests'. Prudently, this legislation does not make this obligation mandatory. But the real damage can be seen in the application that such standards of disinterested political conduct can have at the other end of the regulatory spectrum, in the operations of zealous anti-corruption bodies. Again, an Australian example can reinforce the risks of overreach that can come from unrealistically high standards. I refer to the New South Wales (NSW) Independent Commission Against Corruption (ICAC) inquiry that effectively brought down Greiner, the state's chief political executive (Uhr, 2000).

I emphasize that this case is not evidence against the ethical merits of 'selflessness' or of any defective contribution made by the original Nolan Committee. But the Greiner case does provide something of a warning of the potential misapplication of a 'selflessness' standard when joined to bureaucratic capacity to ferret out failures of allegedly self-interested political leadership. Carping critics aside, I have no evidence that the Nolan principles have done anything other than enliven public debate over appropriate standards (see, for example, Neill, 2000, pp. 12–16). But such an orientation to personal virtue might at some point tempt regulators of political conduct to transform their opposition to political vice into a campaign to weed politics of anything less than selfless political conduct. That such a potential exists can be seen in the Greiner case where an anti-corruption agency came to be seen as a moral crusader for a politics of selflessness.

The traditional anti-corruption approach has been reformed to reflect the kind of virtue ethics found in the experience of the NSW ICAC (see Fleming, Chapter 11). This new wave of anti-corruption strategies calls on ministers and other high public officials to guard against undue partiality in the exercise of public office. At its best, the policy intention of this fencing-in of partiality is to protect public integrity in the processes of public decision making. But the external ethics community seems to be redefining 'integrity', changing its essentially negative orientation to a new and ambitious positive orientation. This new orientation invites integrity commissioners to go beyond tests of procedural justice to experiment with tests of policy substance, at the risk of imposing their standards of social justice on those devised by duly elected representatives.

Premier Greiner defended his offer in parliament of a government job to an independent member of the legislature as 'normal politics', and attacked the charge of partiality based corruption as ushering in 'the death of politics' (ICAC, 1992a, p. 92). Acknowledging that 'this is a very difficult philosophical matter', Greiner defended the practice of political appointments to the public service, claiming that this went to 'the very nature of politics itself — that is, the conflict between the demands of politics and the demands of public office'. The political system 'is about what is in many ways a largely private interest in terms of winning or holding a seat or holding office'. The alternative was the system of what he called 'disinterestedness' where elected officials 'act only in what they considered to be the national interest'. This he condemned as inimical to 'a workable system of democracy' (ICAC, 1992a, pp. 92–3).

Clearly, part of the ICAC problem is the broad sweep of the legislative definition of 'corruption' which the parliamentary oversight committee is currently working to keep the term 'corruption' for the most serious forms of official misconduct and to label lesser forms simply as official misconduct. Without defending the political scheming associated with the Metherell affair it is important to recognize this instance of institutional over reach and subsequent roll-back, reflecting as it does uncertainty over how much political partiality is acceptable in what Greiner called 'a workable system of democracy'.

Promoting Parliamentary Regulation

One of the unacknowledged problems with ministerial ethics is that parliaments themselves resist declaring appropriate standards for ministerial conduct, even though parliaments reserve to themselves the right to judge in particular circumstances whether individual ministers deserve to lose their office of high responsibility. One requirement of moderating ministerial ethics is moderating the usual partisanship excited by the chase of ministerial resignations. This reform requires greater parliamentary involvement in the declaration of appropriate standards for ministerial conduct and in the determination of disputed cases.

The most positive step taken by a Westminster-derived parliament was modelled by the House of Commons public service committee just before the election of the Blair Labour government. The House of Commons committee looked beyond the conventional debates over ministerial resignation as the primary test of ministerial responsibility: 'Proper and rigorous scrutiny and accountability may be more important to parliament's ability to correct error than forcing resignations' (House of Commons Parliamentary Committee (HCPC), 1996, para. 26). Ministers for their part must take personal responsibility for their obligations of accountability, including the obligation to provide public explanations of government performance, which is an issue that goes to the core of 'democratic control of government' (HCPC, 1996, para. 28). The Committee reformulated the 'theory of Ministerial responsibility' to require that executive governments be 'less coy' in their 'definition of what Ministerial responsibility means' (HCPC, 1996, para. 32). Accordingly, the committee devised its own working definition of this core term. The political executive are 'obliged to give an account — to provide full information about and explain its actions'; and the executive is also 'liable to be held to account' in order to retain the confidence of parliament (HCPC, 1996, para. 32). With this new parliamentary definition of responsibility, the committee set out to bring greater parliamentary control, not simply over the conduct of ministers but also over the appropriate public definition of the duties of ministers (see Tomkins, 1998, pp. 49–52).

Challenging the political executive's monopoly of control over what constitutes the proper role of ministers, the committee successfully called on parliament to resolve in its own terms the institutional requirements of ministerial responsibility (HCPC, 1996, para. 60; cf. HCPC, 1997, annex 2). This resolution was carried in the House of Commons in March 1997 (HC Parliamentary Debates, 19 March 1997, pp. 1046–47; Tomkins, 1998, pp. 60–3; Neill, 2000, paras 4.62–4.63). From a parliamentary perspective, the practical core of ministerial responsibility is not the norm of collective support for cabinet, however important that might be to the everyday operation of responsible government, but the surprisingly negative norm of not misleading parliament. The resolution on accountability notes that failure to provide information to parliament cuts across the duty of ministers not to 'obstruct or impede' the prior duty of parliament to carry out its own functions. The accountability obligation of ministers requires that they provide 'full and accurate' information to parliament, even to the point of not letting 'any inadvertent errors' remain uncorrected. It is for this reason that the vice of misleading parliament is serious enough to deserve the penalty of resignation, which the committee noted was (strictly speaking) beyond parliament's power to effect (Tomkins, 1998, pp. 41–5).

Rights give rise to responsibilities. The committee's contention was that ministerial responsibilities flowed from the rights of parliament to set terms and conditions on those enjoying executive office. These terms and conditions were not in the nature of employment obligations, because the chief political executive has effective authority to hire, move and remove ministers and by extension to establish any code of conduct expressing the ideals of ministerial conduct expected of members of the executive team. The ethic of accountability to parliament covers a complementary set of expectations deriving from parliament and expressing its expected standards, designed to facilitate the work of parliament rather than the somewhat separate work of the political executive. The basis of the proposed obligation was that its breach would constitute a contempt of parliament, a view that British political executives have refused to accept (HCPC, 1997, paras 7–10; cf. Tomkins, 1998, pp. 57–63).

The proposers of the parliamentary resolution hoped that it would make ministers 'think carefully before withholding information' from parliament (HCPC, 1996, para.

61). The fact that the relevant sanctions are political rather than legal tells us much about the nature of this dimension of ministerial ethics. We are dealing with political morality for which Westminster-derived parliaments have no agreed institutional framework other than the usual checks and balances of government and Opposition (Reid, 1980). The committee was very conscious that this aspect of ministerial responsibility 'is a political activity, conducted between politicians', and therefore of the need not 'to confuse a political activity with a judicial (or quasi-judicial) one' (HCPC, 1996, para. 67).

Modest Hopes

To their credit, political executives are now responding to public calls for standards appropriate to ministerial officers. But the political executive model suffers from persistent doubts about the ability of chief political executives to put aside the partisan interests of the serving government when judging allegations about self-serving ministerial colleagues. Independent expert models can suffer from the opposite problem — what the report of the 1979 Bowen Inquiry termed the 'danger to good government' from 'moral escalation': raising expectations so high that ethics offices cannot sustain the higher standards of public interest they are established to help generate (Bowen, 1979, para. 3.10). Hence the importance of exploring the potential of the parliamentary model to moderate ministerial ethics, including the moderation of unrealistic expectations about the personal qualities of elected public office holders.

Putting political ethics in its place means finding a greater role for parliaments as standards setters. The Bowen Inquiry provides a model of best policy practice. Bowen recommended that a Public Integrity Commission be established with powers akin to those of a royal commission and with the obligation of conducting its proceedings publicly, reporting directly to parliament on matters of parliamentary and ministerial ethics (Bowen, 1979, paras 12.41–12.43). Should such an investigative body act on ministerial or alternatively parliamentary direction? Developments since 1979 have shown the advantage for high officials like the Auditor-General of reporting directly to parliamentary committees as distinct from ministers. Australian debate over how best to regulate ministerial standards should relearn the policy lessons, conceptual and institutional, that are evident in the Bowen design for moderating ministerial ethics.

An example of the Bowen approach is the Bill for a Charter of Political Honesty sponsored by Australian Democrats senator Andrew Murray. The fact that the Bill comes from a minor party and one in the Senate itself tells a larger tale. The Bill is designed to establish a Commissioner for Ministerial and Parliamentary Ethics to implement a code of conduct. A parliamentary committee would take responsibility for preparing a new code of conduct covering ministers and, probably separately, backbenchers. Parliament, through the power of the two presiding officers, would appoint the new commissioner, responsible for the practical implementation of the code. Duties range from post-election education to investigation and report of alleged breaches of the code. The proposed commissioner is more of an investigator than a judge. The Murray Bill has been introduced into the Senate but not yet debated. It stands as a useful reminder of the responsibility parliament must face up to if it wants to re-establish its own credibility by restoring its ethical standards as well as those of ministers.

Conclusion

Although ethics is about right or virtuous conduct, I have argued that there are good public policy reasons for targeting vice (e.g. misuse of public office) ahead of virtue (e.g. personal moral excellence among public officials). The debate over whether to prioritize vice or virtue was argued out over 50 years ago in the classic Friedrich–Finer debates over the relative merits of internal and external protections against maladministration and defective discretion in democratic governance (see, for example, Friedrich, 1966; Finer, 1966; and more generally Uhr, 1989). Finer warned about the dangers to democratic governance of over-reliance on the 'internal checks' of private ethics compared to the 'external checks' of public accountability. In Finer's terms, what is of interest is ministers' ability to manage their accountability obligations, and their personal qualities are relevant to the extent that these qualities help or hinder the proper management of these parliamentary obligations (Finer, 1966, pp. 251–6). To oversimplify: individuals devoid of personal virtue might still make worthy ministers if they are committed to the professional management of their obligations of public accountability and prepared to marshall their personal qualities to do justice to their obligations of office. Just as clearly, individuals with outstanding personal qualities might make unworthy ministers, particularly if their 'overfeasance' gets in the way of their routines of responsibility to parliament.

My fear is similar to the one Finer raised against Friedrich, or indeed at the practical policy level, similar to Bowen's fears of 'moral escalation' and the rise of intrusive 'censorial authorities' (Bowen, 1979, para. 3.10). Friedrich was prepared to trust to the policy discretion of officials, including officials working in bureaucratic watchdogs designed to promote public integrity. By contrast, Finer called for renewed legislative scrutiny of bureaucracy, particularly of bureaucratic guardians of the public interest. Many of the core issues about the best balance of internal responsibility and external accountability remain with us. The modern ethics movement can be seen as an extension of Friedrich's position, which is yet to face its Finer-like challenge and be required to defend its call for new expert institutions to protect political life against partisan excesses.

In that spirited academic debate of old both protagonists recognized that under contemporary social conditions the rule of law required ever-expanding spheres of official discretion, exercised by unelected officials as well as ministers. Both accepted ministerial and official discretion had come to stay; what divided them was how best to regulate or control discretionary decision making to make it compatible with the norms of responsible democratic governance. Friedrich was 'the modernist': the advocate of reliance on the inner check of the personal ethics of public officials, safeguarded by greater community participation in government decision making. Finer was 'the traditionalist': the advocate of reliance on the external checks of public accountability, particularly the accountability of the executive to the legislature.

Friedrich's case was a version of the argument commonly made against external accountability. That is, that the great ideal of parliamentary government rarely if ever matched political practice, where legislative oversight either drains official discretion of its motivating qualities or is itself driven and distorted by partisan interests, with norms of party government trumping parliamentary independence (Friedrich, 1966, pp. 227–32; cf. Woodhouse, 1994, pp. 16–8). For Friedrich, it made better sense to prepare, educate and train public officials (including ministers) in the arts of responsible public decision making and to trust to their good sense and good will, subject to the checks and balances of open government and public criticism.

Finer's response was more than simply a restatement of the traditional ideals of responsible parliamentary government, with administrative officials accountable to ministers who in turn are accountable to parliament. Finer's critique became a larger concern about the pretensions of officials, particularly unelected officials, to exercise their ethical superiority to protect the wider public interest of society, even protecting society against the law and policy as determined by the legislature. His special contribution to this classic debate was to draw attention to the hazards to democratic governance of what he termed 'overfeasance, where a duty is taken beyond what law and custom oblige or empower'. Overfeasance might arise from dictatorial temper, or from bureaucratic ambition, or from 'genuine, sincere, public-spirited zeal'. Finer's case was that virtue itself has need of limits, to save society from 'public-spirited zeal' (Finer, 1966, p. 252).

Today we can say that both were right in their own terms. Contemporary democratic governance requires both the public official's individual sense of responsibility and the institutional capacity of accountability agencies: that is, both internal and external checks, with motivation through the personal ethics of public officials as well as the safeguards of external checks of public accountability (Uhr, 1999a). The real challenge is to get the balance right. Both sides of this classic debate linger on today, with now rather dated versions of the Friedrich line on the need for greater virtue in executive officials and the Finer line on the need for greater legislative oversight to restrain the political executive from misplaced zeal. What is long overdue is a blending of these two perspectives, particularly an exploration of the inner checks that should motivate legislators when managing the system of external accountability.

Note

1   Thanks to Adam Tomkins, Geoff Stokes, Bernard Wright and Richard Mulgan for helpful comments on earlier drafts.

Chapter 16

Advancing Ministerial Ethics

Ian Holland and Jenny Fleming

During the mid-1990s, Australian government minister Peter Reith, then an Opposition frontbencher, breached the guidelines for the use of his parliamentary entitlements by giving his parliamentary telephone card (telecard) service number and security code to his son. It was only in October 2000, however, that the consequences of Mr Reith's breach emerged in the press and the parliament. It transpired that his son had made around $1 000 of calls using the minister's phone access. More significantly, the telecard had been used by others whose identities were never positively determined by the Australian Federal Police. These other individuals charged over $45 000 of calls to the card from locations around the world, creating a scandal that was dubbed the telecard affair. The prime minister refused to sack his minister or to require that he take responsibility for the debt, but Peter Reith was eventually forced by popular pressure to personally repay the $50 000 phone bill that had been incurred in his name.

Following the telecard affair, the Opposition introduced a Bill into parliament aimed at increasing the scrutiny of parliamentarians. The Auditor of Parliamentary Allowances and Entitlements Bill 2000 was necessary, Labor said, 'to help restore community confidence in the way in which Members of the Commonwealth Parliament use their various entitlements' (Beazley, 2000, p. 1). The Bill contained the core elements of one of Labor's 1998 election policy planks. It proposed the creation of an independent officer, with similar powers to the Auditor-General and the Ombudsman, whose responsibility would be to advise parliamentarians on the use of their allowances. The office would also audit the use of these entitlements and investigate complaints about their use.

The government, however, disagreed with Labor's proposal. They pointed out that to pursue this institutional reform was 'to suspect every member and senator' of rorting the entitlements system (Australia, Senate, 9 November 2000, p. 19594). The conservative government mocked the Opposition's stance, pointing out that it implied they thought their own members of parliament could not be trusted and that the Opposition was 'smearing every MP in this house' (Australia, House of Representatives, 31 October 2000, p. 21707).

The government also pointed out that the parliament was in danger of using a sledge-hammer to crack a walnut. The cost of the proposed institutional arrangements, they reasoned, would be huge compared to the cost of any malfeasance they might reveal. An audit of travel entitlements administration in 1997 showed an error rate in the claiming of entitlements of less than 2 per cent, not always to the detriment of the public purse (Australia, Senate, 9 November 2000, p. 19577). Thus, despite the telecard scandal, Labor's proposal is likely to be defeated on party lines.

As details about Mr Reith's phone bill materialized in the media, some may have gained the impression that there were no systems in place either to guide or monitor the use of entitlements by politicians, but as the previous chapters have shown this is not the case. Monitoring systems have been in place, not only in Australia but elsewhere, sometimes for many years. They have worked in large measure to keep politicians out of trouble and the burden on the public purse to reasonable levels. Indeed, an array of structures is used to encourage politicians generally, and sometimes ministers in particular, not to abuse the privileges of public office.

As Uhr (Chapter 15) has indicated, some of these monitoring systems emphasize the role of the executive, some the role of parliament and some the role of extra-parliamentary institutions. The first group includes:

- Westminster conventions of ministerial responsibility;
- Written and unwritten norms within the cabinet, policed by the head of the executive (Australia before the 1980s, UK before the 1990s);
- A written code, known to all and policed by the head of the executive (Australia since 1996);
- A combination of a published prime minister's code of conduct and a parliamentary commissioner for public standards (UK since mid-1990s); and
- A written code, supported by an adviser to the head of the executive (Canada since 1994, Queensland since 2000).

The second type is exemplified by the Canadian provincial mechanisms:

- Parliamentary legislated code, under which a commissioner is appointed to advise MPs and recommend to parliament corrective courses of action (most Canadian provinces).

The third approach can take two distinct forms, with a constitutional basis or an extra-parliamentary institutional basis:

- A statutory authority which may initiate its own investigations, independent of the government, answerable to an all-party committee of the parliament (Western Australia and New South Wales since 1988 and Queensland since 1989);
- Appointment of a sitting judge as a conflict of interest commissioner, with powers to impose penalties or refer matters to the provincial courts (Nova Scotia since 1991); and

- Constitutional frameworks, under which aspects of parliamentary or executive conduct are constitutionally specified and thus judicially enforced (elements of the German party law).

Despite the existence of these institutional arrangements, the motivation of ministers remains the subject of proposals for reform. In some cases this is because most arrangements are targeted at parliament generally, and not designed specifically with ministers in mind. Few of these institutions, including those that do deal with ministers directly, have been without controversy. Some are periodically reported to be either in crisis or in danger of disappearing altogether, such as the increasingly tenuous link between Westminster conventions of responsibility and ministerial resignation as evidenced by Woodhouse (Chapter 4). Other elements of the machinery of government have proven decidedly reluctant to impinge upon the special jurisdiction of the executive — for example, the Auditor-General in Australia (Wanna and Gash, Chapter 12). At the same time, few doubt that there must be some sort of institutional capacity to guide ministers and sanction them if they stray too far. The problem will not go away, as citizen confidence in politicians continues to decline (McAllister, 2000) and the media respond by attempting to ensure these issues remain in the public eye (Tanner, 1998, Chapter 13). The only way forward would seem to be to enhance the institutional framework that might motivate ministers to do the right thing, but this is not an easy task.

Tensions at the Centre of Power

As Sutherland wrote a decade ago, when it comes to ethics in parliament 'every reform is its own problem' (Sutherland, 1991, p. 91). There are tensions in all processes of political reform, and the studies in this volume have highlighted how acute these tensions can become when they are interventions at the centre of power in modern democracies. These tensions and contradictions define the constraints under which practical attempts at reform must be undertaken, and are outlined here.

First, institutions that further fix the body politic under the public gaze are almost inevitably going to give the public new scandals to observe. Institutions that promote ethical political behaviour will also reveal discourses of moral failure in politics and are likely to trip up more MPs, further alienating the public even as rorts are successfully eliminated. The NSW ICAC, for example, sharpened the knife of 'corruption'. Its emphasis on treating unethical behaviour as corruption, together with its considerable powers as an anti-corruption watchdog, combined to cut short the careers of two NSW MPs (see Fleming, Tanner, Chapters 11 and 13).

John Howard's code of conduct similarly reduced the discretionary space in which ministers might operate. It set out rules for ministers in writing, in a very public and readily accessible form, and with more comprehensive coverage than before. This increased the chance that ministers would be criticized or sacked without there necessarily being any change in the actual standard of ministerial conduct. As Weller and Tiernan document, this is exactly the situation that eventuated. Similarly, the proximity of the Ethics Counsellor to the Canadian prime minister has allowed the public to superimpose a sceptical discourse about the integrity of the counsellor on top of their existing perceptions of conflict of interest and patronage among MPs (Jackson, Chapter 9). Any mechanism for motivating ministers to higher ethical standards has to balance a competing need not to motivate voters to greater moral outrage.

Second, any institution that attenuates the power of the executive becomes a target of the executive. Yet, many of the institutional mechanisms for motivating ministers to ethical conduct necessarily attenuate executive power. Thus any reform in this area risks executive opposition. Sometimes the hostility of governments to ethics is evident in their resistance to proposed institutional reforms. This is exemplified by the British government's rejection of the British Committee on Standards in Public Life's proposals for amendments to the *Questions of Procedure* (now *Ministerial Code*; see Baker, 2000; Nolan, Woodhouse, Chapters 2 and 4) and by the tortuous process in NSW by which party commitments to a code of conduct took the best part of a decade to translate into an actual document. At other times the hostility is evidenced by governments restraining or ignoring ethics advisers. The Canadian federal arrangement that keeps the Ethics Counsellor's advice confidential and the legislative amendments in Queensland that constrain the parameters within which the CJC operates are examples of this (Jackson, Fleming, Chapters 9 and 11).

There are ways in which executive resistance may be mitigated. As Fleming showed with the ICAC and CJC, strong media and public support for watchdog organizations can provide some balance against governments that want to curb institutions they believe infringe on executive authority. Even with that support, however, the ICAC and CJC have been to varying degrees restrained from exercising their original mandate. Part of the issue here is the challenge of avoiding ethics institutions becoming casualties of an issue attention cycle, when governments start to realize the complexity and cost of ethics support, and public interest in the last scandal wanes (Downs, 1972).

Another way to entrench support for the institutions is to focus on their effort in helping ministers rather than investigating them — on prior advice rather than subsequent investigation (Preston, Sampford, Chapters 10 and 14). The exemplar for this might be the way in which conflict of interest commissioners and the like have worked in the Canadian provinces (as distinct from the federal arrangement) to assist MPs, based on a parliamentary mandate (Greene and Shugarman, 1997). Difficult as the task may be, attempts to motivate ministers must be organized either to prevent ministers from wanting to turn against them, or to have the institutional authority and capacity to resist the pressure when it comes. Furthermore, this balance has to be struck in a way that produces some sort of credible enforcement mechanism.

The question of how to avoid simply engendering executive opposition immediately reveals a *third* constraint on finding mechanisms to motivate ministers.

There is always a balancing act required between institutionalizing ethics on an equitable basis across the parliament or public sector, and having regard to the special circumstances of the executive that were set out in Chapter 1. Parliamentary institutions, like the Canadian provincial commissioners, work with all MPs rather than just ministers. Any institution that supports all MPs has in its scope members of all parties, and can be seen to be even-handed as a consequence. Translating this structure to one that deals only with ministers presents a problem for any party that finds its ministers getting into trouble over an extended period of government. It is relatively easy for a government to introduce standards for ministers at the time of their election, because they use this as a vehicle for establishing a contrast between themselves and the previous, inevitably 'corrupt', administration. But as time goes by they develop a sense of being unfairly persecuted. This is because, although parliamentarians come from every party, ministers are, at any given time, from only one party or governing coalition. There are never ministers on the Opposition benches.

This produces a degree of 'ethics fatigue'. Nowhere was this more evident than in the case of Australia's Prime Minister Howard, who endured two turbulent years of being hammered by the Opposition with the government's own code of conduct. Eventually, defending the latest minister to run into difficulty, Howard effectively ended up arguing, as the Opposition leader put it, that 'the ministerial guidelines are a guide: they are not a death sentence' (Australia, House of Representatives, 2 November 2000, p. 19997). The public response to this was again cynicism that apparently 'the only rule for determining when ministers resign is when the prime minister decides' (Thompson and Tillotsen, 1999, pp. 52–3, Weller, Chapter 5).

There is thus an important limit to what lessons can be distilled from the cases of the Canadian provincial conflict of interest commissioners. Any institution that monitors only ministers scrutinizes only one side of politics for long periods of time, and has to walk a fine line between being a captive of the government and being its persecutor. It is the line between being Howard Wilson, Canadian federal Ethics Counsellor — criticized for being an instrument of the government — and being Kenneth Starr, US special prosecutor — criticized for being a partisan enemy of the executive (Jackson, Chapter 9).

Fourth, there are dilemmas about what might comprise helpful ethical guidance for ministers. Every scandal that gets blamed on ambiguity in guidelines encourages greater articulation of ethical standards, yet community standards are constantly evolving. Thus attempts to set clear and explicit goals may attempt to fix standards that are in a state of flux, or clash with other community standards and mores. An example of this can be found in the issue of the regulation of ministerial interests and those of their spouses. Ministers are generally expected to meet very high standards of disclosure of their personal financial and business arrangements, and are often called upon to alter those arrangements — through the disposal of shares, for example — in order to hold ministerial office. These standards are to a great degree extended to ministers' spouses and in some instances other immediate family members. Yet at the same time, the community supports rights to privacy and the autonomy of spouses, who may have business interests in their own right. Every time the rules governing disclosure and divestment are extended to deal with the latest outrage the rules risk violating evolving community standards about the independent nature of family members. This led, for example, to a spouse withholding for a year information demanded under the disclosure rules in Newfoundland (Greene, 1997). Thus attempts to focus on being comprehensive in articulating rules for conduct, while temporarily comforting for both politicians and their constituents, also risk failure because they are not flexible enough as community expectations evolve.

This problem of articulating ethical standards is further complicated by divergent opinions about just what is appropriate conduct in political life. There is a great temptation to assume that everyone in the community shares the same moral code, and that politicians are ordinary people who function off the same ethical template as others in the community. Yet clearly this is not the case.

There are differences between the views of citizens and their representatives about what constitutes ethical conduct (Mancuso, 1995; Jackson and Smith, 1996; Smith, 1998). Several studies found that the ethical standards of elected representatives were both lower and more diverse than those of voters. Parliamentarians were likely to believe it was ethical for them to do things that advantaged citizens in their electorates, but those citizens were likely to disagree. Assuming that voters care about the ethics of their representatives, the ultimate check on how far the morals of elector and elected can diverge is the electoral process. Yet little has been said about how any institution other than the ballot box can address this. MPs claim they are comfortable having voters judge their ethics at the ballot box, and do not want the help of ethics 'experts'. It seems that, while research reveals differences between MPs and citizens, the MPs resolutely want to believe they hold the same values as their constituents. Yet, given that politicians seem to have ethical views somewhat different from those of the electorate as a whole, this approach is likely to see the persistent emergence of scandals, as MPs periodically fail to notice what they do not want to see: that their ethical choices are not the same as those their citizens would make. The treatment of euthanasia laws in several countries is evidence of this, as parliaments have blocked the liberalizing of laws governing the right of citizens to seek assistance in ending their own lives, while most citizens support law reform. Ministers as a subset of MPs are likely to share the ethical perspective of their parliamentary colleagues, but the situation is more pressing here because their power to act on their own ethical views is so much greater. Motivating ministers to morality is contentious because it admits this ethical divergence that politicians want to deny.

The other reason that it is not safe to assume that politicians should work off the same ethical premises as their constituents is that parliamentary life creates different ethical choices from those faced by private citizens. Hayden refers to the examples of politicians finding themselves in situations where they have power to make choices that can mean lying can save a life, or more extreme still, where sending one person to his/her death may save many lives (Hayden, 1998). Far less extreme, however, are the never-ending stream of compromises negotiated between competing interests that are called for during the process of government. In these situations, what might be seen as corruption in other contexts becomes a sanctioned, if not warmly embraced, way of solving problems (Philp, 1997). The subtle dividing line between these things is evident in the case of NSW Premier Greiner and the ICAC (Fleming, Tanner, Chapters 11 and 13). These remarks are not intended to endorse 'corrupt' practices because they are necessary to the politics of 'dirty hands' (Rynard and Shugarman, 1999). Rather, the point is that because these situations arise, it is not fair to expect ministers to know the right thing to do by reference to the moral frameworks of their constituents, or to what they might regard as their own 'private' moral values. Members of the executive have role responsibilities that put them in a unique ethical position that means that they require moral reference points to guide them, external to their own ethical knowledge. Once again, however, this is not something politicians want to admit, and every attempt at intervention to provide this framework risks enforcing unrealistically inflexible standards on the one hand, or inappropriately vague guidance on the other.

Fifth, as the telecard affair has highlighted, there is the question of the cost effectiveness of change. Some institutions cost millions to run, yet may hunt down malfeasance costing just thousands. Some assessments need to be made of what is in reality the greater cost to society. Yet the capacity to see institution formation as a waste of money is limited by citizens' (and the media's) insistence on scandalizing any abuse of privilege. A proposed office of an auditor of parliamentary entitlements, for example, has the potential to create a financial cost that may seem out of proportion to the errors it is designed to remedy. The counter-argument is that restoring public faith in politicians is worth far more than the potential savings in parliamentary expenditure. The most important role these institutions play is not in preventing malfeasance but in increasing confidence in democratic institutions. Few would disagree with this reasoning, if parliamentary debates in recent times are anything to go by, but this brings us to a *sixth* issue: the capacity of *any* ethics reforms to cause a net improvement in the way citizens regard their government, and therefore to make ministers believe that such improvements are worthwhile.

Attempts to motivate ministers to higher standards of conduct risk degenerating into counter-productive trade-offs between the frequency of scandals and the levels of public outrage that they generate. It is worth considering why the growth of ethics institutions has so far coincided with continuing decline in community confidence in politicians. In the past we relied on the ballot box as the most 'formidable method of accountability' (Australia, Senate, 12 October 2000, p. 18441), and politicians continue to attach great importance to this. At the same time, more and more guidelines, scrutineers, checks and balances are established. These mechanisms mean that each subsequent ministerial error is magnified in significance. Media and parliamentary opponents are more ruthless in their attacks on MPs' mistakes because, they argue, ministers had clear guidelines and institutional support. Encouraged by the increasingly hysterical attacks of rival political parties, channelled through the media, the electorate then may express greater outrage at the ballot box.

There is thus a risk that all of this is at best a zero-sum game. Fewer guidelines and less transparency might mean ministers are more willing to do the wrong thing or make bad judgements, but might also mean the electorate is more willing either to forgive or at least vote out of office and forget. High levels of scrutiny of and support for ministers may attenuate misbehaviour but increase the levels of disaffection and punishment prompted by those misdemeanours that are detected. Media commentators made exactly these sorts of observations when both the Major government in the UK and the Howard government in Australia placed an emphasis on 'clean' government and enhanced standards of conduct from MPs. When each of these governments had MPs in trouble, public and media criticism was particularly harsh, as in the British case was the judgement of the electorate at the subsequent general election. The extent of this phenomenon may be difficult to assess, but its implications for reform are obvious.

Finally, tackling ministerial ethics requires not only recognizing the diversity of ethical views mentioned previously, but also recognizing the differences between types of ethical risk. The differences between the problems with party donations evident in Germany (Seibel, Chapter 7) and the problems of conflict of interest in Canada or Australia (Jackson, Tiernan, Chapters 9 and 8), for example, lead to the question of whether different institutions might be necessary — or more effective — for dealing with different ethical problems. The many ethical pitfalls for ministers have different institutional origins. Greene and Shugarman (1997), for example, distinguish between patronage, conflict of interest and undue influence, the latter covering both problems presented by lobbyists (exemplified by the UK 'cash for questions' affair) and by party and election financing. The roots of patronage lie in the executive's authority over appointment processes, which can be constrained by the parliament. Conflict of interest is more a product of the relationship between the individual minister's circumstances and his/her portfolio responsibilities, while party financing issues arise not out of the executive's power *per se*, but out of the overwhelming importance of parties to the electoral system, and ministers' dependence upon them. As Seibel shows in the German case, it is the weakness of party laws that render German ministers vulnerable to ethical failure.

Overlaying the diverse institutional origins of ethical issues are differences between political cultures and the way citizens respond to political indiscretions. Thompson (2000) distinguishes between three different types of scandal in the political field: sex scandals, financial scandals and power scandals. He notes that while these basic types have distinguishing features, they all involve 'the transgression of norms or conventions [and] the kinds of norms vary from one type of scandal to another' (p. 120). In Thompson's terms the defining feature of financial scandals, for example, generally involves 'an infringement of rules governing the acquisition and allocation of economic resources' (p. 121). What is important for our purposes is that we recognize that what matters ethically in one jurisdiction may not be considered an issue or a dilemma in another. In other words, we need to identify what constitutes an ethical danger in these various jurisdictions. Seibel's rendition of the Kohl scandal in Germany, for example, depicts an entirely different public response to a financial scandal from the Australians' reaction to the 'telecard' affair or the travel entitlement rorts. Another example is that of sexual indiscretion. Sex scandals have long provided material for the media, but as an example of unethical behaviour the issue has much more salience in the UK and the USA than it does, for example, in Australia (see Gaster, 1988; Silverstein, 1988; Thompson, 2000, pp. 124–58).

These diverse ethical challenges may demand diverse institutional reactions. The sort of structure that might deal with conflict of interest may not be very effective in tackling party and election financing questions. It is similarly not clear that a body charged with preventing official misconduct generally is going to handle patronage cases arising in the executive. The administration of parliamentary entitlements is an area in which the main requirements are meticulous administration and effective audit; the requirements of preventing ministers from giving lobbyists undue access to decision processes would seem altogether different.

We have described a range of parameters that constrain institutional changes that might enhance the ethical motivation of ministers. There is the need to avoid reforms that create more scandals purely by raising standards, without there being any actual deterioration in ministerial conduct. There is the difficulty of designing any institution so that those it both supports and regulates do not simply turn on it and try to dismantle or stymie the apparatus. There is the challenge of having to regulate or advise only one 'side' of politics for long periods of time. There is the problem of trying to define appropriate ethical standards that reflect community values and to get parliamentary support for such a process. There is the possibility that change will cost more than it will benefit the community. There is the risk that enhanced transparency will lead to greater electoral alienation, as new scandals come to light. There is a need for multiple responses to the very diverse nature of the ethical questions that ministers face. What can be achieved in the face of all these constraints?

Prospects for Motivating Ministers

There is a point too easily forgotten amidst the scandals portrayed in the media and the declining respect citizens have for their elected representatives. It is that many countries experience affluence, the rule of law, an effective separation of power, liberal democratic values, an educated electorate, a free press and a competitive political process. These have ensured a remarkable equality of access to political life, a great degree of transparency of parliamentary and executive processes, and a high degree of integrity among the vast majority of participants, many of whom could attempt to extract great personal or partisan benefit from the system but who choose not to do so.

Ethics in politics is nevertheless an increasingly important issue, as electorates become more educated and less tolerant of waste and abuse of office. However, it is important not to get this out of perspective. The February 2001 state election result in

Queensland, Australia, for example, saw a political party that had suffered significant damage, as a result of a very public and damaging vote rigging scandal (CJC, 2000a) and conflict of interest allegations, returned to power with a massive majority. The result suggests citizens remained focused on stable government and policy issues more than ethical questions when they judged alternative governments. Perhaps they were mostly satisfied that unethical conduct in politics had not developed on a scale so serious as to be damaging the fabric of democratic political life.

Beyond this key point several observations may be made. There are structural tensions between the desires of heads of government and parliaments to be the primary reference point for ministers and their conduct (Uhr, Chapter 15). These tensions are evident in the balancing act in Westminster-influenced jurisdictions, between reliance on conventions of ministerial responsibility and other parliamentary or extra-parliamentary institutions. By and large, however, parliaments have only been successful in gaining some ascendancy over premiers and prime ministers in settings where parliaments have a power base potentially separate from the government itself. This has been most evident in 'strong' bicameral systems (e.g. Australia, the USA) and situations where governing parties have a slim grip on power. In the former, different electoral systems often apportion party power differently between the Houses. The resulting differences create a potential site for critique of cabinet only partly dependent on the Opposition. It also leads to the possibility of ministers being censured by one House, even though the government may have a majority in the other. This, together with an active committee system, increases the need for ministers to defend credibly their conduct to other than their head of government and their party room.

Minority governments, governments created through the formation of *ad hoc* coalitions and governments with very small majorities can all find parliament to be more activist in the judgement of ministers. Non-aligned MPs or disaffected backbenchers may have sufficient power in such a parliament that even the threat of defection against a government can bring a minister down (Fleming, Chapter 11; Finer, 1956; Woodhouse, 1993). Coalition partners themselves may want ministers to maintain traditional lines of accountability to parliament (Shephard, Chapter 6). In these jurisdictions parliaments have been able to breathe more life into conventions of ministerial responsibility. The stronger the government's control of the parliamentary process, the less likely ministers are to be motivated by anything other than their loyalty to their leader, prompting pessimism about accountability (Woodhouse, Chapter 4). The challenge is to balance the need to motivate ministers in new ways in such jurisdictions against the reluctance of all parties to undertake major institutional reforms at the centre of political power.

Increased public scrutiny of ministerial actions is only going to strengthen the credibility of the executive if there is increased institutional capacity for a well-intentioned minister to work out how to stay out of trouble. There has been a persistent failure of ministers to avoid conflict of interest allegations in many countries including Australia, New Zealand, the UK, Germany, the USA and Canada despite the existence of conventions and norms maintained by presidents, prime ministers and premiers.

Conflict of interest scandals relating to ministerial share holdings, insider trading, trusts, private companies and partnerships have been regular features of politics for over a century, yet despite prime ministerial pronouncements, refined guidelines and disciplinary action they continue to reoccur. This suggests that, whatever the reasons, internal structures are not adequate if unsupported in other ways. In this regard, the Australian federal arrangement put in place by John Howard in 1996 has brought together the worst of both worlds (Uhr, 1998c; Weller, Chapter 5). On the one hand, it has exposed the executive to enhanced scrutiny, increasing the likelihood that the government might lose ministers, thus further disillusioning the public. On the other hand, by keeping the enforcement of the code entirely in the PM's hands it has maximized the likelihood that ministers will be defended, enhancing the crises that ultimately engulf the government. A system such as this maximizes the chance that ministerial conduct will become an issue (by focusing increased attention on the 'bar': the standards of conduct) while not providing the institutional support which will actually either prevent the conduct or expedite the removal of offending ministers.

We recognize that a number of initiatives appear to have been successful in dealing with some ethical problems experienced in the parliamentary democracies discussed in this book, particularly in relation to conflict of interest and the use of entitlements. The prior advice of various agencies seems to have significantly reduced the number of ethical problems faced by parliamentarians. This is the case whether the advice is purely internal (as in the Canadian federal case) or has a parliamentary mandate (as in the Canadian provinces) or is a mixture of these (as in the USA). The important first step is that advice comes from someone other than the head of the executive. Criticism of Canada's federal Ethics Counsellor, however, suggests that while some advice is better than none, the provision of advice by a parliamentary office rather than an executive one is a good idea. Parliamentarians seem to seek advice from professionals if those professionals are available. Whether their underlying motive is desire for the public good or desire to retain power (Patapan, Chapter 3), they do appear by and large to be motivated to seek advice if it is confidential and offers them some 'insurance'.

Nevertheless, when it comes to regulating the executive, one of the most intractable problems remains the third constraint mentioned above: that in any given period all members of an executive are usually from the one party or coalition, which can lead either to governments perceiving a regulator as their enemy, or Oppositions perceiving it as a government's captive. The difficulty of persuading governments to address this issue is apparent when we consider the likely reaction to one approach to this challenge. It is possible to speculate that the problem of the executive being from one side of politics could be tempered by processing certain aspects of ministerial conduct through a federal institution. This would be feasible in cases where several jurisdictions are able to collaborate in creating such a structure on a constitutional basis, such as the Australian states or Canadian provinces.[1] It would require parallel legislative action by participating jurisdictions (as is used to govern competition policy and non-bank financial institutions in Australia). Its purpose would be to advise or investigate ministers in a way that some institutions currently advise or investigate parliamentarians. It could be overseen by a multi-party parliamentary committee. The legislation would create an office of a commissioner as currently operates in most Canadian provinces. The frame of reference for such an organization would be set by legislation, as is the case for virtually all the parliamentary and extra-parliamentary institutions discussed in this book.[2]

Perhaps the issues most amenable to being dealt with in such a forum are those least effectively dealt with by prime ministerial codes of conduct: conflict of interest issues. There is no evidence from the case studies that the use of parliamentary entitlements should be taken outside the arena of parliamentary and government departments, while party and election financing problems can be processed effectively under financing and criminal laws — provided the laws are adequate (which they are not in Germany: Seibel, Chapter 7). Conflict of interest issues, however, while successfully dealt with for MPs generally by existing mechanisms, remain troublesome for the executive. Bringing several jurisdictions' ministers under the one institution would increase the likelihood that at any given time governments of different ideological orientations would be simultaneously under the authority of the monitoring or advisory body. Such an arrangement would have the advantage that it would be complex to dismantle and therefore more able to resist the depredations of the occasional disaffected cabinet. The institutional design would use the engagement of multiple jurisdictions as a 'buffer' against partisan executive attacks.

While an arrangement like this might help deal with conflict of interest, it might suit only some jurisdictions. Furthermore, as we reasoned in the first chapter and also above, the great power of the executive is likely to make it both willing and able to resist proposals such as this. Why would a cabinet voluntarily cede power in this sort of way? It is possible that one state or province, its government destabilized or its parliamentary majority eroded by a major scandal, might consider such a scheme as a way of restoring credibility and perhaps thus salvaging government. But the strength of such an institution is also its weakness: it is unlikely that several jurisdictions would be troubled by such serious scandal at one time. It is thus improbable that several governments would simultaneously be motivated to make such significant changes to how their ministers were motivated. Yet such a mechanism may be the only avenue by which conflict of interest within the executive could be addressed while avoiding the constitutional dilemmas that come with attempts at extra-parliamentary regulation of the executive in states that operate under cabinet government.

As suggested in Chapter 1, ideas such as this need to be considered in the context of a suite of institutions that create the motivational context for ministers. In this regard, one problem to which several contributors have drawn attention, and which warrants further analysis, is the role of political parties. Parties are ubiquitous to modern political systems. They get ministers to the pinnacle of power, and ministers in return are to a significant degree loyal to the interests of their parties. Yet there is ambivalence about what is expected of parties when it comes to ethics in politics. On the one hand, their centrality to most political systems has seen aspects of their operations both regulated and given state support. On the other hand, they remain private organizations which are not required to operate according to public sector norms or under public sector scrutiny. The close relationship between members of the executive and their parties has played a role in the disgrace or downfall of ministers (Gaunt, 1999; Smith, 1999; Seibel, Tiernan, Chapters 7 and 8), yet citizens seem relatively unconcerned about the conduct of party officials outside the parliamentary arena.

As parties increasingly dominate the executive and the parliament they could also become the subject of closer scrutiny and regulation, so that ministers are not tempted to carry service to their party too far. This would seem particularly relevant to questions of party donations and undue influence such as in the case of the 'cash for questions' affair. Parties, however, also play a broader role in the ethical motivation of ministers, through their contribution to the culture of politics, and it is far less apparent how this might be addressed without impairing the vigorous party competition that is an important part of democracy. Some political parties have adopted codes of conduct and their own internal mechanisms for policing these. Whether this sort of strategy can contribute to large-scale changes to political culture that might ultimately modify the ethical world view of ministers in a positive way remains an open question. It is clear, however, that only a suite of arrangements is likely to come to grips with the most important and difficult challenge to ethics in politics: the special circumstances of the executive.

Notes

1 This approach might also be feasible in other settings in which multi-levelled governance takes place, such as the European Union.
2 Such an arrangement could also be implemented through jurisdictional reference of power to a national court of appeal (the High Court in Australia) rather in the manner of the existing arrangement in Nova Scotia.

Bibliography

Abbott, T. (1997), 'Unelected powers behind the throne', *The Australian*, 20 October.
Allars, M. (1997), *Administrative Law: Cases and Commentary*, Butterworths, Sydney.
Anson, Sir W. (1935), *Law and Custom of the Constitution*, 4th edn, Clarendon Press, Oxford.
Applbaum, A.I. (1999), *Ethics for Adversaries*, Princeton University Press, Princeton.
Aristotle [350 BC] (1984), *Politics*, Lord Carnes (trans.), University of Chicago Press, Chicago.
Aristotle [350 BC] (1985), *Nicomachean Ethics*, T. Irwin (trans.), Hackett Publishing Company, Indianapolis / Cambridge.
Australian National Audit Office (ANAO) (1993), *Department of the Environment, Sport and Territories, Community, Cultural, Recreational and Sporting Facilities: Facilities Program*, Efficiency Audit Report, 16 November, Australian Government Publishing Service, Canberra.
Australian National Audit Office (ANAO) (1997), *Ministerial Travel Claims*, Performance Audit Report No. 23, Commonwealth of Australia, Canberra.
Australian National Audit Office (ANAO) (1999–2000), *Examination of the Federation Cultural and Heritage Projects Program*, Audit Report No. 30, Commonwealth of Australia, Canberra.
Australian National Audit Office (ANAO) (2000), *Magnetic Resonance Imaging Services — Effectiveness and Probity of the Policy Development Processes and Implementation*, Performance Audit Report No. 42, 10 May, Commonwealth of Australia, Canberra.
Bailey, S. (1964), 'Ethics in the Public Service', *Public Administration Review*, Vol. 24, pp. 234–43.
Baker, A. (2000), *Prime Ministers and the Rule Book*, Politico's, London.
Barker, A. (1998), 'Political Responsibility for UK Prison Security: Ministers Escape Again', *Public Administration*, Vol. 76, pp. 1–24.
Barton, R. (1997), 'Canberra closeup: Blood on the carpet', *Reuters News Service*, 26 September, cited: http://www.business.reuters.com/.
Beazley, K. (2000), *Auditor of Parliamentary Allowances and Entitlements Bill 2000 Explanatory Memorandum*, Parliament of the Commonwealth of Australia, Canberra.
Becker, G.S. (1968), 'Crime and Punishment: An Economic Approach', *Journal of Political Economy*, Vol. 76, pp. 169–217.
Beiner, R. (1992), *What's the Matter with Liberalism*, University of California Press, Berkeley.
Bennett, W.L. (1988), *News: The Politics of Illusion*, 2nd edn, Longman, New York.
Berlin, I. (1996a), 'The Sense of Reality', in H. Hardy (ed.), *The Sense of Reality: Studies in Ideas and their History*, Farrar, Straus and Giroux, New York, pp. 1–39.
Berlin, I. (1996b), 'Political Judgement', in H. Hardy (ed.), *The Sense of Reality: Studies in Ideas and their History*, Farrar, Straus and Giroux, New York, pp. 50–3.

Blick, B. (1999), 'Ministerial Responsibility in Practice: a Commentary', *Australian Journal of Public Administration*, Vol. 58(1), pp. 58–61.
Blondel, J. (1991), 'Cabinet Government and Cabinet Ministers', in J. Blondel and J.-L. Thiébault (eds), *The Profession of Government Minister in Western Europe*, Macmillan, London, pp. 5–18.
Bogdanor, V. (1997), 'Ministerial Accountability', in B. Thompson and F.F. Ridley (eds), *Under the Scott-Light: British Government Seen Through the Scott Report*, Oxford University Press, Oxford.
Bovens, M. (1998), *The Quest for Responsibility: Accountability and Citizenship in Complex Organisations*, Cambridge University Press, Cambridge.
Bowen, N. (1979), *Public Duty and Private Interest: Report of the Committee of Inquiry*, Australian Government Publishing Service, Canberra.
Boyce, P. (1994), 'The Three Monkeys Syndrome and Possible Remedies', in *Proceedings of the Fourth Conference of the Samuel Griffith Society*, cited: http://www.samuelgriffith.org.au/
Boyken, F. (1998), *Die Neue Parteienfinanzierung*, Nomos, Baden-Baden.
Brien, A. (1998), *A Code of Conduct for Parliamentarians?* Parliamentary Library Research Paper 2, 1998–99, Commonwealth of Australia, Canberra.
Burch, M. and Holliday, I. (1999), 'The Prime Minister's and Cabinet Offices: An Executive Office in All But Name', *Parliamentary Affairs*, Vol. 52(1), pp. 32–45.
Burgmann, M. (1998), 'Constructing Codes: Pitfalls and Challenges', in N. Preston and C. Sampford with C.-A. Bois (eds), *Ethics and Political Practice: Perspectives on Legislative Ethics*, The Federation Press / Routledge, Sydney / London, pp. 118–26.
Butler, D. (1973), *The Canberra Model: Essays on Australian Government*, Macmillan, Melbourne.
Butler, D. (1997), 'Ministerial Accountability: Lessons of the Scott Report', in *Papers on Parliament*, Vol. 29, Department of the Senate, Canberra, pp. 1–17.
Butler, Sir R. (2000), 'Foreword', in A. Baker, *Prime Ministers and the Rule Book*, Politico's, London.
Cabinet Handbook (1988), *Cabinet Handbook*, Australian Government Publishing Service, Canberra.
Cabinet Office (1992), *Questions of Procedure for Ministers*, Cabinet Office, London.
Cabinet Office (1993–94), *Memorandum to Treasury and Civil Service Committee: The Role of the Civil Service*, HC 27-II, HMSO, London.
Cabinet Office (1995), *Response to Committee on Standards in Public Life, First Report*, Cm. 2931, HMSO, London.
Cabinet Office (1996), *Civil Service Code*, Cabinet Office, London.
Cabinet Office (1997), *Ministerial Code: A Code of Conduct and Guidance on Procedures for Ministers*, Cabinet Office, London.
Cabinet Office (1999), *Modernising Government*, Cabinet Office, London.
Canada (1984a), *Conflict of Interest and Post-Employment Code for Public Office Holders*, Supply and Services, Ottawa.
Canada (1984b), *Task Force on Conflict of Interest: Starr-Sharp Report*, Supply and Services, Ottawa.
Canada (1987), *Commission of Inquiry into the Facts and Allegations of Conflict of Interest Concerning the Honourable Sinclair M. Stevens: Report*, Supply and Services, Ottawa.
Chaples, E. and Page, B. (1995), 'The New South Wales Independent Commission Against Corruption', in M. Laffin and M. Painter (eds), *Reform and Reversal: Lessons from the Coalition Government in New South Wales, 1988–1995*, Macmillan, Melbourne, pp. 55–72.

Chapman, J. and Galston, W. (eds) (1992), *Virtue*, New York University Press, New York.
Christensen, J.P. (1999), *Ministerial Responsibility — Is There Such a Thing: Annual Report 1997-98*, Universitas Arhusiensis, Denmark.
Clair, F. (1997), Criminal Justice Commission Media Release, *Clair condemns move to reincarnate the Connolly-Ryan Inquiry*, 12 October, cited: http://cjc.qld.gov.au/cjc/1210medi.shtml.
Clemens, C. (2000), 'A Legacy Reassessed: Helmut Kohl and the German Party Finance Affair', *German Politics*, Vol. 9, pp. 25-50.
Cockerell, M. (2000), 'The secret world of Tony Blair', *New Statesman*, 14 February, pp. 13-14.
Committee of Independent Experts (CIE) (1999), *Second Report on Reform of the [European] Commission*, Committee of Independent Experts, cited: http://www.europarl.eu.int/experts/pdf/rep2-1en.pdf.
Constant, B. [1819] (1988), 'The Liberty of the Ancients Compared with that of the Moderns', in B. Fontana (ed. and trans.), *Political Writings*, Cambridge University Press, Cambridge, pp. 309-28.
Craik, D. (1980), *Minutes of Evidence to House of Commons (UK) Committee of Public Accounts*, 11 June, HMSO, London.
Criminal Justice Commission (CJC) (1991), *Report of an Investigation into Possible Misuse of Parliamentary Travel Entitlements by Members of the 1986-1989 Queensland Legislative Assembly*, CJC, Brisbane.
Criminal Justice Commission (CJC) (1996), *Report on an Investigation into a Memorandum of Understanding Between the Coalition and QPUE and an Investigation into an Alleged Deal Between the ALP and the SSAA*, CJC, Brisbane.
Criminal Justice Commission (CJC) (1996-97), *Criminal Justice Commission Annual Report Summary*, CJC, Brisbane.
Criminal Justice Commission (CJC) (1997), *Submission to the Attorney-General on the Draft Criminal Justice Legislation Amendment Bill 1997 and the Draft Misconduct Tribunals Bill 1997*, September, CJC, Brisbane.
Criminal Justice Commission (CJC) (2000a), *Allegations of Electoral Fraud: Report on an Advice by P.D. McMurdo QC*, CJC, Brisbane.
Criminal Justice Commission (CJC) (2000b), *Public Attitudes to the CJC*, CJC, Brisbane.
Davis, G. (1995), 'The Public Sector Ethics Movement: Guest Editor's Introduction', *Australian Journal of Public Administration*, Vol. 54(4), pp. 437-41.
della Porta, D. and Mény, Y. (1997), 'Conclusion: Democracy and Corruption: Towards a Comparative Analysis', in D. Della Porta and Y. Mény (eds), *Democracy and Corruption in Europe*, Pinter, London, pp. 166-80.
della Porta, D. and Vannucci, A. (1999), *Corrupt Exchanges: Actors, Resources, and Mechanisms of Political Corruption*, Aldine de Gruyter, New York.
Dicey, A. V. (1959), *Introduction to the Study of the Law of the Constitution*, 10th edn, Macmillan, London.
Dickie, P. (1999a), 'The crime-fighters', *Courier-Mail*, 13 March.
Dickie, P. (1999b), Interview with ABC Radio, 4QR Brisbane, 21 July.
Downs, A. (1972), 'Up and Down with Ecology: The Issue Attention Cycle', *The Public Interest*, Vol. 28, pp. 38-50.
Dunn, D.D. (1995), 'Ministerial Staff in Australian Commonwealth Government', *Australian Journal of Public Administration*, Vol. 54(4), pp. 507-19.
Efficiency Unit (1988), *Improving Management in Government: The Next Steps*, HMSO, London.

Ellis, D.L. (1989), 'Collective Ministerial Responsibility and Collective Solidarity', in G. Marshall (ed.), *Ministerial Responsibility*, Oxford University Press, Oxford, pp. 46–56.

Encel, S. (1974), *Cabinet Government in Australia*, 2nd edn, Melbourne University Press, Melbourne.

Epstein, D. (1984), *The Political Theory of The Federalist*, University of Chicago Press, Chicago.

Evans, H. (1999), 'Parliamentary and Extra-Parliamentary Accountability Institutions', *Australian Journal of Public Administration*, Vol. 58(1), pp. 87–9.

Evans, H. (2000), 'The Howard Government and the Parliament', in G. Singleton (ed.), *The Howard Government: Australian Commonwealth Administration 1996-1998*, University of New South Wales Press, Sydney, pp. 26–36.

Festinger, L. (1957), *A Theory of Cognitive Dissonance*, Stanford University Press, Stanford.

Finer, H. [1941] (1966), 'Administrative Responsibility in Democratic Government', in P. Woll (ed.), *Public Administration and Policy: Selected Essays*, Harper Torch Books, New York, pp. 247–75.

Finer, S.E. (1956), 'The Individual Responsibility of Ministers', *Public Administration*, Vol. 34, pp. 377–96.

Finn, P. (1990), 'Myths of Public Administration', in J. Power (ed.), *Public Administration in Australia: A Watershed*, Hale and Iremonger, Sydney, pp. 41–56.

Fitzgerald, G.E. (1989), *Report of a Commission of Inquiry Pursuant to Orders in Council: Commission of Inquiry into Possible Illegal Activities and Associated Police Misconduct*, Government Printer, Brisbane.

FitzGerald, V. (1996), 'Advice on Public Policy: The Changing Balance Between the Public Service and Political Advisers', in J. Disney and J.R. Nethercote (eds), *The House on Capital Hill: Parliament, Politics and Power in the National Capital*, The Federation Press, Sydney, pp. 119–32.

Forward, R. (1977), 'Ministerial Staff Under Whitlam and Fraser', *Australian Journal of Public Administration*, Vol. XXXVI(2), pp. 159–67.

Frankena, W. (1973), *Ethics*, 2nd edn, Prentice Hall, New Jersey.

Franks, Lord O. (1983), *Report by a Committee of Privy Councillors: The Falklands Islands Review*, Cm. 8787, HMSO, London.

Friedrich, C. [1940] (1966), 'Public Policy and the Nature of Administrative Responsibility', in P. Woll (ed.), *Public Administration and Policy: Selected Essays*, Harper Torch Books, New York, pp. 221–46.

Funnell, W. (1994), *An Historically Informed Episodic Study of State Audit Independence* — PhD thesis, University of Wollongong, Wollongong.

Furness, G. (1994), 'The Independent Commission against Corruption, An Insider's View', in P. Weller (ed.), *Royal Commissions and the Making of Public Policy*, Macmillan, Melbourne, pp. 198–209.

Garland, V. (1976), 'Relations between Ministers and Departments', *ACT RIPA Newsletter*, Vol. 3(3), pp. 15–35.

Gaster, R. (1988), 'Sex, Spies, and the Scandal: The Profumo Affair and British Politics', in A.S. Markovits and M. Silverstein (eds), *The Politics of Scandal, Power and Process in Liberal Democracies*, Holmes and Meier, New York, pp. 62–88.

Gaunt, C. (1999), 'Sports Grants and the Political Pork Barrel: An Investigation of Political Bias in the Administration of Australian Sports Grants', *Australian Journal of Political Science*, Vol. 34(1), pp. 63–74.

Gay, O. (2000), *Advisers to Ministers*, Research Paper 00/42, Parliament and Constitution Centre, House of Commons Library, London.

Gleeson, M., Allen, T., and Wilkins, M. (1992), 'An act of corruption? Nick Greiner's years in power and his unorthodox demise', ABC, Sydney.

Goodin, R.E. (1992), *Motivating Political Morality*, Blackwell, Cambridge, Mass.

Gordon, M. (1997), 'Government incompetence and stupidity', *The Australian*, 27–28 September.

Goward, P. (1996), 'The Medium, not the Messenger', in *Reinventing Political Institutions: Papers on Parliament*, Vol. 27, Department of the Senate, Canberra, pp. 49–62.

Grattan, M. (1998), 'The Politics of Spin', *Australian Studies in Journalism*, Vol. 7, pp. 32–45.

Greene, I. and Shugarman, D. (1997), *Honest Politics: Seeking Integrity in Canadian Public Life*, James Lorimer, Toronto.

Gregory, R. (1998), 'Political Responsibility for Bureaucratic Incompetence: Tragedy at Cave Creek', *Public Administration*, Vol. 76(3), pp. 519–38.

Greiner, N. (1993), 'The Smart-alec Culture: A Critique of Australian Journalism', *Australian Studies in Journalism*, Vol. 2, pp. 3–10.

Halligan, J. and Campbell, C. (1992), *Political Leadership in an Age of Constraint: Bureaucratic politics under Hawke and Keating*, Allen & Unwin, Sydney.

Hamilton, A., Madison, J. and Jay, J. [1788] (1982), *The Federalist Papers*, G. Wills (ed.), Bantam, New York.

Hart, H.L.A. (1961), *The Concept of Law*, Clarendon Press, Oxford.

Hart, H.L.A. (1968), *Punishment and Responsibility: Essays in the Philosophy of Law*, Clarendon Press, Oxford.

Hayden, W.G. (1998), 'Politics, Public Responsibility and the Ethical Imperative', in N. Preston and C. Sampford with C.-A. Bois (eds), *Ethics and Political Practice: Perspectives on Legislative Ethics*, The Federation Press / Routledge, Sydney / London, pp. 52–65.

Headey, B. (1974), *British Cabinet Ministers: The Roles of Politicians in Executive Office*, George Allen & Unwin, London.

Hennessy, P. (1989), *Whitehall*, Martin Secker & Warburg Ltd, London.

Hennessy, P. (1999a), *The Importance of Being Tony: Two Years of the Blair Style*, Guy's and St Thomas' Hospital Trust, London.

Hennessy, P. (1999b), 'Tony's bane', *The Guardian*, 9 July.

Hobbes, T. [1651] (1968), *Leviathan*, C.B. Macpherson (ed.), Penguin, Harmondsworth.

Hollway, S. (1996), 'Departments and Ministerial Offices: An Essential Partnership', in J. Disney and J.R. Nethercote (eds), *The House on Capital Hill: Parliament, Politics and Power in the National Capital*, The Federation Press, Sydney, pp. 133–48.

Home Affairs Select Committee (1998-99), *Home Affairs Annual Report*, HC 653, HMSO, London.

Homel, R. (1997), *Political Control of the Queensland Criminal Justice Commission*, CJC, Brisbane.

House of Commons, Canada (1995), *Second Report of the Special Joint Committee on a Code of Conduct of the Senate and the House of Commons*, House of Commons, Canada.

House of Commons Parliamentary Committee (HCPC) (1996), *Ministerial Accountability and Responsibility*, Report from Public Service Committee, House of Commons, London.

House of Commons Parliamentary Committee (HCPC) (1997), *Ministerial Accountability and Responsibility*, Report from Public Service Committee, House of Commons, London.

Howard, J. (1996a), *A Guide on Key Elements of Ministerial Responsibility*, Tabled in the House of Representatives, 30 April, Canberra.

Howard, J. (1996b), 'Transcript at the Launch of Paper: Ethical Standards and Values in the Australian Public Service', 9 May, Canberra.

Howard, J. (1998), 'Sir Robert Garran Oration: A Healthy Public Service is a Vital Part of Australia's Democratic System of Government', *Australian Journal of Public Administration*, Vol. 57(1), pp. 3–11.

Independent Commission Against Corruption (ICAC) (1990a), *Report on Investigation into Silverwater Filling Operation*, ICAC, Sydney.

Independent Commission Against Corruption (ICAC) (1990b), *Report on Investigation into the Walsh Bay Redevelopment Project*, ICAC, Sydney.

Independent Commission Against Corruption (ICAC) (1990c), *Report on Investigation into the North Coast Land and Development*, ICAC, Sydney.

Independent Commission Against Corruption (ICAC) (1991a), *The First Two Years*, ICAC, Sydney.

Independent Commission Against Corruption (ICAC) (1991b), *Report on Investigation concerning Neal and Mochalski*, ICAC, Sydney.

Independent Commission Against Corruption (ICAC) (1992a), *Report on the Investigation into the Metherell Resignation and Appointment*, June, ICAC, Sydney.

Independent Commission Against Corruption (ICAC) (1992b), *Second Report on Investigation into the Metherell Resignation and Appointment*, ICAC, Sydney.

Independent Commission Against Corruption (ICAC) (1998–99), *Annual Report: Commissioner's Review and Highlights*, Government Printer, Sydney.

Independent Commission Against Corruption (ICAC) (1998a), *Investigation into Parliamentary and Electorate Travel: First Report*, ICAC, Sydney.

Independent Commission Against Corruption (ICAC) (1998b), *Investigation into Parliamentary and Electorate Travel: Second Report*, ICAC, Sydney.

Independent Commission Against Corruption (ICAC) (1999), *Investigation into Parliamentary and Electorate Travel: Third Report*, ICAC, Sydney.

Jackson, M. and Smith, R. (1995), 'Everyone's Doing It! Codes of Ethics and New South Wales Parliamentarians' Perceptions of Corruption', *Australian Journal of Public Administration*, Vol. 54(4), pp. 483–93.

Jackson, M. and Smith, R. (1996), 'Inside Moves and Outside Views: An Australian Case Study of Elite and Public Perceptions of Political Corruption', *Governance*, Vol. 9, pp. 23–42.

Jaensch, D. (1997), *The Politics of Australia*, Macmillan, Melbourne.

Jennings, Sir I. (1959), *The Law and the Constitution*, 5th edn, Cambridge University Press, Cambridge.

Johnson, N. (1977), *In Search of the Constitution*, Methuen, London.

Jones, G.W. (1984), 'The Prime Minister's Aides', in A. King (ed.), *The British Prime Minister*, Macmillan, London.

Kant, I. [1795] (1963), *Perpetual Peace*, in L. White Beck (ed. and trans.), *On History*, Macmillan, New York.

Kennedy, P. (1998), *Public Service Act 1922: Report by Authorised Officer into Advice Given in Relation to Tabling of Material in the House of Representatives on 29 May 1997*, Released under Freedom of Information Act by Australian Department of Finance and Administration, Canberra.

Kerin, J. (1996), 'Ten Years a Minister', in J. Disney and J.R. Nethercote (eds), *The House on Capital Hill: Parliament, Politics and Power in the National Capital*, The Federation Press, Sydney, pp. 15–32.

Kernot, C. (1998), 'Codes and their Enforcement: Necessary but not Sufficient for Ethical Conduct', in N. Preston and C. Sampford with C.-A. Bois (eds), *Ethics and Political Practice: Perspectives on Legislative Ethics*, The Federation Press / Routledge, Sydney / London, pp. 134–42.

Kilfoyle, P. (2000), 'Minister heads for heartlands', *BBC News Online*, 31 January, cited: http://news.bbc.co.uk/hi/english/uk_politics/newsid_62500/625784.stm.

Kohl, H. (2000), *Mein Tagebuch: 1998–2000*, Droemer Knaur, München.

Kultgen, J. (1998), 'The Ideological Use of Professional Codes', in R.N. Stichler and R. Hauptman (eds), *Ethics, Information and Technology: Readings*, McFarland, Jefferson, NC, pp. 273–90.

Lehmbruch, G. (2000), *Parteienwettbewerb im Bundesstaat*, 3rd edn, Westdeutscher Verlag, Opladen.

Lewis, C. (1999), *Complaints Against Police: The Politics of Reform*, Hawkins Press, Sydney.

Lewis, D. (1996), *Hidden Agendas*, Hamish Hamilton, London.

Liberal Party of Canada (1993), *Creating Opportunity: The Liberal Party Plan for Canada*, Liberal Party of Canada, Ottawa.

Locke, J. [1689] (1992), *Two Treatises on Government*, 2nd edn, P. Laslett (ed.), Cambridge University Press, Cambridge.

Lucas, J.R. (1995), *Responsibility*, Clarendon Press, Oxford.

McAllister, I. (2000), 'Keeping them Honest: Public and Elite Perceptions of Ethical Conduct Among Australian Legislators', *Political Studies*, Vol. 48, pp. 22–37.

MacIntyre, A. (1981), *After Virtue*, University of Notre Dame Press, Notre Dame, Ind.

Machiavelli, N. [1513-15] (1985), *The Prince*, H.C. Mansfield, Jr (trans.), University of Chicago Press, Chicago.

Machiavelli, N. [1513-17] (1996), *Discourses On Livy*, H.C. Mansfield Jr and N. Tarcov (trans), University of Chicago Press, Chicago.

Management Advisory Board and Management Improvement Committee (1996), *Ethical Standards and Values in the Australian Public Service*, Australian Government Publishing Service, Canberra.

Mancuso, M. (1995), *The Ethical World of British MPs*, McGill-Queen's Press, Toronto.

Mancuso, M. (1998), 'Politicising Ethics: Scandal and the American Experience', in N. Preston and C. Sampford with C.-A. Bois (eds), *Ethics and Political Practice: Perspectives on Legislative Ethics*, The Federation Press / Routledge, Sydney / London, pp. 66–80.

Mancuso, M. (2000), 'Implementing Ethics Programs: Issues and Challenges', paper presented at the International Institute of Public Ethics conference, September, Ottawa.

Mancuso, M., Atkinson, M., Blais, A., Greene, I. and Nevitte, N. (1998), *A Question of Ethics: Canadians Speak Out*, Oxford University Press, Toronto.

Mansfield, H.C. Jr (1994), 'Separation of Powers in the American Constitution', in B. Wilson and P. Schramm (eds), *Separation of Powers and Good Government*, Rowan & Littlefield, Lanham, pp. 3–15.

Marshall, G. (1986), *Constitutional Conventions*, Clarendon Press, Oxford.

Marshall, G. and Moodie, G. (1959), *Some Problems of the Constitution*, Hutchinson, London.

Mather, G. (1996), 'Clarifying Responsibility and Accountability', in Chartered Institute of Public Finance and Accountancy (CIPFA) (ed.), *Government Accountability*, CIPFA, London, pp. 21–5.

Maxwell Fyfe, Sir D. (1954), *House of Commons Debates*, 20 July, col. 1290, HMSO, London.

Members' Ethics and Parliamentary Privilege Committee (MEPPC) (2000), *Report on a Code of Ethical Standards for Members of the Queensland Legislative Assembly*, Report No. 44, Parliament House, Brisbane.

Menadue, J. (2000), *Morality and Public Life* [Lenten Lecture], 25 August, cited: http://www.abc.net.au/rn/relig/enc/stories/s125998.htm.

Mény, Y. (1996), '"Fin de siecle" Corruption: Change, Crisis and Shifting Values', *International Social Science Journal*, Vol. 48, pp. 309–20.

Meyrowitz, J. (1993), 'Images of Media: Hidden Ferment — and Harmony — in the Field', *Journal of Communication*, Vol. 43(3), pp. 55–66.

Montesquieu [1752] (1989), *The Spirit of the Laws*, A.M. Cohler, B.C. Miller and H.S. Stone (eds and trans), Cambridge University Press, Cambridge.

Moore, M. (1993), 'More to Blame than the Media', *Australian Quarterly*, Vol. 65(2), pp. 97–104.

Mosher, F.C. (1979), *The GAO: the Quest for Accountability in American Government*, Westview Press, Boulder.

Mulgan, R. (1997), 'The Processes of Public Accountability', *Australian Journal of Public Administration*, Vol. 56(1), pp. 25–36.

Mulgan, R. (1999), *Have New Zealand's Political Experiments Increased Public Accountability?*, Discussion Paper No. 59, Public Policy Program, Australian National University, Canberra.

Neill, Lord (2000), *Reinforcing Standards: Sixth Report of the Committee on Standards in Public Life*, cited: http:www.public-standards.gov.uk.

New Zealand Treasury (1987), *Government Management: A Brief to the Incoming Government*, New Zealand Treasury, Wellington.

Nicholson, I.F. (1986), *The Mystery of Crichel Down*, Oxford University Press, Oxford.

Nolan, Rt Hon. Lord (1995), *First Report of the Committee on Standards in Public Life*, Cm. 2850-1, HMSO, London.

Norton, P. (1993), *Does Parliament Matter?*, Harvester Wheatsheaf, London.

Norton, P. (2000), *Strengthening Parliament*, The Report of the Commission to Strengthen Parliament, The Conservative Party, London.

Office of Government Ethics (OGE) (2000), *Ethics in the Executive Branch of the United States Government*, OGE, Washington DC.

Oliver, D. and Austin, R. (1987), 'Political and Constitutional Aspects of the Westland Affair', *Parliamentary Affairs*, Vol. 40, pp. 20–41.

Packenham, R. (1970), 'Legislatures and Political Development', in A. Kornberg and L.D. Musolf (eds), *Legislatures in Developmental Perspective*, Duke University Press, Durham NC, pp. 521–37.

Page, B. (1990), 'Ministerial Resignation and Individual Ministerial Responsibility in Australia: 1976-1989', *Journal of Commonwealth and Comparative Politics*, Vol. 28(2), pp. 141–61.

Parliamentary Joint Committee (PJC) (1999a), *Parliamentary Joint Committee Report: General Meeting with the Commissioner of the ICAC: 24 September*, New South Wales Government, Sydney.

Parliamentary Joint Committee (PJC) (1999b), *Parliamentary Joint Committee Report: General Meeting with the Commissioner of the ICAC: 12 November*, New South Wales Government, Sydney.

Parliamentary Joint Committee (PJC) (2000), *Parliamentary Joint Committee Report – Review 11: Jurisdictional Issues*, New South Wales Government, Sydney.

Patapan, H. (1999), 'Separation of Powers in Australia', *Australian Journal of Political Science*, Vol. 34(3), pp. 391–407.

Peters, B.G., Rhodes, R.A.W. and Wright, V. (2000), *Administering the Summit: Administration of the Core Executive in Developed Countries*, Macmillan, London.
Philp, M. (1997), 'Defining Political Corruption', *Political Studies*, Vol. 45, pp. 436–62.
Plowden, W. (1987), 'Relationships Between Advisers and Departmental Civil Servants', in W. Plowden (ed.), *Advising the Rulers*, Basil Blackwell, Oxford, pp. 170–3.
Polybius [150 BC] (1979), *The Histories*, W.R. Paton (trans.), Harvard University Press, Cambridge, Mass.
Preston, N. (1998), 'Legislative Ethics: Prospects and Challenges', in N. Preston and C. Sampford with C.-A. Bois (eds), *Ethics and Political Practice: Perspectives on Legislative Ethics*, The Federation Press / Routledge, Sydney / London, pp. 143–52.
Preston, N., Sampford, C. with Bois, C.-A. (eds) (1998), *Ethics and Political Practice: Perspectives on Legislative Ethics*, The Federation Press / Routledge, Sydney / London.
Prior, J. (1983), *House of Commons Debates*, 24 October, cols. 23–4, HMSO, London.
Public Administration Committee (2000-01), *The Ministerial Code: Improving the Rule Book*, HC 235, HMSO, London.
Public Service Committee (1995–96), *Second Report: Ministerial Accountability and Responsibility*, HC 313, HMSO, London.
Public Service Committee (1996–97), *First Special Report: Government's Response to Public Service Committee's Report on Ministerial Accountability and Responsibility*, HC 67, HMSO, London.
Queensland Audit Office (1999), *Audit of Certain Matters Associated with the Issue of an Interactive Gambling Licence*, Report to Parliament, No. 1, Brisbane.
Queensland, Parliamentary Debates (1997), *Queensland Parliamentary Debates*, Government Printer, Brisbane.
Rawls, J. (1971), *A Theory of Justice*, Belknap Press, Cambridge, Mass.
Reid, G.S. (1980), 'Responsible Government and Ministerial Responsibility', *Australian Journal of Public Administration*, Vol. 39, pp. 301–17.
Rosenthal, A. (1998), '"Appearance" as an Ethical Standard: Its Consequences for US State Legislatures', in N. Preston and C. Sampford with C.-A. Bois (eds), *Ethics and Political Practice: Perspectives on Legislative Ethics*, The Federation Press / Routledge, Sydney / London, pp. 24–40.
Rousseau, J.-J. [1762] (1968), *The Social Contract*, M. Cranston (trans.), Penguin, Harmondsworth.
Roy Morgan (1998), *Politicians fall to low levels of honesty and ethics*, Roy Morgan Research Centre, Finding No. 3088, May, cited: http//www.roymorgan.com.au/polls/1998/3088/index.html.
Royal Commission on Australian Government Administration (1976), *Report* and four *Volumes of Appendices*, Parliamentary Papers No. 185-89, Australian Government Publishing Service, Canberra.
Rynard, P. and Shugarman, D.P. (eds) (1999), *Cruelty and Deception: The Controversy Over Dirty Hands in Politics*, Broadview Press, Peterborough, Ontario.
Saalfeld, T. and Muller, W. (1997), 'Roles in Legislative Studies: A Theoretical Introduction', *Journal of Legislative Studies*, Vol. 3(3), pp. 1–16.
Sabato, L. (1991), *Feeding Frenzy: How Attack Journalism has Transformed American Politics*, Free Press, New York.
Sampford, C. (1986), 'The Dimensions of Rights and their Protection by Statute', in C. Sampford and B. Galligan (eds), *Law, Rights and the Welfare State*, Croom Helm, London, pp. 171–99.

Sampford, C. (1992), 'Law, Institutions and the Public Private Divide', *Federal Law Review*, Vol. 20, pp. 185–222.

Sampford, C. (1994), 'Institutionalizing Public Sector Ethics', in N. Preston (ed.), *Ethics for the Public Sector: Education and Training*, The Federation Press, Sydney, pp. 14–34.

Sampford, C. (1997), 'Beyond Best Practice', address to the Premier and Directors-General of Queensland Government Departments, 28 November, Parliament House, Brisbane.

Sampford, C. (1998), 'What's a Lawyer Doing in a Nice Place Like This? Lawyers and Ethical Life', *Legal Ethics*, Vol. 1(1), pp. 35–50.

Sampford, C. and Blencowe, S. (1998), 'Educating Lawyers to be Ethical Advisers', in K. Economides (ed.), *Ethical Challenges to Legal Education and Conduct*, Oxford University Press, Oxford, pp. 315–40.

Sampford, C. and Blencowe, S. (2001), 'Raising the Standard: An Integrated Approach to Promoting Professional Standards and Avoiding Professional Criminality', in R. Smith (ed.), *Crime in the Professions*, Australian Institute of Criminology, Canberra, *in press*.

Sampford, C. and Wood, D. (1993), 'The Future of Business Ethics', in C.A.J. Coady and C. Sampford (eds), *Business, Ethics and the Law*, The Federation Press, Sydney, pp. 2–23.

Sampford, C., Preston, N. with Bois, C.-A. Eds. (1998), *Public Sector Ethics: Finding and Implementing Values*, The Federation Press / Routledge, Sydney / London.

Sandel, M. (1982), *Liberalism and the Limits of Justice*, Cambridge University Press, Cambridge.

Scott, Sir R. (1996a), *Report of the Inquiry into the Export of Defence Equipment and Dual-Use Goods to Iraq and Related Prosecutions*, HC 115, HMSO, London.

Scott, Sir R. (1996b), 'Ministerial Accountability', *Public Law*, Vol. 410, pp. 410–26.

Scottish Executive (1999), *Scottish Ministerial Code: A Code of Conduct and Guidance on Procedures for Members of the Scottish Executive and Junior Ministers*, cited: http://www.scotland.gov.uk/library2/doc03/smic-00.htm.

Seibel, W. (1997), 'Corruption in the Federal Republic of Germany Before and in the Wake of Reunification', in D. Della Porta and Y. Mény (eds), *Democracy and Corruption in Europe*, Pinter, London, pp. 85–102.

Select Committee on the Parliamentary Commissioner for Administration (1994-95), *The Child Support Agency: Third Report*, HC 199, HMSO, London.

Select Committee on Public Administration (2000), *Making Government Work: Minutes of Evidence*, 12 July, Questions 1–47, House of Commons, UK.

Sennett, R. (1977), *The Fall of Public Man*, Alfred A. Knopf, New York.

Shephard, M. (2001), 'Parliament: Calling the Shots for both Scotland and the UK?', in The Constitution Unit (ed.), *Nations and Regions: The Dynamics of Devolution: Quarterly Monitoring Programme*, Scotland Reports, pp. 15–21, cited: http://www.ucl.ac.uk/constitution-unit/leverh/pub.htm.

Sherman, T. (1998), 'Public Sector Ethics: Prospects and Challenges', in C. Sampford and N. Preston with C.-A. Bois (eds), *Public Sector Ethics: Finding and Implementing Values*, The Federation Press / Routledge, Sydney / London, pp. 13–25.

Shklar, J. (1984), *Ordinary Vices*, Harvard University Press, Cambridge, Mass.

Shklar, J. (1992), 'Justice without Virtue', in J. Chapman and W. Galston (eds), *Virtue*, New York University Press, New York, pp. 283–88.

Sigal, L. (1973), *Reporters and Officials: The Organization and Politics of Newsmaking*, Heath and Co., Mass.

Silverstein, M. (1988), 'Watergate and the American Political System', in A.S. Markovits and M. Silverstein (eds), *The Politics of Scandal, Power and Process in Liberal Democracies*, Holmes and Meier, New York, pp. 15–37.

Simms, M. (1999), 'Models of Political Accountability', *Australian Journal of Public Administration*, Vol. 58(1), pp. 34–8.

Sinclair, I. (1996), 'Changes in the Ministry', in J. Disney and J.R. Nethercote (eds), *The House on Capital Hill: Parliament, Politics and Power in the National Capital*, The Federation Press, Sydney, pp. 33–48.

Smith, F. (2000), Forbes Smith, CJC, interviewed by Jenny Fleming, 7 May 2000, Brisbane.

Smith, R. (1998), 'Strange Distinctions: Legislators, Political Parties and Legislative Ethics Research', in N. Preston and C. Sampford with C.-A. Bois (eds), *Ethics and Political Practice: Perspectives on Legislative Ethics*, The Federation Press / Routledge, Sydney / London, pp. 41–51.

Smith, R. (1999), 'Visible and Invisible Cultures of Parliamentary Ethics: The '"Sports Rorts" Affair Revisited', *Australian Journal of Political Science*, Vol. 34(1), pp. 47–62.

Smith, R.F.I. (1977), 'Ministerial Advisers: The Experience of the Whitlam Government', *Australian Journal of Public Administration*, Vol. XXXVI(2), pp. 133–58.

Smith, R.F.I. (1989), 'Working with Ministers', in G.R. Curnow and B. Page (eds), *Politicization and the Career Service*, Canberra College of Advanced Education and NSW Division of the Royal Australian Institute of Public Administration, Canberra, pp. 99–108.

Social Security Committee (1993-94), *The Operation of the Child Support Act: First Report*, HC 69, HMSO, London.

Stathis, P. (2000), Peter Stathis, ICAC, interviewed by Jenny Fleming, 15 July, Sydney.

Sturgess, G. (1994), 'Guarding the Polity, The NSW Independent Commission against Corruption', in P. Weller (ed.), *Royal Commissions and the Making of Public Policy*, Macmillan, Melbourne, pp. 107–28.

Sutherland, S. (2000), 'Retrospection and Democracy', in P. Rynard and D.S. Shugarman (eds), *Cruelty and Deception: The Controversy Over Dirty Hands in Politics*, Broadview Press, Peterborough, Ontario, pp. 207–24.

Sutherland, S.L. (1991), 'Responsible Government and Ministerial Responsibility: Every Reform is its Own Problem', *Canadian Journal of Political Science*, Vol. 24(1), pp. 91–120.

Tanner, S.J. (1998), 'Watchdog or Attack Dog? The Media, Politics and Ethics', in N. Preston, C. Sampford and C.-A. Bois (eds), *Ethics and Political Practice: Perspectives on Legislative Ethics*, The Federation Press / Routledge, Sydney / London, pp. 90–107.

Tanner, S.J. (1999a), *Political Corruption, Accountability and the Media*, unpublished PhD, University of Tasmania.

Tanner, S.J. (1999b), 'The Media as an Anti-corruption Mechanism', in A. Deysine and D. Kesselman (eds), *Argent, Politique et Corruption*, University of Paris X Press, Paris, pp. 173–88.

Tanner, S.J. (1999c), 'The Corruption Watchdog Condemned – the Media Criticised in Letters to the Editor', *Australian Studies in Journalism*, Vol. 8, pp. 60–82.

Taylor, J. (2000), John Taylor, former Auditor-General, interviewed by J. Wanna and C. Ryan, April.

Thompson, D.F. (1987), *Political Ethics and Public Office*, Harvard University Press, Cambridge, Mass.

Thompson, D.F. (1995), *Ethics in Congress: From Individual to Institutional Corruption*, Brookings Institution, Washington DC.

Thompson, E. and Tillotsen, G. (1999), 'Caught in the Act: The Smoking Gun View of Ministerial Responsibility', *Australian Journal of Public Administration*, Vol. 58(1), pp. 48–57.

Thompson, J.B. (2000), *Political Scandal: Power and Visibility in the Media Age*, Polity Press, Cambridge.

Tiffin, R. (1999), *Scandals, Media, Politics and Corruption in Contemporary Australia*, University of New South Wales Press, Sydney.

Tomkins, A. (1998), *The Constitution After Scott*, Clarendon Press, Oxford.

Treasury and Civil Service Committee (1988-89), *The Civil Service Management Reforms: The Next Steps*, HC 494, HMSO, London.

Twining, W. and Miers, D. (1983), *How to do Things with Rules*, Weidenfeld and Nicholson, London.

Uhr, J. (1989), 'Reflections on the State of Executive Development', in A. Kouzmin and N. Scott (eds), *Dynamics in Australian Public Sector Management: Selected Essays*, Macmillan, Melbourne, pp. 269–77.

Uhr, J. (ed.) (1996), *Ethical Practice in Government: Improving Organisational Management*, Federalism Research Centre, ANU, Canberra.

Uhr, J. (1998a), 'Democracy and the Ethics of Representation', in N. Preston and C. Sampford with C.-A. Bois (eds), *Ethics and Political Practice: Perspectives on Legislative Ethics*, The Federation Press / Routledge, Sydney / London, pp. 11–23.

Uhr, J. (1998b), *Deliberative Democracy in Australia: The Changing Place of Parliament*, Cambridge University Press, Cambridge.

Uhr, J. (1998c), 'Howard's Ministerial Code', *Res Publica*, Vol. 7(1), pp. 7–13.

Uhr, J. (1999a), 'Institutions of Integrity: Balancing Values and Verification in Democratic Governance', *Public Integrity*, Vol. 1(1), pp. 94–106.

Uhr, J. (1999b), 'Three Accountability Anxieties: A Conclusion to the Symposium', *Australian Journal of Public Administration*, Vol. 58(1), pp. 98–101.

Uhr, J. (2000), 'Public Service Ethics in Australia', in T. Cooper (ed.), *Handbook of Administrative Ethics*, 2nd edn, Marcel Dekker, New York, pp. 719–40.

UK Parliament, (1998), *Summary of the Nolan Committee's First Report on Standards in Public Life*, cited: http://www.official-publications.co.uk/document/parlment/nolan/nolan.htm.

Verney, D.V. [1979] (1992), 'Parliamentary Government and Presidential Government', in A. Lijphart (ed.), *Parliamentary Versus Presidential Government*, Oxford University Press, Oxford, pp. 31–47.

Walker, J. (1995), *Goss: A Political Biography*, University of Queensland Press, St Lucia.

Walsh, K.-A. and Richardson, N. (1995), 'Politicians: how low can they go?', *Bulletin*, 12 September, pp. 14–17.

Walter, J. (1986), *The Ministers' Minders: Personal Advisers in National Government*, Oxford University Press, Melbourne.

Walter, J. (1989), 'The Evolution of Ministerial Staff in Australia', in G.R. Curnow and B. Page (eds), *Politicization and the Career Service*, Canberra College of Advanced Education and NSW Division of the Royal Australian Institute of Public Administration, Canberra, pp. 109–30.

Walter, J. (1992), 'Prime Ministers and Their Staff', in P. Weller (ed.), *Menzies to Keating: The Development of the Australian Prime Ministership*, Melbourne University Press, Melbourne, pp. 28–63.

Wanna, J. (1991), 'Parliamentary Commissions of Review: The Criminal Justice Commission and the Electoral and Administrative Review Commission', in R. Whip and C.A. Hughes (eds), *Political Crossroads: The 1989 Queensland Election*, University of Queensland Press, St Lucia, pp. 207–24.

Warhurst, J. (1980), 'Exercising Control over Statutory Authorities, A Study in Government Technique', in P. Weller and D. Jaensch (eds), *Responsible Government in Australia*, Drummond Publishing, Richmond, pp. 151–60.

Warn, P. (1996), 'Ministers and Minders', in J. Disney and J.R. Nethercote (eds), *The House on Capital Hill: Parliament, Power and Politics in the National Capital*, The Federation Press, Sydney, pp. 149–64.

Waterford, J. (1996), 'The Minister and His Private Office', in K. Walsh (ed.), *Poets, Presidents, People and Parliament: Republicanism and Other Issues: Papers on the Parliament*, Vol. 28, Department of the Senate, Canberra, pp. 83–103.

Weller, P. (1999), 'Disentangling Concepts of Ministerial Responsibility', *Australian Journal of Public Administration*, Vol. 58(1), pp. 62–4.

Weller, P. (2001), *Australia's Mandarins: The Frank and the Fearless?*, Allen & Unwin, Sydney.

Weller, P. and Grattan, M. (1981), *Can Ministers Cope? Australian Federal Ministers at Work*, Hutchinson, Melbourne.

Weller, P. and Jaensch, D. (eds) (1980), *Responsible Government in Australia*, Drummond Publishing, Richmond.

Western, J. (1987), 'The Role of the Media in Politics', *Current Affairs Bulletin*, Vol. 63(9), pp. 14–23.

White, D.M. (1988), 'Backup for Ministers', *Politics*, Vol. 23(1), pp. 21-31.

White, D.M. (1989), 'Political Communication and Democratic Government', *Politics*, Vol. 24(1), pp. 29–41.

Wilenski, P. (1979), 'Ministers, Public Servants and Public Policy', *Australian Quarterly*, Vol. 51(2), pp. 31–45.

Williams, G. (1999), *Human Rights under the Australian Constitution*, Oxford University Press, Melbourne.

Wilson, H.R. (1998), 'Ethics Counsellor to the Government: The Canadian Experience', in N. Preston and C. Sampford with C.-A. Bois (eds), *Ethics and Political Practice: Perspectives on Legislative Ethics*, The Federation Press / Routledge, Sydney / London, pp. 81–9.

Wilson, H. (1999a), 'Ethics and Government: The Canadian Case', in *Australia and Parliamentary Orthodoxy*, Department of the Senate, Canberra.

Wilson, H. (1999b), 'Ethics and Government: The Canadian Experience', unpublished paper delivered at the Australian Senate, 19 February, Canberra.

Wintour, P. (2000), 'MPs look into Blair's "secret department"', *The Guardian*, 2 June.

Woodcock, Sir J. (1994), *Report on the escape from Whitemoor Prison*, Cm. 2741, HMSO, London.

Woodhouse, D. (1993), 'Ministerial Responsibility in the 1990s: When Do Ministers Resign?', *Parliamentary Affairs*, Vol. 46(3), pp. 277–92.

Woodhouse, D. (1994), *Ministers and Parliament: Accountability in Theory and Practice*, Clarendon Press, Oxford.

Woodhouse, D. (1999), 'Individual Ministerial Responsibility and a "Dash of Principle"', in D. Butler, V. Bogdanor and R. Summers (eds), *The Law, Politics, and the Constitution: Essays in Honour of Geoffrey Marshall*, Oxford University Press, Oxford, pp. 102–30.

Yack, B. (1999), 'Putting Injustice First: An Alternative Approach to Liberal Pluralism', *Social Research*, Vol. 66(4), pp. 1103–20.

Index

Abbott, Tony 94
Accountability 46
    governmental 5
    ministerial 5, 8, 42–43, 46, 112, 119, 130, 155, 169, 180, 196, 211
    parliamentary 157–58
Administrative Law 8
Advice to ministers about ethical issues 10, 119–28
    prior advice 171–84, 202
Ahern, Mike 120
Aitkin, Jonathan 38
Anti-corruption legislation 15
Aristotle 21–24
Audit Act 1901 (Commonwealth of Australia) 147–48
Auditor of Parliamentary Allowances and Entitlements Bill 2000 (Commonwealth of Australia) 201
Auditor-General 10, 39, 98, 115, 121, 124, 131, 138, 145–57
    and ministerial ethics/behaviour 145–57, 203
    and prime ministers 151, 155
    role and powers 147–50, 201
Auditor-General Act 1997 (Commonwealth of Australia) 149, 152, 154,
Australia 3, 21, 41, 111, 148, 208–11
    Australian Broadcasting Corporation (ABC) 161
    Australian Securities Commission 166

Bowen Inquiry 193–94, 198, 199
Constitution 29–32
Department of Finance & Administration 152
Department of Prime Minister & Cabinet 50, 54, 59, 119
House of Representatives 95, 98–100
Ombudsman 201
Remuneration Tribunal 95
Royal Commission into Australian Government Administration (RCAGA) 153
Senate 95, 98
Australian Democrats 198
Australian Labor Party 96, 120, 127, 175

Baumeister, Brigitte 83
Beattie, Peter 120, 121
Berlin, Isaiah 107
Bingham, Sir Max 130, 131
Bisshop, Philomena 100
Bjelke-Petersen, Sir Joh 120
Blair, Tony 9, 45, 54, 92, 192
    Blair government 38, 45, 92, 196
Blondin-Andrew, Ethel 113
Boothroyd, Betty 65
Borbidge, Rob 120, 122, 126, 135, 142
Bouchard, Lucien 114
Britain (see United Kingdom)
Brittan, Leon 39, 46
Brown, Gordon 65
Brown, Michael 38
Burkhard, Hirsch 83

Cabinet
  collective responsibility 6, 56, 58, 66, 193
  conventions 6, 146, 193, 202
  decisions 6
  handbook 45, 50–51, 54–57
  rules 9, 50, 67, 203
  secrecy 6
Cabinet Office 51, 54, 61
Canada 3, 21, 29, 120, 145, 177, 204, 208, 210
  British Columbia 110
  Canadian Radio-Television Corporation (CRTC) 113
  Canadian Security Intelligence Service 115
  code of conduct 111, 202
  ethics/integrity advisers/counsellors/commissioners 107–18, 122, 179–81, 202–5, 211
  Newfoundland 206
  Ontario 110
  Parker Commission 109
  Taskforce on Conflict of Interest (Starr-Sharp Report) 109, 179
Carrington, Lord 39, 40, 46
Carruthers, Ken 133
Chrétien, Jean 111, 115, 116
Civil/Public Servants/Civil Service Code 13, 45, 59, 71, 92–93
  relations with ministers 69–70, 97–98, 102
Clair, Frank 134
Clermont, George 113
Clinton, Bill 3
Codes of Conduct (see also Ministerial Codes of Conduct) 12, 16, 30–31, 44–46, 191, 198, 211
Collenette, David 113
Colston, Mal 95
Committee on Standards in Public Life (Nolan Committee; Neill Committee) 4, 9, 11–20, 44–45, 55, 61, 65, 91, 93, 192, 194–96
  Seven Principles of Public Life 194–95, 204
Conflict of interest 38, 202, 204, 208, 210–12
Connolly, Peter 133
Cook, Robin 38
Cooper, Russell 133, 135
Copps, Sheila 113
Criminal Justice Act 1989 (Queensland) 131
Criminal Justice Commission (CJC) 10, 31, 45, 121, 124, 129–35, 140–43, 167, 184–85
  Carruthers Inquiry 133, 135
  community/stakeholder support for Connolly-Ryan Inquiry 129, 133–35, 142–43, 204
  legislation, role and powers 130–32, 204
  Parliamentary Criminal Justice Committee (PCJC) 132, 134
  relationship with governments 129, 132–35, 140–43
  Shepherdson Inquiry into Electoral Rorting 141–42
  Travel Entitlements investigation 130, 133–35, 184
Currie, Edwina 37

Deacon, Susan 69
DeBane, Pierre 113
Denmark 46
Dewar, Donald 69
Downey, Sir Gordon 19
Dugdale, Sir Thomas 39
Dupuy, Michel 113

Elf-Aquitaine 81, 83
Ellis, David 66
Ethical culture/norms 94, 116–17, 175, 211
Ethics

classical vs modern perspectives on 21–29, 32
dangers of complacency 14
education 8, 31, 47, 177, 199
institutionalising 9, 17, 21–33, 77–90, 107–18, 120, 173, 187, 200
legislative mechanisms 5, 14, 30, 107, 109, 112, 119–28, 175, 202
parliamentary 4, 15, 43, 187, 196–98, 209
personal morality and 77–78, 86–90, 189
political 4, 5, 77–78, 187–200
in public life 4, 107
regulation 8, 188, 190, 196–98
Ethics Advisers/Counsellors 21, 31, 173, 178–79
Canada 10, 107–18, 122, 177
Queensland 10, 119–28, 177
United Kingdom 18
Ethics/Integrity Regimes 173–87

Falkland Islands 40, 46
Faulkner, John 99
Filkin, Elizabeth 19
Fitzgerald Inquiry 120–21, 130, 132–33, 184
Fraser Government 92
Freedom of Information (FOI) 6, 8
Fritchie, Dame Rennie 16

Galbraith, Sam 69
Geißler, Heiner 80
Germany 3, 77–90, 208, 210
Christian Democratic Union (CDU) 9, 78–90
financing rorts scandal (see Political scandals — Germany)
Free Democratic Party (FDP) 82
powers of Federal Chancellor 85
Social Democratic Party (SDP) 84
Gibson, Brian 38
Godfrey, Brendan 96

Greiner, Nick 137–38, 160–65, 167–68, 184, 195, 207
Grey, Deborah 114
Guide to Key Elements of Ministerial Responsibility (see Ministerial codes)

Hamilton, Alexander 28–29
Hamilton, Neil 38
Harman, Harriet 65
Hennessy, Peter 54, 56
Heseltine, Michael 40
High Court 30
Hobbes, Thomas 26
House of Commons 11, 16–17, 19, 43–44, 65, 192, 194, 197
House of Lords 17
Howard, John 52–53, 56, 58, 99–100, 119, 175, 205, 211
Howard government 127, 175, 208
Howe, C.D. 108
Hughes, Carolyn 100
Hughes, Robert 38
Hürland-Büning, Agnes 83, 84

Independent Commission Against Corruption (ICAC) 7–8, 10, 31, 45, 129, 135–43, 161, 164, 167, 175, 184, 195, 203, 207
community/stakeholder support for 142–43, 204
legislation, role and powers 136, 139–40
Neal Report 137
North Coast Land Development Investigation 136
Parliamentary Joint Committee (PJC) 136, 140, 142
relationship with governments 136–40, 142–43
Silverwater Filling Operation 136
Travel Entitlement Investigation 138–39
Irish Republican Army (IRA) 41

Jull, David 38, 95–103

Kant, Immanuel 32
Kanther, Manfred 82
Kelly, Ros 39, 155
Kennett, Felicity 161
Kennett, Jeff 161–62, 165–67, 168–70
Kiep, Walter 80
Kilfoyle, Peter 66
Kirch, Leo 83
Koch, Roland 81, 82
Kohl, Hannelore 83
Kohl, Helmut 10, 78–90, 208

Labour Party (UK) 61, 69, 71
Le Grand, Mark 133
Lewis, Derek 41
Liberal Democrats 69, 71
Liberal Democrats (UK) 69, 71,
Liberal Party/Liberal-National Coalition (Australia) 132,
Locke, John 26, 27, 29
Lyell, Sir Nicholas 43

MacEachen, Allan 110
Machiavelli 22, 25–26, 32, 119
Madison, James 27
Major, John 18, 45, 54, 61, 68
    Major government 38, 45, 208
Mandelson, Peter 38
Manning, Preston 114
Marchi, Sergio 113
Martin, Paul 113
Mathieson, Bruce 166
Maucher, Helmut 83
Mayne, Stephen 161–63, 166
Maze Prison 41
McGauran, Peter 38, 99
McKenna, Fiona 99–100
McMurdo, P.D. QC 141
Media
    and ethical conduct of ministers 159–70, 173, 202
    and politicians 10, 12, 139, 141, 160, 207
Mellor, David 38
Mellors, John 99
Members of Parliament (Staff) Act (Commonwealth of Aust) 92–93, 147, 149
Merkel, Angela 82–83
Merz, Friedrich 83
Metherell, Terry 137, 160–65
Ministerial Codes of Conduct 44–46, 49–60, 181, 191–93, 202, 211
    compliance 73, 109, 116, 175
    enforcement 53, 59–60, 73, 109, 113, 116
    interpretation 53, 55, 72, 111, 116, 175
    monitoring 72–73, 119
    prime ministers and 52–53, 55–56, 71, 108–116, 181, 192–93, 202, 211
    publication 45, 49–50, 55, 57, 125, 175, 203
    Australia
        Guidelines on Key Elements of Min. Responsibility 45, 52–53, 56–57, 99, 193–95, 202–3
        Ministerial Handbook (Queensland) 125
    Britain (*Questions of Procedure for Ministers — QPM)* 17–19, 44–45, 47, 54–57, 61–74, 192, 204
    Canada 108–9
    Scotland 61–74
Ministerial responsibility 5–6, 8–9, 37–49, 65, 190–92, 196–97, 210
Ministerial Staff 8–9, 53, 91–103, 147, 149, 151
Ministers
    accountability 5, 8, 42–43, 46, 112, 119, 130, 138, 155, 181, 190–91, 196
    censure 47, 210
    and Civil Servants (see Civil Servants & Ministers) behaviour 9,

18–19, 30, 38–39, 49–60, 63–65, 72, 110–12, 147, 163–68
  ethical dangers faced by 6–8, 93–94, 101, 110, 183, 190, 206, 208
  ethical obligations 6, 17, 30, 191, 196, 199, 205
  ethical outlook/logic 93, 101, 108, 180, 206
  motivating 5, 19–20, 47–48, 72, 182, 186, 203, 206, 209–10
  pressures on 10, 94, 101, 201, 204
  resignations 37–44, 46–48, 53, 66, 99, 100, 113, 132, 135, 137, 141–42, 159, 164, 193, 196, 203, 205
  scrutiny by independent/external bodies 129–143, 202, 211
  special responsibilities of 5–8, 57–58, 64, 91, 191, 205
Misuse of public office 15–16, 39, 189–90
Montesquieu 26–27, 29
Moore, Clover 162
Moore, John 45
Moore, Tim 161–62, 165, 169
Morality (see Ethics)
Morris, Grahame 99–100
Müller, Herbert 81
Mulroney, Brian 109, 116
Mundingburra By-Election 132–33, 141
  Memorandum of Understanding (MOU) 132
Murray, Andrew 198

National Health Service (NHS) 14, 16
Neill Committee (see Committee on Standards in Public Life)
New Zealand 41–42, 144
Nicholls, Lord 15
Nolan Committee (see Committee on Standards in Public Life)
Nolan, Lord 45, 59, 61, 73–74
Northern Ireland 61
Norton, Lord of Louth 66

Oakes, Laurie   99

Palestinian Liberation Organisation (PLO) 38
Parer, Warwick 45, 53
Parkinson, Cecil 38
Parliament/legislatures
  accountability mechanisms 187–88
Parliamentary Privileges Act 1987 (Commonwealth of Australia)   149
Pearson, Lester 108
Political corruption 4, 196, 203, 205
Political executive 5–8, 16, 62–74, 197, 198, 209–11
Political institutions
  declining public confidence in 3, 11, 30, 188, 192–93, 203, 207
Political parties 30
  influence on ethical behaviour 9, 79–90, 94, 208, 211–13
Political scandals 3–4, 208–9
  media handling of 159–70
  preventive strategies 173–86
Australia
  Kennett Share Deal 161, 165–70
  Magnetic Resonance Imaging (MRI) Audit 152–53
  Marshall Islands Affair 44
  Metherell Affair 137–38, 160–65, 167, 170, 196
  Mundingburra 132–33, 141
  Net Bet Affair 121, 127
  Sports Rorts 39, 154
  Telecard affair 201–2, 207, 209
  Travel Rorts 91, 95–103, 151–52, 209
Britain
  Arms to Iraq (Matrix Churchill Affair) 43
  Cash for questions 13, 15, 38, 208, 213
  Crichel Downs 39, 43, 191
  Ministerial employment post-retirement 13

Westland Affair 40, 46
Canada 109–110, 208
   Job Creation 114
Germany
   Financing rorts 3, 77–90, 212
   Flick Affair 85
New Zealand
   Cave Creek Tragedy 3, 40, 42
United States
   Whitewater 3
Politicians
   behaviour 3, 11, 12
   ethical behaviour/outlook of 4, 79–90
   media scrutiny 10, 12, 139, 159–70, 202, 207
   and parliamentary entitlements 3, 38, 95–98, 138–39, 152–53, 209, 211
   public attitudes towards 3, 11–13, 30, 108–9, 131, 135, 167, 173, 205, 208
   unpopularity 11–13
Preston, Peter 20
Prime Ministers
   and ethical conduct of ministers 6, 9, 38–39, 44–45, 49, 53, 55, 58–60, 68, 182–83, 210–11
   and ministerial codes (see ministerial codes)
Prior, James 41
Prosser, Geoff 38
Public Sector Ethics Amendment Act 1999 (Queensland) 121, 195
Public Service Act 1996 (Queensland) 121

Quangos 13–14
Queensland 119–28, 202, 204, 210
Questions of Procedure for Ministers (QPM) — see Ministerial Code of Conduct — UK

Ray, Robert 98
Reid, John 65
Reith, Peter 201–2
Richards, Rod 38
Robinson, Geoffrey 38

Saudi Arabia 80
Schäuble, Wolfgang 82–83
Schmidt, Helmut 85
Schreiber, Karlheinz 80
Schwarten, Robert 141
Scotland 9, 61–74
Scott, Andy 114
Scott, Bruce 97
Scott, Sir Richard 43
Sharp, John 38, 96, 99, 151
Sharp, Mitchell 111–12
Short, Jim 38, 177
Smith, Forbes 131
Smith, Tim 38
Snedden, Billy 193
Special Advisers 19, 68–71, 91–93, 102
Standards of Conduct
   institutions and procedures 5
   perceptions about 108, 125, 131, 167, 173, 190, 205
   political 9, 77–78, 190, 206
   public attitudes/expectations in public life 11–12, 16, 111, 206
Starr, Kenneth 205
Steel, David 65
Stevens, Sinclair 109
Stewart, Jane 114
Stockdale, Alan 161
Stokes, Kerry 166
Sutherland, John 96–100

Temby, Ian 137
Thatcher, Margaret 46, 54
Thyssen-Henschel 80
Trend, Burke 56
Trudeau, Pierre 108, 110
Turner, John 113

United Kingdom 21, 41, 144, 210

Business Appointments Committee 17
Child Support Agency 41, 65
Commissioner for Public Appointments 16–17, 19
Parliamentary Commissioner for Standards 15–17, 19, 73, 194
Prison Service Agency 41
Register of Members' Interests 73
Strategic Defence Review 65
United States of America 3, 21, 210–11
constitution 22, 27–29
Office of Government Ethics (OGE) 176–77

Voters/voting 4, 47, 59, 167, 204–6

Waldegrave, William 43–44
Welsh Assembly 47
Western Australia — Commission on Government 45
Western Australian Commissioner for Public Sector Standards 45
Westminster systems/conventions 6, 29–30, 129, 193–94, 196–97, 203, 210
Weyruch, Horst 80
Whistle Blowers 19
White, Dennis 92
Whitlam Government 56, 92
Wiggenstein, Casimir Prinz Zu Sayn 81
Wilson, Harold 92
Wilson, Howard 111, 113, 115–16, 124, 205
Woolridge, Michael 151–53

Yeo, Tim 38
Young, Doug 114